"Trauma Recovery and Empowerment is an enormously important resource. It is not a 'must-read' book, it is a 'must-do' book. Maxine Harris and the Community Connections Trauma Work Group have laid out a step-by-step guide for working with women survivors based on the most important principle of all—that every woman carries the seed of healing within her."

> —BONITA VEYSEY, The National Gains Center for People with Co-Occurring Disorders in the Justice System

"This manual is a long-overdue and essential resource for clinicians who wish to help women clients recover from traumatic abuse histories. I know of no other manual that presents detailed interventions aimed at both those women who are in beginning states and those in advanced stages of recovery. Dr. Harris and her colleagues truly have made a significant contribution to the recovery movement."

> —JESSICA A. JONIKAS, author of *Safe, Secure, and Street Smart: Empowering Women with Mental Illness to Achieve Greater Independence in the Community*

"Maxine Harris and the Community Connections Trauma Work Group are to be commended for their clear dedication to creating conditions through group process that allow women to bear witness to one another. Built on principles grounded in strength-based approaches, empowerment, and validation, their book should be required reading for all concerned with assisting women on the long journey back from the margins and home to themselves."

> —LAURA PRESCOTT, Independent Consultant, Women, Violence and Mental Health

TRAUMA RECOVERY AND EMPOWERMENT

A CLINICIAN'S GUIDE
FOR WORKING WITH WOMEN IN GROUPS

Maxine Harris, Ph.D.

and

The Community Connections Trauma Work Group

Jerri Anglin,
Editorial Coordinator

THE FREE PRESS
NEW YORK   LONDON   TORONTO   SYDNEY

*f*P

THE FREE PRESS
A Division of Simon & Schuster, Inc.
1230 Avenue of the Americas
New York, N.Y. 10020

THE FREE PRESS and colophon are trademarks
of Simon & Schuster Inc.

Designed by Michael Mendelsohn of MM Design 2000, Inc.

Manufactured in the United States of America

10 9 8

Library of Congress Cataloging-in-Publication Data

Harris, Maxine.
    Trauma recovery and empowerment : a clinician's guide for working
with women in groups/Maxine Harris and the Community Connections
Trauma Work Group.
        p.   cm.
    1. Psychic trauma—Treatment—Handbooks, manuals, etc. 2. Abused
women—Counseling of —Handbooks, manuals, etc. 3. Abused women—
Mental health—Handbooks, manuals, etc. 4. Compulsive behavior—
Treatment—Handbooks, manuals, etc. 5. Post-traumatic stress
disorder—Treatment—Handbooks, manuals, etc. 6. Group
psychotherapy—Handbooks, manuals, etc.   I. Community Connections
(Washington, D.C.).   Trauma Work Group   II. Title
    RC552.T7H37   1998
    616.85'2106'082—dc21   98–23590
                                                                          CIP

ISBN 0-684-84323-4

THE COMMUNITY CONNECTIONS TRAUMA WORK GROUP

Catherine Anderson

Jerri Anglin

Ellen Arledge

Deborah Bankson

Lori Beyer

Katherine Chiocchio

Carolyn Duca

Marlene Dunsmore

Mary Beth Flournoy

Liz Gregg

Maxine Harris

L. Joy Hayden

Margaret Hobbs

Mirta Jones

Christine Landis

Asta Lynch

Colleen Mahoney

Sharon Miller

Bronwen Millet

Nora Rowny

Sally Sargent

Heather Stowe

Rebecca Wolfson

Evelyn Zephirin-Atkins

ACKNOWLEDGMENTS

This manual would not have been possible without the many women who participated in the intervention itself. They shared their stories and gave of themselves, and for that we thank them. We also thank the men who participated in focus groups to discuss the relevance of the intervention to their experiences.

As we worked on this manual, we also received institutional support from many program managers at Community Connections who did not themselves work on the manual but who allowed their staff to do so. In particular Helen Bergman, Marlene Desmond, Jack Kline, and Felicity Swayze deserve our thanks.

Program directors at other agencies made it possible for us to run groups at their facilities. Janet Harris, Steve Lucente, Crystal Nichols, Henry Richards, and Sheila Snowden all opened their doors to us.

We relied on work done by others as we developed our manual. The theoretical work of Judith Herman, Christine Courtois, Marsha Linehan, and Carol Gilligan inspired our work. The movement and dance innovations of Deborah Riley were adapted for some of our exercises. We read with care the work on personal safety developed by Judith Cook and Jessica Jonikas.

Our early work was supported in part by a grant from the Substance Abuse and Mental Health Services Administration. Special thanks to Susan Salasin, James Pitman, and Bernard Arons, whose early belief in our work was much appreciated. Colleagues Ann Jennings, Bonnie Veysey, and Mary Ann Reilly offered support and encouragement.

We owe a particular note of thanks to our agent, Leslie Breed, who believed in the merits of this project. Our editor, Philip Rappaport, offered thoughtful suggestions that have made this a much better manual. His support has been invaluable.

Our partners and friends have been there for us as we have listened and learned from the stories and the pain of so many.

CONTENTS

PART III: ADVANCED TRAUMA RECOVERY ISSUES

PART IV: CLOSING RITUALS

PART V: MODIFICATIONS OR SUPPLEMENTS FOR SPECIAL POPULATIONS

PART VI: APPENDIX

INTRODUCTION

After reading a sampling of all the books written about sexual abuse and post-traumatic stress disorder, most clinicians are still left with one overpowering question: How do I intervene to help women recover from the aftereffects of trauma?

Clinicians may appreciate broad-based discussions about recovery; it gives them a framework and theory to understand their clients. But what they also need is a very practical, step-by-step guide to help them carry out a recovery intervention. This manual gives practicing clinicians just such a hands-on guide to doing recovery work with women. It is a product of work that has been done during the past 13 years at Community Connections, a private, not-for-profit mental health clinic in downtown Washington, D.C.

Since its establishment in 1984, Community Connections has delivered mental health, residential, vocational, and addictions services to hundreds of men and women in the Washington, D.C., metropolitan area. As a private, non-profit clinic, our mandate has been to serve people who survive on the economic and social margin. Like so many public and private clinics around the country, when we first opened our doors, we did not envision that we would be doing trauma recovery work. And like so many others, we found that we could not effectively deliver the services we were mandated to provide without addressing the often overwhelming histories of physical and sexual abuse that our clients have suffered and survived. Most importantly for the creation of this manual, we found that we needed an approach very different from that described in the current literature on trauma recovery. Much of the ground breaking literature, such as Judith Herman's *Trauma and Recovery* (1992), Christine Courtois' *Healing the Incest Wound* (1988), and Ronnie Janoff Bulman's *Shattered Assumptions* (1992) provide the reader with a sound theoretical understanding of how trauma impacts an individual's life and a broad guide for how treatment should proceed. The existing literature, however, cautions the clinician about doing work with highly vulnerable women.

For several very important reasons, women who have experienced sexual, emotional, and/or physical abuse in childhood, and who live on the social, emotional, or economic margin as adults, rarely fit neatly into existing treatments for trauma recovery. These women almost always lack the economic resources needed to participate in individual therapy; they are judged to be too emotionally fragile or disruptive for most group therapies; and they do not have the social supports needed to sustain participation in standard self-help formats. Yet, these women present themselves for treatment at public clinics, through employee assistance programs, and at nonprofit social service agencies in ever-increasing numbers.

We needed an intervention that dealt with the fact that many of the women themselves did not view abuse—either past or present—as their primary problem. They had come to label themselves and their problems in other ways. They had come to accept the often inaccurate labels given to them by other people.

Some women call themselves sad. They feel depressed and empty. They may be unable to summon the energy to accomplish small tasks much less to maintain a home or pursue a career. Feeling depleted can lead to self-attributions of incompetence. Women believe themselves to be failures; they cannot understand why it seems so much harder for them to cope than it does for "normal" women. Sadness can drift to despair and a feeling that life is not worth living, placing such women at an increased risk for suicide. Mental health workers come to notice these women when they appear at emergency departments or mental health clinics or when employers or teachers become concerned about their absenteeism or spotty work performance and refer them for counseling.

Other women are thought of as bad. They are angry and easily provoked. They drive too fast, scream too loud, and drink too much. They rebel against and have contempt for rules and regulations. Sometimes they commit crimes because they feel that they deserve to have what they need, perhaps as compensation for some past misfortune. Sometimes their crimes are against abusive partners and are attempts to defend themselves against more abuse. These women seem to care little for others and to view the world as a ruthless, unforgiving place. They come to the attention of mental health counselors when they commit crimes that send them to prison, when they are referred for substance abuse treatment, or when someone complains to child protective services that they are mistreating their children.

Finally, some women have been labeled as mad. They may be diagnosed as having a serious mental illness. Their symptoms often have been treated with medication and they have spent some time in psychiatric hospitals. A few have been confined involuntarily in state institutions and have endured being managed with chemical and physical restraints. After a while, these women come to doubt their judgments as well as their perceptions. They no longer feel certain that they can tell what is real and what is not. They often feel confused and distant from others. Their overwhelming concern about being harmed and damaged may be viewed as paranoia. They are frequently referred for mental health services by family members, friends, and general practitioners.

Regardless of whether they have been labeled as sad, bad, or mad, most women who have been overwhelmed by their histories of trauma do not identify trauma as their main problem when they request or are referred for treatment. Rather, they may complain of depression or anxiety. They may suffer from physical ailments such as headaches, muscle pains, or stomachaches. Sometimes they reveal that they have had difficulty forming relationships or that they drink more than they feel comfortable admitting. Occasionally, they report having been victimized by current domestic partners and having experienced brief bouts of homelessness. Almost never do these women link current difficulties to past abuses. In part this is because the link has never been made for them. Then was then and now is now, and they have not been encouraged to see any connection between the two. For many, dissociative defenses have served to keep the past tightly locked away.

The trauma recovery approach that we have developed is based on four core assumptions:

1. Some current dysfunctional behaviors and/or symptoms may have originated as legitimate coping responses to trauma.
2. Women who experienced repeated trauma in childhood were deprived of the opportunity to develop certain skills necessary for adult coping.
3. Trauma severs core connections to one's family, one's community, and ultimately to oneself.
4. Women who have been abused repeatedly feel powerless and unable to advocate for themselves.

Building upon these assumptions, we have developed a model of recovery that includes the following elements:

1. Basic education about physical and sexual abuse and how current behaviors are linked to past abuses.
2. A reframing of current symptoms as attempts to cope with unbearable trauma.
3. An appreciation of the problem-solving attempts locked and hidden in certain repetitive behaviors.
4. Education focusing on basic skills in self-regulation, boundary maintenance, and communication.
5. Basic education about female sexuality, correcting misperceptions and misconceptions.
6. Creation of a healing community by providing recovery services within a group format.
7. Rediscovery of and reconnection to lost memories, feelings, and perceptions.
8. An opportunity for women to experience a sense of competence and resolution as they face the demons from the past.
9. An opportunity for women to trust their own perceptions about reality and to receive validation from others for those correct perceptions.

For many reasons, some very practical and logistical (e.g., we could serve more women at less cost) and some more abstract and intuitive (e.g., our belief that broken connections can only heal in the context of new connections) we came to believe that recovery should occur in a group format. Many clinics and practice groups must rely on the talents of one or two clinicians to provide all the trauma recovery services. These clinicians can serve more women when services are made available to a group. Spotty attendance on the part of one or two women does not cancel the intervention. The group still can meet with as few as two or three members present. A group format also allows women to create important connections with other women. So often, a trauma survivor feels like the consummate outsider. She has felt outside her family, estranged from peers, outside her community, and dissociated from her very self. Healing connections are an essential part of any recovery and can happen naturally as a group evolves and coalesces.

In keeping with the underlying philosophy of the intervention itself, this trauma manual was developed by a community of women. For almost five years, 27 clinicians and more than 500 participants developed and refined the interventions contained in this manual. Thousands of hours of recovery work and clinical discussion went into producing the final version of the manual. This manual has no single author. The writing was done over several years by a group of clinicians. The editing also was done as a group project. No doubt a manual like this could have been produced more quickly if a single author had sat down and written it. Instead we chose to produce a work that reflects the ingenuity, the experience, and the struggles of many women, just as we believe that true healing must reflect the collaboration of many individuals. The group of 27 clinician-authors included experienced practitioners and novice therapists; it contained providers and consumer-providers. We struggled with issues of vulnerability, trust, security, and aggression, just as women in recovery must do. We bore witness to one another's struggles and pain, just as we shared each other's strengths and wisdom. Women in recovery must learn that the female spirit contains great possibility for triumph and accomplishment. We learned this ourselves as we worked together to create this manual.

We have produced what we felt we needed when we began our exploration—a very practical, hands-on guide for how to do trauma recovery work. The manual covers 33 topics that we believe need to be addressed in the process of recovery from trauma. Each topic is presented with a clinical rationale, a set of goals, a series of questions to be posed to the group, and an experiential exercise.

For each question that we suggest be posed to the group, we have included a set of typical responses. These responses were drawn from the many women who have participated in our groups and shared their stories with us. They provide a good idea of what to expect in response to a particular question. Other responses are possible, but those included here represent the broad range of responses that might be heard. We have followed these typical participant responses with a discussion of how to frame the leaders' response to them. The discussion suggests ways to make the most of members' responses and guides leaders in structuring the overall topic. We have attempted to anticipate as many questions that leaders might have as we can.

As we have introduced this intervention to women in a variety of settings, we have learned that some women, because of their special circumstances, appreciate a somewhat modified format. Women with serious mental illnesses, those who are parenting children, those who themselves have committed abuse, and women who are incarcerated all benefit from participating in some additional or slightly modified sessions that directly relate trauma and recovery to their most pressing concerns. Consequently, we have included modifications for each of these subpopulations of women.

Although this intervention was designed specifically for women survivors of abuse, we frequently speak with clinicians who ask, "What about men?" Can this recovery program be used with male survivors of abuse? Several clinicians at Community Connections asked the very same question. They convened focus groups of male survivors and asked men what issues they would like to see addressed in a recovery group. Using the core manual as a guide and adapting 16 of the sessions for male survivors, these clinicians have created a recovery intervention specifically for men. That intervention is included in the section addressing the needs of special populations.

We hope that this manual presents a clear guide for how to proceed with recovery and empowerment work. Most of all, we hope this manual functions as a "friend in the room" when you begin helping women through the process of recovery. We have certainly found that having a friend to consult with makes the process of helping others much easier.

GENERAL INSTRUCTIONS
TO GROUP LEADERS

GROUP FORMAT AND STRUCTURE

The following skills training manual addresses issues of sexual, physical, and emotional abuse in a population of overwhelmed and vulnerable women who have histories of trauma. The manual is divided into five parts and an appendix. Part I consists of 11 separate topics and introduces themes of gender identity, sexuality, interpersonal boundaries, and self-esteem without specifically addressing abuse issues. Part II consists of 10 topics and focuses on sexual, physical, and emotional abuse and their relationship to psychiatric symptoms, substance abuse, and current relationships. Part III consists of nine topics that further examine trauma issues such as blame, responsibility, and the role of forgiveness in recovery. Part IV consists of three sessions and serves as the conclusion to the intervention. Part V consists of modifications or supplements for special populations.

Each group meeting is designed to take 75 minutes; group meetings are to be conducted on consecutive weeks. Each topic should take one week to discuss, but leaders have the option of continuing for a second week if they and the members so choose. Leaders should not feel bound to answer every question under each topic if members are accomplishing the goals for the session. Group meetings should be conducted as structured conversations. The questions included in each session are intended as prompts to guide and facilitate the discussion. Each topic also includes an experiential exercise. The exercises promote group cohesiveness and allow for the inclusion of less verbal members. Exercises that allow participants to move around or to experience poetry, singing, drawing, and storytelling are preferable to those that are more abstract and strictly verbal. Leaders also should participate in the exercises.

This intervention functions best when conducted in the context of supportive case management or therapy. Each group member ideally should have a case manager or therapist to help her process the material of the group and deal with any upsetting feelings that may arise between group meetings. A woman who does not have any outside mental health support still can participate in the group, but leaders should be prepared to give her extra time if necessary.

PRACTICAL STRATEGIES TO REINFORCE GROUP STRUCTURE   Beyond having a set starting and stopping time and a consistent meeting place, leaders can define the structure of the group and bolster group cohesiveness in any of the following ways:

1. Leaders can use a flip chart or chalkboard to record member responses, but should avoid a format that feels overly didactic and bookish. Some group members report feeling emotionally validated or becoming clearer about their own thoughts when they see their responses or ideas written down on the chart.
2. Each woman can be given a group notebook she can take home with her or leave with the leaders for safekeeping between sessions. At the beginning of each session, you can add a page to each woman's notebook that summarizes the themes of the previous session and also provides blank spaces for her to add thoughts or reflections. When the skills manual is complete, each woman will have a substantial record of the group's work that contains both group themes and personal observations. (See Appendix Item A)
3. The group might keep a communal journal in which any member can write before or after each meeting. The journal entries can be anonymous or signed.
4. Each member might make a name tag to be worn during the group. The name tags are distributed at the beginning of the group and collected at the end. This process becomes a way to mark group boundaries and to recognize the community members share each week.
5. Announce the topic for next week's discussion at the end of each session.

REFERRAL TO THE GROUP

Referring clinicians begin by discussing possible group participation with clients who acknowledge a history of trauma. Childhood sexual or physical abuse, institutional abuse, rape in adulthood, and domestic violence all qualify as trauma. Together, client and clinician decide if a referral to the group is appropriate. Any woman who expresses some interest in attending a trauma recovery group should be given a chance to do so.

MEMBERSHIP

Pay attention to issues of addiction, character style, level of education, and psychosis when selecting members.

ADDICTION A woman currently addicted to drugs or alcohol may attend the group. While she is attending, her case manager or therapist should meet with her individually to suggest that she begin to consider how her addiction might be related to her trauma history. Some correlations to consider are as follows:

1. Drugs or alcohol may have been part of the abuse experience (i.e., either she or the abuser was drunk or high).
2. Drugs or alcohol may be a way to avoid feeling her pain or losses.
3. Drug and alcohol use subject a woman to higher rates of revictimization.
4. The uncertain street life of an addict is itself traumatizing.

A woman addicted to drugs or alcohol may need periodic detoxification during the life of the group. It is also possible that a woman in recovery may relapse given the emotional intensity of the group. As the group develops cohesiveness, members may grow increasingly disturbed by the self-destructive aspects of a group member's continuing addiction. Members may choose to confront an addicted member as their initial compassion grows into frustration with her behavior.

A group member high on drugs or alcohol at the time of the group meeting should not be allowed to attend that session. By setting this limit, leaders model appropriate boundaries and provide a safe environment for the other group members.

Women who are involved in continuous drug-seeking behavior often drop out of the group because they have little time in their lives for any activity other than satisfying their drug cravings. Women who are using episodically seem better able to maintain their attendance even though they are continuing to use substances.

CHARACTER STYLE A woman may find it difficult to tell her story within a group format if her abuse history has left her with an extreme sensitivity to any criticism, an aggressive desire to monopolize the conversation, or hair-trigger and diffuse anger. Groups of 8 to 10 women can, however, incorporate a maximum of 1 or 2 women with the above responses if leaders take the initiative to do the following:

1. Limit air time—Members with a tendency to monopolize the group are given two or three time-limited periods each group meeting, during which time they can tell their stories. Once these periods are used, however, monopolizing members can still make relevant comments to other group members.
2. Ensure safety—Caution all women that they may express anger but that they may not frighten or bully other members of the group. Ridiculing or screaming at another group member should never be tolerated. A woman may need to leave the group temporarily to regain her composure. Be mindful that members need to feel emotionally as well as physically safe. Emotional safety is established when members listen respectfully and courteously to one another. Be quick to stop any verbal or nonverbal expressions of scorn or ridicule.
3. Reframe comments to acknowledge a woman's strength—Group members often are better able to hear limit-setting or confrontational comments that begin by acknowledging their strengths and their value to the group. For example, "You are such a compassionate woman, why do you think you are having trouble listening to Jane's story?" or "You obviously care about this group, why do you think you have trouble coming on time?" Comments that begin by bolstering self-esteem are easier to hear for a woman with a tenuous sense of self-worth.
4. Ensure that group members have the capacity to manage their anxiety or to recognize when their anxiety is overwhelming and are able to ask for help— Some women feel very fragile and doubt their capacity to contend with strong feelings and disturbing content. Emphasize that group members can choose to excuse themselves for a time-out from the session and can return

when they feel comfortable. Women who do not have that ability often self-select to leave the group.

5. Group leaders or individual case managers should be prepared to provide one-to-one time for vulnerable members after the group time ends. Limit the amount of time to 10 or 15 minutes.

LEVEL OF EDUCATION Because the groups emphasize skill development and psychoeducation, a woman's education level and comfort in a learning environment are important factors in her successful participation. Leaders must assess each woman's vocabulary, abstract reasoning, attention span, and general literacy. When women exhibit learning deficits, leaders should make attempts to use concrete examples, define any difficult words, and rely less on written charts and instructions.

PSYCHOSIS A woman diagnosed with psychotic symptoms may attend the group. Generally, these women either remain silent in the group or else become somewhat more organized in response to a structured and relevant agenda. Many women appreciate the chance to talk honestly about long-silenced abuse issues. Do not attempt to form a group that consists only of women with psychotic symptoms. Heterogeneous groups, by and large, function better.

GROUP ATTENDANCE AND PARTICIPATION

ATTENDANCE You must be willing to grant some leniency with respect both to regular attendance and to punctuality, especially during the early stages of group development. Nonetheless, women must attend two of the first four sessions to continue with the group. Highly anxious women may need to have some extra support and control over their attendance until they are certain that the group is a safe place. Members should be given a grace period of up to 15 minutes before the doors close for any given session. Late members should be welcomed, but take no more than a few seconds to bring late arriving members up to date.

Group leaders can improve attendance by as much as 50 percent by making weekly telephone calls to all members just prior to the group to remind them of the meeting time. The regular calls serve several functions:

1. They remind members of the meeting time.
2. They demonstrate the concern and interest of the group leaders.
3. They establish a healthy ritual of connection to the group.

If reminder phone calls become an expected part of the group, you will need to do them weekly. You should discuss, however, the benefits and liabilities of reminder phone calls. While they do increase attendance, they may be experienced by some as intrusive or controlling. They also shift responsibility from client to clinician, a shift that may be at odds with the goal of empowerment.

You can structure the group to include a procedure to allow group members to inquire after those who were absent from a given meeting. When participants assume responsibility for contacting absent members, group cohesiveness and a sense of shared responsibility develop in the group. Group members also can contact one another before meetings so they can plan to arrive together or to share transportation.

Standard group rules that exclude women unable to manage the time and attendance boundaries are often too inflexible for women who feel overwhelmed by past and present abuse. At the same time, an individual's need for flexibility must be balanced by the group's need to maintain its boundaries. Often the leaders designate a specific date, perhaps three or four weeks after the group begins, when the early phase of group formation is considered complete. A woman who has missed the beginning sessions designed to socialize members to the group model and promote cohesiveness often is unable to become part of the group. After that time of initial group formation, members must commit to regular and timely attendance. Recognize, however, that some women will continue to miss an occasional session. Group members who attend only one of every three sessions can still benefit from the group.

ATTRITION Even when care is taken to select group members well, 30 to 40 percent of the women who begin the first session may eventually drop out of the group. Some of the reasons for dropping out include the following:

1. Finding the content of the group too upsetting
2. Deciding that what they experienced was not trauma or that the past does not affect their current lives
3. Believing they have already done recovery work

4. Feeling too uncomfortable in a group setting
5. Believing the intervention is too long and not wanting to make a several-month commitment
6. Feeling uncomfortable in an all female group with only female coleaders
7. Uncontrolled drug use

Occasionally, a member will require extra support, such as a short hospitalization or a course of medication, during the life of the group. These actions need not jeopardize her participation in the group. If her absence is prolonged, however, she may want to begin her recovery work again with a newly forming group.

CONFIDENTIALITY

Inform members that material shared in the group will remain confidential with the following exceptions:

1. A woman reports a desire to and a plan for killing herself or someone else.
2. A woman reports abuse of a dependent child.

Leaders are ethically and professionally bound to take action in these cases.

Also ask prospective members about their ability to maintain confidences that might be shared by other group members. Any woman who feels unable to respect confidentiality should be referred to individual therapy.

Group members should be instructed that material discussed within the group will remain within the group. Members may choose to share their personal stories with people outside the group; they may not, however, disclose the stories of other members. Group members should develop a policy for extra-group contacts. Generally, in the early stages of group development, members welcome a prohibition on member to member contact outside the group. As the group coheres, members may request that this ban be lifted.

THE ROLE OF GROUP LEADERS

A central role for the group leaders is to allow group members to be heard and understood and to encourage the development of empowerment skills. As group leaders demonstrate genuine and empathic responses, group members feel increasingly safe and capable of working on the issues related to their trauma experiences.

A group should be facilitated by at least two and sometimes three coleaders. This is recommended for several reasons:

1. To provide support for leaders while dealing with difficult emotional material that may arise during the group.
2. To prevent clinician burnout.
3. To ensure group continuity in case of an absent leader.
4. To lend additional ego strength to the group for discussion, problem solving, support to members, and the fostering of empowerment related ideas and goals.

In small clinics or practices where it is not possible to have coleaders, a group leader should meet regularly with peers who are leading groups at other agencies for support and collaboration. Leaders also can ask a member who has completed the group to repeat the intervention as a cofacilitator.

Follow the session agenda and only address group process when the process prevents the group from doing its work. Ideally, one leader will keep the group on topic or task according to the outline of the manual; another leader will be the timekeeper for the group and will write responses on the flip chart or chalkboard.

Coleaders should spend 20–30 minutes before the group to prepare the group's agenda and the same amount of time after the group to process the group's work. When leaders work as a team, group members feel more secure and the group's agenda proceeds more smoothly. Women feel enriched and empowered when they work with competent female leaders who can demonstrate problem-solving skills. Moreover, it is affirming to work with and get to know female leaders who are comfortable with their own power and knowledge and who present an enthusiastic and hopeful view of a woman's life.

LEADER DISCLOSURE

You may want to share some personal material where appropriate; however, complete disclosure about one's own trauma history is inappropriate.

Humanity is revealed when honest and empathic responses are made by group leaders. Group members report that this is essential to making the group work. If group members inquire as to a leader's personal history, leaders should respond by saying "most women in this society have encountered some form of abuse (domestic violence, harassment, rape or assault, and/or sexual or physical abuse) but that this is not a place or time for me to tell my story but rather for me to listen to your story and to help you." When leaders are unsure about whether to reveal part of their personal histories, they should err on the side of not disclosing. Some routine disclosure occurs for all leaders during their participation in the weekly exercises.

LEADER PAIRING

Because of the emotional nature of the work, leaders should pair with someone they know and trust. Ideally, one leader should focus on the topic and the discussion questions. The other leader should monitor the process of the group and be mindful of any member who might be having difficulty with the topic and need extra support. Two leaders who have worked successfully and comfortably with one another may add a third leader who is being trained to do trauma recovery work.

LEADER SELF-CARE

In the course of doing trauma recovery work, you may feel emotionally vulnerable. Because some leaders may remember traumatic experiences of their own, ongoing supervision and peer support should be available to all group leaders.

HOW TO USE THIS MANUAL

Trauma Recovery and Empowerment was written for practicing clinicians. It is a step-by-step guide for running recovery groups with traumatized women. It is not our expectation, however, that leaders will be rigid in their adherence to the manual. The goals at the beginning of each topic let the leaders know the intent of the session. If the goals have been well served after discussing only one or two of the main questions, you may choose to skip the remaining questions. If leaders prefer some of the additional questions to the main questions, they may make substitutions. In general, we believe the exercises add a unique dimension to the discussion. You may not, however, feel comfortable or skilled at using all the exercises. Omitting an occasional exercise still maintains the integrity of the intervention.

The intervention should be conducted using all of the topics in the prescribed order. If, however, clinicians are mandated by funding sources to limit their interventions, they can delete Part III, Advanced Trauma Recovery Issues, without violating the spirit and intent of the intervention. This manual is not solely a how-to book. It represents a specific philosophy about recovery in general and about pacing in particular. Selecting one or two topics for a psychoeducational presentation or attempting to shorten the intervention by omitting a number of sessions from Parts I and II are both ill-advised.

PART I

Empowerment

TOPIC 1 Introductory Session

SESSION RATIONALE

1. Members need a nonthreatening first group to help them adjust to the group format.
2. Even though members have been introduced to the group format and rationale in the referral and intake process, this session gives members a chance to ask any questions or clarify any concerns they may have.

GOAL 1: Each member will understand the format and agenda of the group.

GOAL 2: Each member will introduce herself to the group.

AGENDA

1. Group leaders should explain the rationale for the group and discuss the prevalence of trauma among women in general and among the population of women receiving services in public clinics (25–90% depending on reporting mechanisms and population characteristics).
   - Despite the fact that the group deals with histories of trauma, its mission is to address a woman's current functioning. Group leaders should suggest that there is a relationship between low self-esteem, a sense of disempowerment, and a history of trauma. When women deal with their pasts in healthy ways, they are bound to benefit from enhanced functioning in the present.
2. Group format and agenda are presented.
   - Leaders should tell members how the group differs from both traditional therapy groups that are more open-ended and process focused and 12-step recovery programs emphasizing self-disclosure and adherence to a formulaic script. The group discussion is not open-ended, but relies on a clear structure and a question and answer format; it is educational without being didactic.

3. Group rules are presented.
   - Leaders should emphasize that rules allow the group to do its work and help keep members safe.
   - Leaders should instruct members that group discussions are confidential.
   - The group requires that members respect one another's experiences and listen while others speak. Violence and aggression are not tolerated.
   - Leaders should explain that the group begins and ends on time each week and terminates at the end of a prespecified time, no less than 6 months and no more than 12 months.

EXERCISES

1. Each group member and each leader makes a name tag. Leaders should provide poster board, stickers, markers, feathers, beads, glitter, and so on. Participants are instructed to make name tags that say something about who they are. After the name tags are completed (about 15 minutes), each participant takes a turn at explaining her name tag (and thereby herself) to the group.
2. Leaders should ask members to go around the circle and introduce themselves and state what they hope to get out of the group.

LEADERS' NOTES

Present information, rationale, and group rules as outlined in the agenda.

EXERCISE 1

Prepare for the name tag exercise with the following materials:

    4" × 8" heavy paper, cardboard, or poster board
    Magic Markers, stickers, feathers, glitter, ribbons
    glue and scissors

All materials should be laid out on a table of sufficient size for the group members to gather around while making their name tags.

TYPICAL RESPONSES	Name printed and flowers drawn around the member's name
	Animals, special interests, or hobbies drawn on the name tag
	Tag may be covered with glitter and name written in Magic Marker

Occasionally a member will make a particularly disturbing name tag—one that expresses her pain, anger, or disorganization. You might acknowledge the message of the name tag while being careful not to be stigmatizing or too intrusive.

EXERCISE 2

At times, Exercise 1 may seem inappropriate, either because the meeting space cannot accommodate a crafts exercise or because the members seem unreceptive to making name tags. You may choose to use the following activity:

Ask members to go around the circle and introduce themselves and state what they hope to get out of the group.

TYPICAL RESPONSES	Letting go of anger
	Learning positive coping strategies
	Developing personal strength
	Learning about my true self
	Regaining self-esteem
	Becoming less eager to please and submit to the wishes of others
	Feeling alive again

Remember, this exercise is designed to help members introduce themselves to one another. You will want to discourage too much self-disclosure during this exercise and keep the conversation at an appropriate introductory level.

Ideally, provide a format during the first session that is both nonthreatening and inviting. During the introductory session more than at any other time, you will need to act as salespeople to increase the likelihood that women will return for subsequent sessions.

You also may find that you do more talking during the initial sessions of the group. Above all, you should convey a sense of hope and articulate the importance of what will be learned from this group.

Group members may be experiencing anxiety and may be reluctant to discuss the topic of trauma and their feelings surrounding their own trauma experiences. Communicate to the group that these feelings are normal and directly related to their trauma experience and assure members that they can participate as they feel ready. Members may present their concerns in one of several ways:

1. Group members may avoid the topic by being quiet, passive, or minimizing their experience. They may talk about related issues such as substance use, parenting, current relationships, or self-destructive behaviors in a manner that avoids looking at the relationship between such activities and their trauma experience. For example, by focusing on her substance use or her anxiety about being a mother, a woman can avoid dealing with the central issue of trauma.

   You may be tempted to use confrontation as a way to deal with the member's minimizing of behavior or feelings. However, confrontation of any sort by a leader should be avoided in this first session. It may come across as moralizing, punishing, shaming, or attacking. Instead, make a comment that addresses the topic by saying, "We will be talking about drug addiction, relationships, and so forth later on in this group and how each relates to trauma." If the member denies that trauma has had any effect on her life, leaders can comment, "Some people feel that way at the beginning of the group but often see things differently later on. Let's see how it goes for you."

2. Group members may be ready to talk and disclose prematurely. This may happen by a member's presenting a confession: "If I tell my story today, I'll feel much better and I won't have to deal with it anymore." This premature disclosure also may be the result of unintentional prompting by the referring clinician in an effort to prepare the member for the group. Once again, empathize and acknowledge the member's contribution but be prepared to contain her contribution to some extent so that it will not make other members overly anxious.

During the introductory session, you need to assess the readiness and needs of individual group members. Be on the lookout for members who present evidence of having difficulty with:

1. Maintaining boundaries
2. Monopolizing group time
3. Participating verbally
4. Staying focused and concentrating
5. Disrupting the group process

Once a thorough assessment is done, the group leaders need to develop a plan to deal with a member who needs assistance in one of the above ways. For example, if a member verbally monopolizes group time in a tangential manner, a leader may limit the number of contributions made by the member or the amount of time used during the group by saying, "Hold on Diane, let's hear from Vivian for a moment." or "Diane, let's give Vivian a chance to say something."

Another example applies to the group member who monopolizes group time with on target contributions. At first, such a member may seem like an ideal group participant. She has much to say, all of which is relevant. What you will eventually realize is that this star member intimidates other members, making it difficult for less articulate members to contribute. Leaders can contain the contributions of such a member by supporting the contributions of other members.

At times, you will have someone in a group whose story you already know. Do not pressure such a member to speak before she is ready to do so.

LENA'S STORY

They started the group by asking us to make name tags. I made a pretty one with flower and bird stickers circling my name written in fancy script. I thought it would be good to introduce myself as being nice, so that the other women would like me.

One of the other women didn't feel that way. Her name tag was ugly and almost scary. It was covered mostly in black, and it made me really nervous to look at it. I wonder what I have gotten myself into. I am not sure I want to tell about some of the things that have happened to me. And I am afraid that people will get angry or cry in this group. The leaders tried to reassure us and tell us that we would be all right in the group. I want to feel better, but I am not sure I can do this group.

TOPIC 2 What It Means to Be a Woman

SESSION RATIONALE

1. This session serves to identify common experiences among group members other than their trauma histories.
2. This session serves as a reference point for the remainder of the skills module. During subsequent sessions leaders will encourage women to reflect on how (and if) their attitudes and beliefs about being a woman have changed.
3. This session establishes a feminist context for the recovery work.

GOAL 1: Each member will begin to explore the personal and cultural meanings of being a woman.

GOAL 2: Each member will think about how being a woman has affected her life.

QUESTIONS

1. When you think about being a woman, what are the first words and images that come to your mind?
2. What are your feelings about being a woman?
3. How did your family treat boys and girls differently?

EXERCISES

PERSONAL MYTHS AND STORIES

1. Each woman is asked to remember when she first began her menstrual cycle. Women who feel comfortable sharing their menstruation stories with one another are asked to do so. These stories establish sharing of one's history as a group norm.
2. Each member is given a bag containing an identical set of colored shapes.

Each woman is then asked to make her own unique design from the common pieces. The exercise is a metaphor for how we each start with the same raw material and then create unique selves.

CULTURAL IMAGES

3. Members are asked to generate a list of positive and negative images of women from advertising, music, movies, TV, and so on.

LEADERS' NOTES

Start the group by welcoming back all members and providing an opportunity for introductions if there are new members at this week's group.

Remember, a member must attend a minimum of two of the first four sessions to proceed with the group. No one should join the group later than the third or fourth group meeting.

QUESTION 1

When you think about being a woman, what are the first words and images that come to your mind?

To facilitate this discussion, ask members to come up with the one word that comes to mind quickly when they hear the word *woman*.

TYPICAL RESPONSES

Being the strong one
Being a good girl
Being self-protective
Being a doormat
Being assertive = bitch
Being responsible
Menstruating
Being vulnerable with the opposite sex
Being paid less for the same work
Being a mother

Being a caretaker
Being a sex object
Putting others first
Being dumb
Looking good and feeling feminine
Being a good organizer
Staying behind the scene and having difficulty achieving real power

After listing the responses, look for common themes (i.e., nurturing and victimization).

After generating a list of roles and word associations, you can launch into a discussion about distorted images, myths, and attitudes regarding women. Question where and how such attitudes and images are formed. This may lead into a discussion of relationships with one's family of origin. Leaders unfamiliar with the literature on female identity and images of womanhood can refer to any of the following: Andrea Dworkin's *Woman Hating* (1974), Susan Faludi's *Backlash* (1991), Maxine Harris' *Down From the Pedestal* (1994), Carolyn Heilbrun's *Reinventing Womanhood* (1979), Mardy Ireland's *Recovering Women* (1993), and Naomi Wolf's *The Beauty Myth* (1991).

Pay attention to the balance of positive and negative comments being made. If most of the images or roles are negative, ask "Where are the positive pictures of what it means to be a woman?" If most of the images are positive, ask the comparable question about negative images.

If a group member has identified an image such as caretaker, as negative, ask "What would it take for caretaker to shift to a positive image?"

QUESTION 2

What are your feelings about being a woman?

TYPICAL RESPONSES		
Sad	Wished I'd been a man	
Angry	Vulnerable and hurt	
Disgusted	Disillusioned	
Feeling worthless	Frustrated	
Tired	Invisible	
Hostile	Lonely	
Unable to trust	Depressed	
Pleased		

Once again, if the discussion centers around negative feelings, ask "What are the positive aspects of being a woman?"

TYPICAL RESPONSES	Can enjoy friendships with other women
	Easier to communicate feelings

More sensitive and understanding
Know feelings better
More freedom
Insight and foresight
Being a mother and ability to have children
Like the choices I have
Feel strong
More introspective and connected to others
Greater inner strength

This topic often generates discussion about a member's family of origin, especially about a daughter's relationship to her mother. Often, this begins the discussion for many women about their mothers, and what their mothers taught them about life and womanhood, as well as whether their mothers protected them or abused them. This content may come up during the discussion and is appropriate. The leaders should allow this material to be introduced but should be mindful about staying on topic. Therefore, after an appropriate amount of time for discussion, group members should be redirected back to the main topic regarding their feelings about being women. The theme of mothers and daughters is one that recurs throughout the skills training module.

QUESTION 3

How did your family treat boys and girls differently?

TYPICAL RESPONSES   Girls had to be protected.
Girls had different chores.
Boys had fewer rules and curfews.
Sexuality was more monitored for girls.
Girls had to stay home and baby-sit.
Girls got spoiled.
Boys were expected to be smart and go to college.
Girls were trained to marry and become wives and
mothers.

This question generally leads to a discussion of male and female stereotypes. Ask members how they feel about the differing expectations for boys and girls. Could members have done anything to alter those expectations when they were growing up?

ADDITIONAL QUESTIONS

1. Who defines us as women? (Leaders will discover that this question often is taken as a rhetorical question and leads to a political discussion.)
2. Are there ways in which you have challenged traditional expectations?
3. Who were your primary female role models?
4. Has being a woman held you back? If so, how?

EXERCISE 1

MENSTRUAL STORIES Introduce this topic by saying, "One of the things that all women share is the fact that we all start menstruating. Let's talk about our own stories of when we first started menstruating." Members will go around the circle and tell their stories. This activity builds group cohesion and reveals some of the myths and anxieties women share as they enter into womanhood.

Any member who feels uncomfortable about this exercise or cannot remember her story can opt to pass. Although it is the goal of the group to encourage all women to participate, it is never appropriate to push a woman to speak before she is ready. Because intimidation is central to abuse situations, survivors are especially sensitive to anything that feels like coercion. Therefore, you will want to be careful to avoid any kind of subtle retraumatization that might result from pressuring group members to participate. Be prepared to hear the negative feelings—particularly shame and fear—that often accompany a trauma survivor's passage into womanhood.

EXERCISE 2

The exercise with colored shapes works well for a small group or with members who have difficulty verbalizing.

EXERCISE 3

The exercise using cultural images initiates a general discussion of stereotypes about what is feminine and masculine. Often, group members will discuss stereotypes found in the media, via advertising, television, or through popular music.

TYPICAL RESPONSES	FEMININE	MASCULINE
	Soft spoken	Abusive
	Gentle, dainty	Strong
	Weak	Powerful, physical, and aggressive
	Sex object	
	Understanding	Muscular
	Submissive	Insensitive
	Domestic	Dominant
	Young and beautiful	Money maker
	Sneaky	
	Emotional	

Encourage group members to examine their own ideas and stereotypes about femininity and masculinity. Group members should pay particular attention to the origin of such stereotypes. Members will begin to question some culturally sanctioned stereotypes about what it means to be a woman.

Leaders should preserve the notes from this session. In particular, prepare a hard copy of the responses to Question 1 "When you think of being a woman, what are the first words and images that come to your mind?" These responses will be used as a point of comparison in Part IV when this topic is repeated as part of the closing exercises.

BETH'S STORY

I don't like being a woman. I feel like all it has ever gotten me is pain. When I was a girl, my father used to beat me all the time. I was the youngest and the smallest so I guess he saw me as an easy target. I used to think if I was a boy he wouldn't hit me like that. Being a girl just meant being a victim.

I was determined when I grew up that I was going to get away from him. So I moved in with the first guy who showed me any affection. It was just a few months and my boyfriend was doing the same thing. Only he was worse than my dad. He wouldn't let me go out of the house, he alienated all of my friends, and he told me I was worthless. By that time I was pregnant and trapped. I didn't want to be a mother. I knew it would mean more responsibility than I could handle.

So what is so great about being a woman? You end up being trapped and vulnerable. Whenever things go wrong, it's always your fault.

TOPIC 3 What Do You Know and How Do You Feel About Your Body?

SESSION RATIONALE

Experiences of sexual and physical abuse frequently derail learning in childhood and adolescence. Despite the fact that they are prematurely exposed to sexual realities, abuse survivors are often naive about even the most basic information regarding their own bodies. Because of the shame and disgust survivors experience during the abuse, they often grow up with highly negative and volatile feelings about their bodies.

GOAL 1: Each member will have a clear sense of how to describe a woman's body.

GOAL 2: Each member will have an understanding of her body's cycles and rhythms and a basic understanding of human reproduction.

GOAL 3: Each member will begin to articulate how she feels about her body.

QUESTIONS

1. Do you think you have a good understanding of how your body works? How would you rate your knowledge on a scale of 1 to 10?
2. What were you taught about your body at home? At school? On the streets? From the media?
3. Are there things about your body that confuse you? Are there things that you would like to know better?
4. How do you feel about your body?
5. What are the messages others have given you about your body? What were your reactions?

EXERCISES

1. Leaders will place an outline of a full-size body on the floor and give each member a marker. Members will fill in the outline, drawing and identifying different parts of the female reproductive system.

   After completing the above, the group will use a diagram of the female reproductive anatomy and discuss how conception and pregnancy occur. Members will ask questions and share information as well as misperceptions about conception, contraception, pregnancy, menstruation, and menopause.

2. For each sexual body part, generate a list of commonly used slang terms and discuss how it feels to have one's body referred to in this way.

LEADERS' NOTES

You will need to be knowledgeable about the female reproductive system and the body's organs. A good source of information is *Our Bodies, Our Selves* by The Boston Women's Health Book Collective (New York: Simon & Schuster, 1992).

QUESTION 1

Do you think you have a good understanding of how your body works? How would you rate your knowledge on a scale of 1 to 10?

   Generally, women rate themselves in the mid-range of knowledge. If a member ranks herself at either the top or bottom of the scale, leaders should ask how she came to know so much more or less than the average woman.

QUESTION 2

What were you taught about your body at home? At school? On the streets? From the media?

TYPICAL RESPONSES

From family: Once you start your period, you've really got to watch it because now you can go out and get your self pregnant.

My mom wouldn't talk to me about my body, my period, or anything . . . it was all shameful and private.

Grandma said if a boy touched me I would get pregnant.

I wasn't taught anything so when I got my period I thought I was going to die.

From school:

I didn't get much from the movies they showed us in school.

I had a Girl Scout leader who told me about my period and what I should do about it.

I learned what I needed to know from Health Ed.

From the streets:

I didn't know much about my body until I got pregnant at age 13.

My friends told me some stuff but I wasn't sure how much of it was true.

We played nurse and doctor.

From the media:

Women need to be young, beautiful, and thin.

Women are naturally unclean and need to pay special attention to their feminine hygiene.

Blonde, sexy, big-breasted women can get anything they want.

These questions should prompt members to distinguish between how much "mislearning" and misinformation they share with other women as a part of the collective female knowledge base and how much of this faulty information is acquired as a part of growing up in an abusive household.

This discussion also may raise questions about the extent to which abuse affects learning. As a result of abuse experiences, many survivors rely on defenses such as dissociation and denial that can have a significant impact on learning in general. A survivor who dissociated during classroom time missed vital opportunities for learning. She may label herself as dumb or forgetful when in fact she was absent from class when important material was being taught. This can be an important insight, especially for a woman who has experienced barriers to learning during her past.

QUESTION 3

Are there things about your body that confuse you? Are there things that you would like to know better?

TYPICAL RESPONSES   I don't understand what menopause is or when it happens.

I had a hysterectomy but I'm not completely sure what the doctor did.

I had a tumor in my uterus and I didn't know how it got there.

How does a diaphragm work?

What exactly is an orgasm?

When do I need a mammogram?

Questions concerning bladder infections, vaginal infections, birth control, conception, giving birth, and hygiene also are common. We have found that most of the confusion has to do with birth control and reproduction.

Once again, you will want to emphasize the strong connection between abuse experiences and a woman's lack of information about her own body.

QUESTION 4

How do you feel about your body?

TYPICAL RESPONSES   Ashamed.

Angry.

Disgusted.

Disappointed.

Embarrassed, because I've never looked good.

> Mad, because I'm never thin enough.
>
> I wish I were invisible.
>
> Mad, because my body is misshapen—I never had
> the right shape.
>
> Sad, because people always have said negative
> things about my body—that I'm a butterball or
> too fat.
>
> Ashamed, because all anyone ever wanted me for
> was my body.
>
> I've never wanted breasts because I was raised that
> men want big-breasted women for sex.

Not only do survivors of abuse fail to accurately process information about their bodies, they also feel bad about what information they do have. As women share their feelings about their bodies, they may become angry that past traumas have left them with such scars. Women should be told that a degree of anger and sadness are normal responses to old conflicts.

QUESTION 5

What are the messages others have given you about your body? What were your reactions?

TYPICAL RESPONSES	MESSAGES	REACTIONS
	Too muscular	Disgust.
	Too fat	Self-hatred.
	Too tall	Shame.
	Too big breasted	Secrecy.
	Too small breasted	Confusion about my body.
	Too much or too little rear end or thighs	I do not want to be a woman.
	Too hairy	I dislike having a woman's body. I hate having my period. I hate having breasts.

Sexual and physical abuse are traumas that assault the body. Not only is the body harmed but the survivor also is made to feel that her body is bad. Women often feel a great deal of self-loathing about their bodies.

ADDITIONAL QUESTIONS

1. Who or what was most helpful in teaching you about your body? (This question encourages storytelling and reminiscing.)
2. Do you remember when your body first started developing and changing?
3. Why do you think knowing about your body matters?

EXERCISE 1

Prior to the group, prepare a life-size outline of a woman's body. This can be done by having one leader lie down on a 6-foot-long piece of paper while the other leader draws an outline of her body. Leave the inside of the outline blank. During the group, members will fill in the outline, using Magic Markers to draw and identify different parts of the reproductive system. Ask members to use colors of Magic Markers that best portray the way they feel about specific body parts. They also may wish to use more metaphorical choices of color to draw a body part. For example, members may choose cool colors for body parts where they have felt some self-recovery and hot colors for areas they feel they have not yet been able to reclaim.

As group members informally gather around the drawing and write in the body parts, a sense of collaboration and cohesiveness is fostered. The goal is to identify female body parts. If women respond quickly, there is no need to prolong the exercise.

TYPICAL QUESTIONS How do you get pregnant?
When do you ovulate?
How do your breasts fluctuate in size and feel?
What is menopause and when does it start?
What does it mean to have your tubes tied?
Why do I have irregular periods?
Do you bleed when you lose your virginity?

EXERCISE 2

Ask group members, "What words have people used in reference to your body that made you feel bad about your body?" These slang words can be printed in a different color marker on the life-sized outline used in Exercise 1. Often, teasing in childhood or adolescence is based on some perception of body image that others use as the source of taunts and ridicule. Ask members if they were ever called names because of their bodies and how they felt as a result of being called such names. Members may remember being called "fat stuff" because they were overweight; "ugly" or "odd" because they were not regarded as pretty or cute; "werewolf" or "mannish" because they had a lot of facial hair; and so forth.

If members have difficulty with the above exercise, you can ask members to generate a list of slang terms for various body parts. Follow up by asking members how they felt when others used slang words to describe their bodies.

TYPICAL RESPONSES   Breasts: tits, boobs, knockers.
                     Vagina/Pubic area: pussy, snatch, cunt.

A group whose members are somewhat shy, shame prone, or tentative with one another may have difficulty with the exercise using slang words. This activity tends to work best with a high-energy, highly verbal group. You will need to be sensitive to group composition and appropriateness when choosing either exercise.

Often, discussion about disrespectful terms for a woman's body will prompt stories of abuse. Redirect group members to look at how such misunderstanding and disrespect for a woman's body contributes to her poor self-image and feelings of shame. This may be a place where some members begin to tell some of their abuse stories.

This topic frequently foreshadows some of the themes that will be developed further in the session on self-esteem. Ask group members about what happens when their own sense of who they are does not match society's ideal. Members will respond by describing how they feel and what they think when they experience themselves as being different from the ideal woman.

TYPICAL RESPONSES   Depression.
                     Competition.

Jealousy.

Self-abuse.

Then, I must not be a woman.

Constantly trying to reach that ideal image by dieting, overattention to certain cosmetic concerns
(hair, make-up, clothing), and so on.

I won't be accepted.

I have to scale down my ambitions.

This topic may generate feelings of anger for some women and depression for others. During this session, each member should begin to understand what a typical response to an assault on her self-esteem might be. When self-esteem is attacked, people respond differently. Some people respond by withdrawing, others with self-hate, despair, anger, or depression. Each person has her own particular response pattern. Women should be encouraged to self-assess and come to some understanding as to what their own typical responses are and how those responses occur.

JOYCE'S STORY

I didn't used to be fat. When I was in high school I was thin and pretty. I used to get a lot of attention for my looks and felt good about that. Then the rape happened and I stopped looking in mirrors and shopping for clothes. I felt so bad about my body that I started eating a lot. The weight went on quickly and I was happy to hide behind it. I didn't want anyone thinking that I looked good again.

I'm still very heavy. People tend to avoid looking at me when I walk down the street. I don't like the way I look, but I don't want to lose the weight either. When I drop a couple of pounds it makes me nervous and I start eating more again. I feel like my fat protects me. Who would want to have sex with some-one like me?

TOPIC 4 Physical Boundaries

SESSION RATIONALE

Whether it is physical or sexual, abuse violates and intrudes on an individual's personal space. Abuse survivors may find themselves confused about what constitutes safe and appropriate space for them personally and within their peer groups. The session gives members a chance to explore the topic and receive feedback from one another.

GOAL 1: Each member will begin to develop an understanding of her own personal space. She will also learn how her level of personal comfort and safety varies when she respects her need for space versus when she does not.

GOAL 2: Each member will begin to develop a sense of how much or how little control she has over what happens to her body.

Begin the session with Exercise 1.

QUESTIONS

1. How much space do you need? What is the comfortable distance between you and others?
2. Does anyone ever come physically close to you when you do not want to be approached?
3. What constitutes unwanted contact? How do you react to unwanted contact?
4. How does one's body language say stay away or come close?

EXERCISES

1. As group members enter the room, the leaders call their attention to boxes outlined on the floor with masking tape. The boxes are shapes of different

34

sizes. Some are close together, others are farther apart. Group members are asked to stand or sit in a box. The group leaders discuss the boxes and let the members know that they represent boundaries and that the group is going to discuss boundaries.

Each group member should notice what kind of box (size, proximity to other boxes) she selects.

2. Measuring Personal Space: This exercise is designed to measure a woman's need for personal space. Two approaches to the exercise are as follows:

A. Members are arbitrarily paired with one another. Members in each pair stand a comfortable distance from one another. Using a tape measure, leaders measure the distance between members of each pair. Distances are recorded on a flip chart. Members then are asked to stand next to someone they feel could become a friend. This distance is also measured and recorded. Members compare and discuss the two readings.

B. Using a tape measure, each member of the group measures off her own interpersonal comfort zone (the distance that one requires to feel comfortable being with other people). All distances are written on a flip chart next to the appropriate member's name. Members then are asked to adjust the distance (or not) imagining that the other person is someone toward whom they feel close. Members then make the same adjustment for a stranger. All distances are written on the flip chart and members have a chance to discuss their responses.

LEADERS' NOTES

You will need to prepare for the group by having a large roll of 1″ masking tape. You will need approximately 20 minutes prior to the group to prepare the floor by forming various boxes, triangles, and rectangles with masking tape. Prepare at least 12 to 15 boxes for a group of 8 to 10 persons allowing members to have a choice.

The floor of the group room may resemble the configuration at the top of the following page.

As group members enter the room, ask members to choose a box. Begin

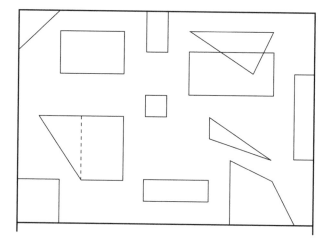

the group by informing members that the boxes represent boundaries and asking members what they mean when they use the word *boundary.*

Once members have selected a box in which to stand, ask members to pay attention to which box they chose, how far or near it is to someone else, and what is the exact location of the box in the room. Additional prompts for discussion may include:

Why did you choose that box?
What part of the box do you feel most comfortable standing in?
Are you in the middle of the room or on the periphery?
Is there room for anyone else to stand in your box?
Are you facing others or is your back to others in the room?
If you could choose another box, which one would you choose? Which one wouldn't you choose?

Sometimes you will need to make a member's strategy explicit. For example, "It looks like you need to have your back to the wall to feel safe." Leaders can be somewhat creative and playful during this exercise.

After the above discussion, members can be seated for discussion of questions 1–3.

QUESTION 1

How much space do you need? What is the comfortable distance between you and others?

Ask members to consider relationships with partners, family, roommates, as well as situations such as riding the bus, sitting in the doctor's office, going to the movies, and being approached by someone unfamiliar.

You will want to emphasize that boundaries may change depending on safety and familiarity with others in the environment. Discussion should be directed to include the strategies a member uses to control her boundaries as well as how she responds when those boundaries are violated.

TYPICAL RESPONSES	I need to keep people at arm's length.
	I don't need any space.
	I need more space.
	I don't like to touch anyone.
	It depends on how well I know them.
	I don't like people to stand over me.

You will need to respect that in addition to individual and family differences, there are also cultural differences in how comfortable people feel with managing personal space. These differences should be acknowledged in the discussion.

QUESTIONS 2 AND 3

Does anyone ever come physically close to you when you do not want to be approached?

What constitutes unwanted contact?

TYPICAL RESPONSES	Someone brushing up against me
	Someone standing too close to me
	Someone forcing sex on me
	Someone touching me when I don't want to be touched
	Someone hitting me
	Someone staring at me
	Someone talking too close to my face

Pay attention to the range of responses. For some women, contact must be forced sex before it is labeled as being unwanted. For others, a simple glance feels like an intrusion when it is unsolicited.

How do you react to unwanted contact?

TYPICAL RESPONSES		
Get angry	Feel anxious	Tune out
Get mad and cuss	Give in	Strike out
Leave the situation	Feel nauseated	Feel indignant
Panic	Get scared	Get intimidated
Get embarrassed	Have difficulty breathing	

Ask members what feelings and defenses occur as a reaction to unwanted contact. Members will discuss whether current responses are a replication of childhood responses or if they are responding as they wished they had during childhood. Once again, encourage members to assess their response patterns and to understand whether or not those patterns are new or old.

QUESTION 4

How does one's body language say stay away or come close?

TYPICAL RESPONSES	STAY AWAY	COME CLOSE
	Folding my arms across my body	Motioning with my hand to come here
	Turning my body away from the other person	Putting my arm around someone
	Turning my head away while someone is talking to me	Standing closer to someone
	Running away from someone	Having open body posture
	Staring back hostilely	Making eye contact
	Looking down and avoiding eye contact	Smiling

This question should enable members to look at the ways they carry their own bodies in the world and to examine their own definitions and behaviors regarding physical boundaries. Women may want to demonstrate the different ways in which they hold their bodies.

ADDITIONAL QUESTIONS

1. Are there times when you need more space than at other times? What cues do you respond to?
2. What happens when you can't get the space you need?

EXERCISE 2A AND B

Exercises A and B are designed to measure a woman's need for personal space. Have a measuring tape available for use in these exercises. Exercise A is done with pairs and may be suitable for an already interactive group. Exercise B may be more appropriate with isolated individuals who seem like loners.

After completing the exercise, ask members "What would you need to shorten the distance?" and "What are the factors that go into feeling more comfort with someone?"

TYPICAL RESPONSES		
Time passing	Familiarity
Gender	Race
Trust	Similarity
Relaxation	Liking and enjoying the person

MARY BETH'S STORY

I really like the physical boundaries session. As a former dancer I have a fondness for open spaces and the room, without the chairs, feels really open and without obstacles.

As I start moving through the room, mingling with others and deciding on a box selection, my excitement begins to turn to anxiety. I suddenly become aware that I will have to disclose why I chose a particular box. I panic and yell to myself in anguish, "I can't possibly be vulnerable in front of this many people!" When I stop moving and settle into my space, my kinesthetic joy is replaced by a series of mental calculations.

I wonder: "How will I protect myself? Can I lie about my choice and still sound convincing?" I decide I can and create escape hatches by making up less revealing reasons why I am in my box.

It is then that I realize that I still have a body attached to this head. That is when I notice that my stomach is tightening; I feel hot. The room that was once so open feels too small as my space needs suddenly become larger. I wonder if there is a way I can quietly, without being noticed, get outside. Surely there is enough space in the outdoors to satisfy my personal needs.

As we all make our choices and come to stillness we look at each other, and I realize I am not going anywhere but here. My anxiety begins to dissolve into a desire to share my experience. I realize that others too have their own obstacles to overcome.

TOPIC 5 Emotional Boundaries: Setting Limits and Asking for What You Want

SESSION RATIONALE

Women survivors of trauma have a history of feeling in jeopardy when they say no to the demands of others. Survivors worry that they will hurt or disappoint others. They also worry that they will be abandoned, attacked, or disliked. Sometimes they become fearful that they themselves will counterattack and be unable to control their own anger. Survivors must learn that:

A. They have a right to say no.
B. They can survive the consequences of saying no.
C. The responses of others may be different from what they expect.

GOAL 1: Each member will be able to form an "I want" statement that is individual and specific to her alone.

GOAL 2: Each member will begin to understand the difference between active and passive strategies to get what she wants.

GOAL 3: Each member will begin to understand what it means to set an interpersonal limit.

QUESTIONS

1. Do you ask yourself what you want when you enter a new situation or a new relationship? If not, why not?
2. Has anyone else ever asked you what you wanted? Did you trust that they meant it?
3. When do you say no to others?
   What things get in the way of saying no?
   How do you feel when you want to say no or actually say no?

4. Have you ever said no in a way that worked? Please share these successful strategies with the rest of the group. What conditions make it easier or harder to say no?

5. What do you think the link is between your trauma experience and the difficulty with saying no?

EXERCISES

1. Each group member frames an I-want statement. Each member is instructed to form her statement so that it is personal, avoiding statements such as "I want world peace." A leader writes the statements down and puts them in a large box. One statement is drawn out at a time. The group brainstorms on how to achieve the goal of the I-want statement and looks for two strategies that will work and for one strategy that is a real loser. Strategies are written on a flip chart and the leaders help the group identify strategies as active or passive. The leader then asks when one might use a passive strategy (looking for issues of safety and fear) as opposed to a more active one.

2. Each member will think of a situation in which she is currently having difficulty setting limits. The group will choose one or two of these situations for shared problem solving.

3. Members will practice saying the word *no*. To begin, each member will say "No" in her everyday voice. Members will raise their voices up one notch at a time until they begin to feel uncomfortable. Members will do this one at a time and give feedback to each other.

Abuse survivors need to acknowledge their own desires as healthy and legitimate.

LEADERS' NOTES

QUESTION 1

Do you ask yourself what you want when you enter a new situation or a new relationship? If not, why not?

> TYPICAL RESPONSES   No, I assume they're only willing to take . . . not give.

No, I don't always know how to get my needs met.
No, because I'm happy with whatever I get.
No, no one listens to me anyway.
No, because then I will be too vulnerable.
No, I wait and see what happens.

This question encourages members to develop awareness of their internal state when asking themselves what they want in specific situations, especially during important events. Some women may be surprised to realize that what they want never enters their minds when entering a new relationship. Many women are merely passive players who drift into relationships with little or no self-awareness.

QUESTION 2

Has anyone else ever asked you what you wanted? Did you trust that they meant it?

TYPICAL RESPONSES   No.
Not really.
I'm suspicious of them and their motives.
Yes, but I'm very honest . . . maybe too trusting.
Yes, but I hold back.
Yes, but it didn't make any difference.
No, because I thought the information would be used to control me.

This is not a question generally posed to women. Even so, group members should ask themselves whether they believe they are asked this question less than the average woman. Members might want to consider why their needs and wants are often ignored.

QUESTION 3

When do you say no to others?
What things get in the way of saying no?

How do you feel when you want to say or actually say no?

As an introduction to the discussion about saying no when setting personal limits, ask members to list what situations prompt members to say no.

TYPICAL RESPONSES   **WHEN DO YOU SAY NO TO OTHERS?**
When someone asks me to lend them money or to
  borrow my car.
When someone asks me if I want to go out partying
  or get high.
When someone wants sex and I don't want sex.
Pressure from my family to do something that I
  don't agree with or don't want to do.
I am never able to say no.

Encourage group members to discuss what gets in the way of saying no and how it feels to say no. It is useful to stress the link between trauma experiences and the difficulty women have saying no.

TYPICAL RESPONSES   **WHAT THINGS GET IN THE WAY OF SAYING NO?**

Feeling guilty	Being disliked
Feeling hurt	Needing to keep the
Being afraid of the	peace with family or
repercussions	friends
Being rejected by others	Feeling pressure from
Someone getting angry	someone to say yes
or mad at me	Being manipulated
Hurting the feelings of	Having the other person
others	be my lover or mate
Being stunned	Not wanting to disap-
Wanting to fit in	point the other
Wanting to be liked	person

TYPICAL RESPONSES   **HOW DOES IT FEEL TO SAY NO?**

Scary	Strong but nervous
Anxious	Guilty

Angry	Relieved
Powerless	Empowered
Ashamed	Fine

Often, this question will provide an opportunity for members to share what happened when they previously reported a trauma. You should not discourage this and should allow members to tell their stories.

QUESTION 4

Have you ever said no in a way that worked? Please share these successful strategies with the rest of the group. What conditions make it easier or harder to say no?

Encourage group members to list both effective and ineffective ways to say no. Strategies should be written on a flip chart so members can consider the pros and cons of the various strategies. For example, members may suggest the following when wanting to say no.

TYPICAL RESPONSES	INEFFECTIVE STRATEGIES	EFFECTIVE STRATEGIES
	Becoming passive	Making clear statements
	Shutting down	Deciding for yourself what you can give or take
	Lashing out in anger	
	Letting the feelings fester inside	Specifying what is good for you
	Directing anger toward someone else such as an innocent bystander	Negotiating
		Communicating what you want and listening to what the other person wants
	Exploding	
	Drinking or using drugs	Keeping self-preservation in mind
	Simply withdrawing from the situation	
		Taking a time out

Help members to examine the possible ramifications of both types of strategies. It is important to understand not only why one has chosen particular strategies in the past but also what the current consequences of particular strategies are.

QUESTION 5

What do you think the link is between your trauma experience and the difficulty with saying no?

TYPICAL RESPONSES   Remembering painful incidents from the past when I couldn't say no makes it difficult to say no now.
Feeling the same fear I did as a child when I couldn't say no to the abuser.
Feeling the emotional pain I did in the past.
It did not matter if I did say no.
My saying no doesn't matter.
Feeling unworthy to say no.
Feeling that I have no power to affect anything.

You can help members to share their own experiences by giving examples of what happens to some people when they say no or stand up for themselves:

The perpetrator may call you crazy.
The abuser may threaten you or someone you care about.
The abuser may threaten a pet or something else you value.
The abuser may threaten suicide.
The abuser may withdraw love and attention.

If the sharing of such experiences has been covered in a previous discussion, do not force a repeat of this material.

ADDITIONAL QUESTIONS

1. Can you distinguish between verbal and nonverbal or active and passive ways of saying no?
2. How do you defend yourself beyond just saying no?

EXERCISE 1

The exercise using I-want statements works best when women have achievable goals such as to:

- Manage my money better
- Communicate with my sister
- Improve my relationship with my brother
- Get enough money to go to the movies
- Get a better job
- Live on my own
- Rely on myself to make decisions

You can point out that some goals are harder to accomplish because they are too vague or unrealistic such as:

- A partner to love me forever
- A million dollars
- Be a success
- Be happy
- Be famous

EXERCISE 2

Women are asked for current examples of where they are having trouble with setting limits. Women may need help from the leaders because they may be unaware of exactly where they are having trouble setting limits. Those who have been taken advantage of repeatedly may not recognize unfair situations until someone else points them out.

EXERCISE 3

The exercise in which women say the word *no* works best when women incorporate movement and body language.

SHANA'S STORY

Nobody ever asked me what I wanted. In my family my mom was the one who told everybody what to do. It was never a choice. Since I became depressed, my sister thinks she can do the same thing—tell me how, where, and when. She's extremely bossy and she's younger than me. But she has a good job, and a car, and a house so everyone in the family thinks it's OK for her to say what she wants.

I have a hard time feeling like I have any choice about anything since it seems like so many things have happened without my wanting them to happen. Even the littlest things leave me feeling like I have to go along with other people or I might get hurt. Like when someone asks me for money, I give it over. Even if it's my last few dollars. Nobody can understand why I don't just say no. It's more complicated than saying no. I get scared, wondering what might happen if I refuse, if they might threaten me, or make trouble for me. It doesn't seem worth it to stick up for myself, since the consequences have been so bad so many times before.

TOPIC 6 Self-Esteem

SESSION RATIONALE

Histories of abuse and years of feeling overwhelmed serve to reduce or destroy one's positive sense of self-esteem. Women need to nurture a positive sense of who they are. By focusing on what they like about themselves and reframing survival skills as positive strengths, a woman can begin to heal the damage caused by years of abuse.

GOAL 1: Each member will begin to develop an inventory of her positive qualities.

GOAL 2: Each member will look at how other people's opinions affect her feelings about herself.

GOAL 3: Each member will develop an understanding of how the abuse in her life has affected her self-esteem.

Each member rates herself on a Self-Esteem Thermometer that the leaders have drawn on a flip chart before the session (see Appendix Item B). Members take turns rating how they feel about themselves and then discuss their ratings.

QUESTIONS

1. What makes you feel good about yourself?
2. What have people in your life said or done to you that has made you feel good or bad about yourself?
3. Have there been times in your life when you have felt better about yourself than at other times? Why do you think that is?
4. To what extent does how you feel about yourself depend on another person's opinion of you?
5. How do you think being abused has affected your self-esteem?
6. Are there certain areas of your life about which you feel better than others? Relationships? Work? Family?

EXERCISES

1. Say something good about yourself to the group. Pay attention to how you feel. Share your feelings with the rest of the group if you feel comfortable doing so.
2. Each woman is given the outline of a Positive Self-Esteem Achievement Chart (see Appendix Items C and D). She is asked to fill in the chart with achievements, things about which she feels good or proud, and things she has learned on her own journey. Group members discuss their achievement charts.

LEADERS' NOTES

Prior to the beginning of group, draw a thermometer on the flip chart with ordinal markings from 0 to 10 (see Appendix Item B). Once the group begins, ask members to rate how they feel about themselves on that particular day (0 = no self-esteem and 10 = extremely high self-esteem). After all members have rated themselves, they should discuss their ratings. You will need to explain that a member's rating may fluctuate within several points from day to day.

Leaders can take this opportunity to educate group members about the relationship between self-esteem and trauma. Most trauma survivors experience low self-esteem.

Ask members how they define self-esteem, how positive self-esteem develops, and encourage them to discuss their individual self-esteem patterns.

TYPICAL RESPONSES	TYPICAL RESPONSES
Definition of self-esteem	**Development of self-esteem**
Belief in one's self	I'm not sure
Liking one's self	Putting value on your abilities
Self-value or self-worth	People giving you good feedback
Self-acceptance	Your parents telling you that you're
Self-respect and self-confidence	worth something
	Parents respecting and honoring your
	needs and wishes

You will want to pay attention to whether members focus on external or internal causes for positive self-esteem. If there seem to be too many external reasons for feeling good about one's self, ask members to speculate about some of the problems that derive from being so dependent on external reinforcement for feeling good about one's self.

QUESTION 1

What makes you feel good about yourself?

TYPICAL RESPONSES

> When someone says something nice about me and I think they mean it
> When I've been respected by someone I care about
> When I've been recognized for something I've done
> When I've accomplished an important goal
> When I feel in control of myself
> When I get through a day without a crisis
> When I am loved or cared for
> When I do something nice for others

This question can be understood by members in one of two ways. Some members will see it as an opportunity to say what they like about themselves. Most members, however, will use the question to identify those external circumstances that give them a sense of well-being. Those members with the most damaged self-esteem may have trouble generating any circumstances that make them feel good and may be more focused on how to avoid any further pain.

QUESTION 2

What have people in your life said or done to you that has made you feel good or bad about yourself?

TYPICAL RESPONSES

Good:
Being complimented
Being recognized for hard work
Being told that someone cares about me

Bad: Being abused
                                Being told I was crazy
                                Being put down
                                Never being believed about the abuse
                                Being called names and being told I would not
                                    amount to anything
                                Being told I caused all the problems
                                Being told I was like the abuser

When considering external sources of reinforcement, members should distinguish between people inside and outside the family. You can prompt discussion by asking members whether they received different responses from inside or outside their families and how that affected their self-esteem. Lastly, underscore, once again, the connection between abuse and trauma experiences and poor self-esteem.

QUESTION 3

Have there been times in your life when you have felt better about yourself than at other times? Why do you think that is?

TYPICAL RESPONSES   Yes, when I started working and earning money
                      Yes, when I finished school
                      Yes, when I had my children
                      Yes, when I stopped using drugs
                      Yes, when I lost weight
                      Yes, when my feelings were validated
                      Yes, when I was in a relationship or married
                      Yes, when I started doing things that were good
                          for me

The intent of this question is to highlight the fact that self-esteem is not necessarily a trait but rather a state. As such, it can fluctuate across time. Members begin to see that feeling bad about one's self today does not necessarily mean that one will feel bad about one's self forever.

QUESTION 4

To what extent does how you feel about yourself depend on other people's opinions of you?

TYPICAL RESPONSES   A lot!

I'm at the point that I don't care what others think about me.

This question repeats the theme of internal versus external locus of control that was touched on in Question 1 and can now be discussed in greater depth.

QUESTION 5

How do you think being abused has affected your self-esteem?

TYPICAL RESPONSES   When you've been abused, you start to think that no one loves you and that you don't deserve to be loved.

You start to become suspicious of others when they compliment you and you believe that there is absolutely no truth to what they are saying about you.

I feel like garbage.

I find it difficult to trust my sense of right and wrong.

I sell myself short and don't take chances.

You stop believing any compliments.

This question gets to the core of why women who have been traumatized suffer poor self-esteem. Make sure that members have a clear understanding of the strong connection between trauma and poor self-esteem.

QUESTION 6

Are there certain areas of your life about which you feel better than others?

TYPICAL RESPONSES   Being in a relationship with an understanding
                    partner
                    Performing well at a job I like
                    Being a good mother, sister, or family member

This question introduces the idea that self-esteem is related to context, underscoring the notion that one can feel good about one's self in one context and feel bad about one's self in another context, even during the same time period. The overall goal is for members to develop a much more complex understanding of what self-esteem is. When women understand that self-esteem is not an all or nothing phenomenon, they will begin to feel more empowered to make changes, beginning in one area of their lives. Step by step, they can begin to make an impact on other areas of their lives in a positive way, thereby contributing to improvements in self-esteem.

ADDITIONAL QUESTIONS

1. Are there actions you could take that would make you feel better or worse about yourself?
2. How does your body feel when you are feeling good or bad about yourself?
3. How does low or high self-esteem manifest itself in the way a person carries herself?

EXERCISE 1

Ask group members to say something good about themselves to the group. Group members are asked to pay attention to how they feel and then to share their feelings with the rest of the group. You should honor a member if she opts not to participate in this exercise.

EXERCISE 2

In preparation for the Achievement Chart exercise, leaders should have a copy of a blank Achievement Chart for each member (see Appendix Items C and D). Members are asked to fill in the chart with achievements, things about which they feel good or proud, and things they have learned on their own journeys in life. Allocate approximately 10 minutes for members to complete their charts. Group members will discuss their Achievement Charts.

TYPICAL RESPONSES   Getting married
Having children
Getting a job
Achieving sobriety
Continuing my education
Learning to relax and enjoy myself
Becoming more creative
Feeling connected to God

If members have difficulty doing the exercise on their own, you can turn this into a communal project and generate one composite chart.

CHARLENE'S STORY

When my dad was messing around with me, he would always tell me that I was asking for what he was doing. I never understood what he meant because although I liked getting attention from him, I didn't want him to touch my body. I've always felt that what happened was my fault. I must have been giving him the message that I wanted his sexual advances.

That has always made me feel terrible about myself. Maybe that's why I don't know what you mean when you talk about feeling good about yourself. When you say those positive things about me, I can't feel it or take it in. It's like I have an inch thick, hard layer of skin that can't absorb compliments or praise.

My life is getting better. I've been completely sober for the last couple of months. I have a really nice apartment and lots of friends. I'm even engaged to be married, although I don't feel like I'm good enough for my fiancé. I have this lingering fear that he will leave me for someone better. One of my goals is to someday truly believe that he loves me for who I am.

TOPIC 7   Developing Ways to Feel Better: Self-Soothing

SESSION RATIONALE

Survivors of trauma are often all too aware of the necessary but less-than-ideal ways in which they have comforted themselves in the past: drugs and alcohol, fantasy, dissociation, overeating, self-cutting, and compulsive activity. They are less aware of benign ways to self-comfort. This session begins to introduce less damaging ways in which members might feel comforted and soothed.

GOAL 1: Each member will begin to understand what it means to comfort herself.

GOAL 2: Each member will begin to develop an idea of what it means for a method of self-comforting to be too costly.

QUESTIONS

1. When you feel bad, how do you take care of yourself? (How do you help yourself feel good, calm, not afraid?)
2. Some strategies are of the "feel good now, pay later" variety. What does it cost you to receive comfort? List your three most used comfort strategies in increasing order of cost. (Leaders may need to give examples to help group members with the idea of psychic cost.)
3. Are there some people you can count on to comfort you? Describe what they do to comfort you or what qualities they have that you find comforting.
4. What do you do for yourself when you are troubled and there is no one available to help you?

EXERCISE

Each woman makes a Comfort Card depicting the things that bring her comfort. In designing the comfort card, a woman can use magazine pictures, draw-

56

ings, writings, or objects from home. Common pictures on the Comfort Cards include nature, relationships, food, home, material goods, cosmetics, pets, and exercise. Women may discuss their cards with one another.

LEADERS' NOTES

QUESTION 1

When you feel bad, how do you take care of yourself? (How do you help yourself to feel good, calm, not afraid?)

TYPICAL RESPONSES

Blocking things out of my mind
Keeping busy
Counting to myself
Going out and enjoying myself
Going to the movies
Using drugs and/or alcohol
Taking a bath
Listening to music
Yelling and letting it all out
Eating
Smoking a cigarette
Praying
Distracting myself
Doing fun things
Reading a book or magazine
Socializing
Meditating
Talking to someone who is calming
Taking medication
Avoiding certain situations
Exercising
Fantasizing
Reading the Bible
Going out to dinner with friends

This question helps members become explicit about the ways in which they care for themselves. Often, women who have been severely traumatized feel bereft of any positive means for making themselves feel better and may even have trouble with the concept of self-soothing. In fact, most women do have some strategies to ease internal anxiety and tension. This question is designed not only to help people to think about new strategies but also to allow them to appreciate the positive strategies they already use and consequently feel more empowered.

This is a good opportunity to begin to distinguish between effective and ineffective strategies, (i.e., Does it work?) and constructive versus self-destructive strategies (i.e., What are the secondary consequences of a particular approach?).

QUESTION 2

Some strategies are of the "feel good now, pay later" variety. What does it cost you to receive comfort? List your three most used comfort strategies in increasing order of cost. (You may need to give examples to help group members with the idea of psychic cost.)

TYPICAL RESPONSES		
Using drugs	Using alcohol
Having sex	Overeating
Smoking cigarettes	Sleeping too much
Fighting	Self-mutilating
Watching too much TV	

Leaders will need to define what *cost* means. First, something costly can lead to negative consequences. Using drugs can result in legal trouble or can impair a woman's judgment, leading her to be retraumatized. A second aspect of psychic cost involves how much energy the strategy exhausts. Denial is a way to deal with stressful events but can use a lot of psychic energy. A third aspect of cost has to do with missed opportunities. For example, someone may use a less healthy strategy and therefore be blinded to healthier options.

QUESTION 3

Are there some people you can count on to comfort you? Describe what they do to comfort you or what qualities they have that you find comforting.

TYPICAL RESPONSES		
Being thoughtful	Checking in with each
Being a good listener	other
Being understanding	Getting a hug
Being helpful and	Being close and
supportive	familiar

Being honest	Having been through
Just being there and	personal recovery
available	Being respectful
Being calm and even-	
tempered	

For many trauma survivors, what they have learned about the interpersonal landscape is how to identify problem people. They are often sensitive to the nuances of negative behavior. However, they have more trouble recognizing the positive qualities of people. Therefore, rather than being hypervigilant or suspicious, the goal for the group member is to identify what it is about another person that is positive.

Many of the initial responses to Question 3 will be vague and abstract. Help members to articulate the behavioral markers of comforting behavior. For example, if members list "being thoughtful" as a comforting aspect of someone else's behavior, ask members to define the specific actions that feel soothing (i.e., the other person calls you back when you've called and left a message).

QUESTION 4

What do you do for yourself when you are troubled and there is no one available to help you?

TYPICAL RESPONSES	Listen to my Walkman	Sleep
	Pray or go to church	Take a shower or a bath
	Watch TV or read	Do my hair, nails, and so on
	Walk, run, exercise	Eat
	Shop	Meditate
	Write a letter	Write in a journal

Often, people feel dependent on others for comfort. Encourage members to identify strategies that go beyond relying on someone else for comfort. If members demonstrate difficulty identifying self-soothing behaviors, go back to the responses in Question 1 and ask members which strategies can be done alone.

Members should perform a self-assessment of the strategies they use. For example, how many of the comforting strategies you use require another person? How many of your self-soothing strategies cost money? How many of your strategies are self-generated? Do you feel too many of your strategies are dependent on other people? Do you want to expand your choice of comforting strategies? What is your first choice when needing to comfort yourself? If that is not a possibility, then what do you choose? Then what choice?

Compile a list of the helpful strategies mentioned by group members. A typed version of comforting strategies can be given to members at the next meeting for their use outside of the group (see Appendix Item E).

ADDITIONAL QUESTIONS

1. Would active problem solving make you feel better? How would this work?
2. How do you get comfort when you know you need soothing but feel too defeated to ask for it or give yourself permission to take care of yourself?

EXERCISE 1

Prepare for the Comfort Card exercise by gathering the following materials:

Numerous magazines that represent women from diverse cultures, nature scenes, animals, food, cigarettes, material goods, cosmetics, pets, and exercise
Glue, scissors
A 26″ × 16″ paper or poster board for each participant
Magic Markers

Instruct group members to design their own Comfort Cards by cutting out pictures from magazines; drawing; or bringing pictures from home of special people, family, pets, or of anything that is especially comforting. Allocate approximately 20 minutes to design the card and a 10–15 minute discussion time for members to share their cards with the group. You may want to play soothing music to help put people in the mood.

You can initiate the discussion by asking each member why certain pictures on the Comfort Card are soothing. Members are encouraged to take their

Comfort Cards home for use if they wish. This exercise is very popular and encourages members to *visualize, remember,* and *imagine* options for comfort. The exercise itself, over and above the strategies generated, reinforces a woman's cognitive abilities.

Any member who does not feel competent to do the exercise should be allowed to sit out or should be given assistance.

JO'S STORY

I guess a lot of the ways I comfort myself are "feel good now, pay later" strategies. I eat too much, I smoke, and I used to drink. I also used to prostitute. I think I prostituted because I was looking for love—even if it was only temporary affection. The other thing I started to realize is that if I'm feeling bad I rock and rock and rock. It makes people nervous because they think I'm going to rock myself numb. I guess that's what I'm doing—trying to make it all go away. I think I started when I was really little when nothing around me was good. It was kind of like I could block out the world.

When I did my comfort card I cut out pictures of kittens and cats. I don't have a cat, but I do have pictures of cats on my bedroom walls and I have a stuffed cat. When I'm feeling down, I hug my stuffed cat. It helps me to feel warm inside and that's a comfort. Even when I'm in the group, I hang onto my card because I can remind myself of something good even when I'm upset.

TOPIC 8 Intimacy and Trust

SESSION RATIONALE

Survivors of sexual abuse often mistake sex for intimacy and emotional closeness. The confusion between sexual and emotional closeness leads some survivors to engage in sex when what they really want is intimacy and closeness. Women often feel disappointed and betrayed when a sex partner fails to treat them with the concern and care they would expect from an emotional intimate. Women need to begin clarifying the difference between sex and intimacy if they are to avoid being revictimized in future relationships.

GOAL 1: Each member will understand what it means to be intimate with another person.

GOAL 2: Each member will be able to articulate the conditions that promote or violate trust, reciprocity, and safety.

QUESTIONS

1. What is intimacy?
2. What is necessary for closeness (intimacy) to occur?
3. What conditions create trust, reciprocity, or safety?
4. What conditions violate trust, reciprocity, or safety?
5. How have substance abuse and other destructive behaviors interfered with connection and intimacy?

EXERCISE

Each woman will draw an Intimacy Network. Placing herself in the center, she will arrange her close relationships on concentric circles at increasing distance from the center (herself) (see Appendix Item F). Women will discuss their networks.

LEADERS' NOTES

QUESTION 1

What is intimacy?

TYPICAL RESPONSES
Sex
Passion
Closeness
Trust
Emotional connection
Relationship with a sex partner
Understanding

Women who have experienced trauma demonstrate significant difficulty defining intimacy. Abusers have violated boundaries and thus left women with poor or nonexistent examples of safe and reciprocal relationships. Group members associate intimacy almost exclusively with sex, and often use the two words interchangeably. Consequently, leaders must reeducate members by helping them to redefine intimacy and underscore that the new definition of intimacy will include *trust, reciprocity,* and *safety.*

QUESTION 2

What is necessary for closeness (intimacy) to occur?

TYPICAL RESPONSES
Trust
Listening and being heard
Understanding
Rapport
Confidentiality
Accepting people as they are
Honesty
Familiarity

Most group members have little or no experience with genuine closeness. Consequently, their responses may reflect an idealized and simplistic view. The discussion will be more productive if members can use examples to illustrate what they mean by some of the more abstract terms. Allow space for members to acknowledge their lack of experience with closeness to other people.

QUESTION 3

What conditions create trust, reciprocity, or safety?

TYPICAL RESPONSES When someone holds your confidences
When someone accepts me the way I am
When I'm there for them and they're there for me
When boundaries are respected
When someone does not try to hurt you or take advantage of you
When someone listens to me and I feel heard
When people make a real commitment to one another
Mutual respect

Responses to this question may represent vague generalizations. Encourage members to provide specific behaviors and examples that create and demonstrate trust, reciprocity, and safety. For example:

- *Constancy over time.* She always returns everything she has borrowed from me. Pam and I have been roommates for eight months. We always let each other know if we're going to be home later than usual so we don't worry each other. She attends the building meeting every week. Consistently, Pam responds to me when I talk with her.

- *Predictability, being able to count on someone to behave in a certain way.* Laura is true to her word. When we work on projects together she always follows through on her part of the job. Every Tuesday, Laura agrees to meet me at the bus stop and she is there. She never verbally abuses me if I upset her.

- *Getting to know someone over a reasonable period of time.* I talked with Bob over the phone for several weeks before I told him my address. I talked with Sarah at school for several months before I agreed to go out with her.

- *Sharing the same values with someone.* I feel safe talking to Stan about my urges to use drugs because he has been there and knows what it is like to want to use. We go to NA every Monday and Saturday. He has been clean for two years and he supports my efforts to stay clean, unlike some of my other friends.

QUESTION 4

What conditions violate trust, reciprocity, or safety?

TYPICAL RESPONSES		
Being let down	Lying
Prejudging	Betrayal
Denial	Deceitfulness
Cheating	Selfishness
Greediness	Abandonment
Boundary violation	Being forced to have sex
Being abused	Getting mixed messages
Being taken advantage of	Not being believed
Unreliability	

Leaders should note that women will have an easier time generating examples of how closeness was betrayed or violated than discussing how closeness can be created and maintained. Regrettably, many women who are multiple trauma survivors only know how relationships end in disappointment. You may want to comment about this lack of balance in women's experiences.

QUESTION 5

How have substance abuse and other destructive behaviors interfered with connection and intimacy?

TYPICAL RESPONSES When someone is using, they are not dependable.
When someone is using, they are unavailable when I need them.
When someone uses drugs or drinks, their judgment is impaired and they do things or say things that

they normally would not do or say. Some of
those things are hurtful or abusive and they
don't contribute to a good relationship.

When someone uses, they're unpredictable and
untrustworthy.

The relationship is never reciprocal when someone
is using.

When someone is craving, they might do anything
for drugs which makes being around them
unsafe.

When I use, I am more sexual.

When someone is using, all they want is money for
drugs.

When I am using, I want to be alone so I don't have
to share.

When I use I am disconnected from my feelings and
I have trouble being really close to anyone.

When I use, I am less inhibited and more sexual.

If the group does not have members who have had problems with alcohol or
drugs, you can ask members about other self-destructive behaviors. You also
can redirect the discussion back to the original incidents of abuse and ask
whether drugs or alcohol were ever involved.

ADDITIONAL QUESTIONS

1. What role has abuse played in your ability to be intimate?
2. Does your comfort differ when you are in a close relationship with a
   woman versus a man? How do you understand the difference?

EXERCISE 1

Prepare for this exercise by having an Intimacy Network form for each group
member (see Appendix Item F). Explain that the center of the network represents the individual group member and that each surrounding ring represents
a level of intimacy within her network. The circle closest to the center repre-

sents her most intimate relationships and each ring thereafter represents a less intimate relationship. Encourage members to consider issues of trust, reciprocity, and safety when examining their relationships prior to placing a name on a specific ring of the Intimacy Network.

Allow approximately 10 minutes for members to complete this exercise. Group members will discuss their Intimacy Networks by explaining the placement of each name.

FERN'S STORY

It took me a long time to reach the level of friendship I have with my best girlfriend. I confide in her and lean on her because I know she won't use my secrets against me. I know I can count on her. I don't think I could ever have the same level of closeness with my boyfriend. It's funny, but sometimes having sex makes you less close, not more. The sex becomes important, and you forget about being open and really intimate. I used to think sex and closeness were the same thing. If you want to be close, have sex. Right? Wrong! Now I feel the opposite. I can't figure out how to be sexual and really close in the same relationship.

TOPIC 9 Female Sexuality

SESSION RATIONALE

The session promotes bonding as women share their uniquely female experiences. Because their first sexual experiences were under someone else's control, many trauma survivors are unaware that they can control their own sexual pleasure. Trauma survivors often see sex as taboo and their own sexual responses as bad. The session allows women to discuss sexuality in an open, nonshaming format. The group allows a woman to see her own responses as normal and to begin the long process of accepting her body and its sensuality.

GOAL: Each member will develop an understanding of female sexuality.

QUESTIONS

1. At what age do you remember first feeling aroused? What do you remember specifically?
2. How do you feel about touching your body to give yourself sexual pleasure?
3. When did you begin to think of yourself as a sexual being?
4. Do you still think of yourself as a sexual being? If not, when did you stop and why?
5. What factors increase (decrease) your sexual desire? Does a history of abuse affect it?

EXERCISE

Leaders will ask group members to join them in a body wake-up exercise. The exercise can be explained as something positive that women can do every morning to wake up their bodies to a new day. Members will discuss their reactions after completing the exercise.

LEADERS' NOTES

QUESTION 1

At what age do you remember first feeling aroused? What do you remember specifically?

TYPICAL RESPONSES   When I first touched myself and felt something
When I slid down the banister
When my stepfather touched my vagina
When I played doctor with my friends
When my friends and I rubbed up against each other
When we all piled on top of each other and it felt good
I used to fall asleep with a towel between my legs

For many women, this may be the first time they have shared early memories of arousal. They may be somewhat tentative or embarrassed as they tell their stories. Women who have experienced trauma often feel doubly ashamed of any sexual feelings at all.

QUESTION 2

How do you feel about touching your body to give yourself sexual pleasure?

TYPICAL RESPONSES   I feel embarrassed thinking about it.
I can't imagine doing that to myself.
I feel comfortable about it and enjoy how it feels.
Guilty.
I'm so closed off about sex with anyone else that I can't think about doing something like that to myself.
I was told it was a sin.
It's something I can control and pace.
When I know how to touch myself, I can tell my partner what I like.
I feel dirty afterwards.
I like to do what I'm told not to do.

Often sexual abuse leaves women believing that touching and arousal in general are forbidden and disgusting. Self-stimulation rather than being a potential source of comfort or pleasure is viewed as a betrayal of the self and a collaboration with the enemy. If they are to have the option of enjoying sexual pleasure, women must see the distinction between stimulation that they control and touching that is forced on them.

QUESTION 3

When did you begin to think of yourself as a sexual being?

TYPICAL RESPONSES   When I started menstruating.
When someone flirted with me.
All the men wanted me so I figured I must be sexy.
I still don't think I'm sexy.
When I got a bra.
When I was a girl, I used to flirt and wiggle a lot.
When I got my period, I became sexual.
After the abuse, I knew I could use my body to get things.
When I started dating, I felt sexy.
When I finally had sex with someone who was caring and kind.

Some women may link becoming sexual with having been abused. You will want to make a distinction between being used sexually and being sexually mature or responsive. You may want to help members define what they mean by being sexual. Members also may distinguish between the act of having sex and feeling sexy or aroused. Accurate labeling helps women to make distinctions about just how they are feeling.

QUESTION 4

Do you still think of yourself as a sexual being? If not, when did you stop and why?

TYPICAL RESPONSES No, I'm not interested anymore.

I'm too old, I'm 46.

I have never felt sexy.

I have outgrown my interest.

When I had children, I stopped wanting sex.

After my hysterectomy my desire went away.

I always feel sexy even when I'm not able to have sex.

I dress myself up to feel sexy.

I feel more asexual than really sexual.

Allow women who still feel sexual to express their feelings. For those who no longer feel sexual, ask what it would take for sexual feelings to return. This is also the opportunity to correct some of the inaccurate stereotypes about female sexuality and aging.

QUESTION 5

What factors increase (decrease) your sexual desire? Does a history of abuse affect it?

TYPICAL RESPONSES

Decrease

Not having any place to do it

No privacy

A bad experience

No partner

Medications (antidepressants, blood pressure medications, steroids, thyroid medications)

Drugs

Stress

Being too busy and exhausted

An abusive partner

Increase

An exciting partner

Setting the mood

Liking how I look

Drugs and alcohol

Feeling safe

Feeling loved and cared about

It is useful to distinguish among those factors that pertain to the individual, the partner, and the context. You also need to be explicit about linking past abuse to changes in sexual desire because the connection may not be obvious.

ADDITIONAL QUESTIONS

1. Can you distinguish between sex and sexuality?
2. If you were alone on a desert island, what do you think your sexuality would be like?
3. How do sex, sensuality, and eroticism differ? (This may work better for groups of women who enjoy philosophical or intellectual discussions.)

EXERCISE 1

Ask group members to join together in a body wake-up exercise. Group members can remain sitting in their chairs. The group starts by rubbing their hands together to create warmth and then placing their warm hands over their eyes. The exercise continues by rubbing the hands together again and then placing the warm hands on both temples; then rubbing again, placing their hands on both sides of the neck, rubbing hands again and then placing hands on their shoulders.

Next, ask members to brush away the stress in their left arm by using their right hand starting at the shoulder and brushing down the arm, thinking about brushing out all the stress in the arm. Repeat this exercise for the right arm. Repeat the same process for both legs by starting at the hip and brushing the stress out and down the legs.

Now start again with arms and knead from shoulder to hand. Begin with the left arm and then right arm. Repeat the same for the legs by kneading each thigh with both hands as if you were kneading bread. Repeat the same for the calf muscles in the lower legs. When you have completed the calf muscles, then place your hands on your toes and run your hands up the front of your legs, the abdomen, chest, neck, and head and then extend both arms to the sky. Sweep arms down to the toes again and repeat the massage up the body for a second time.

Now ask group members how their bodies feel. Do they feel more awake and energized? Suggest doing this simple exercise when women feel tired and need to be awake.

GAIL'S STORY

I was married to Tom for 11 years and I bet we had sex less than 15 times. If Tom had pressured me for sex, the marriage would never have lasted that long. When we did have sex, it was because I felt like I should give him some since he so rarely asked, but I never enjoyed it. Don't get me wrong, I loved Tom. He was a sweet, caring guy who was fairly attractive. But there was nothing about the sex I enjoyed, not the kissing nor the touching nor the penetration. Now I was not laying there crying, I just didn't feel anything. I would be thinking to myself "when will this be over?" Since we've been divorced, I've had sex with three other men. It has been the same with them, too.

TOPIC 10 Sex with a Partner

SESSION RATIONALE

Even if they take self-imposed vows of sexual abstinence, women are confronted with the *possibility* of a sexual encounter or relationship throughout their adult lives. That possibility is something women should learn to greet without fear, anger, or confusion. Throughout the process of empowerment and recovery, the goal should be to help women regain as much control as possible over their bodies and their choices about relationships.

GOAL: Each member will understand what goes into a sexually intimate relationship with a partner.

GENERAL DISCUSSION

Leaders should discuss the following with group members at the beginning of this session: Because of the experience of abuse, survivors often fall into one of two general categories. Those in the first tend to oversexualize all relationships or are indiscriminately sexual, feeling that their only value is as a sexual object. Those in the second category become avoidant or almost phobic of sexual encounters and deal with their fears by shutting down their sexual responses.

Consequently, the discussion of sex with a partner must begin with leaders surveying the group to ascertain how many group members are sexually active. Following the general discussion, leaders should assess the group composition and decide which questions to emphasize.

QUESTIONS

1. What attracts you to another person? How do you determine whether or not someone is sexually attracted to you?
2. How do you and your partner communicate about sex?

3. Do you know what gives you sexual pleasure? Your partner sexual pleasure?
4. What happens when one of you does not want sex?
5. Are there things that might interfere with having an intimate partner?

EXERCISE

What would you want someone to know about you before you agreed to have sex? What would you want to know about the other person? How many of your personal criteria were met in your last sexual encounter? Each woman should make a list of her personal need-to-know criteria.

LEADERS' NOTES

Pay particular attention to member responses and attitudes during the discussion of Question 1 and decide which questions to emphasize.

QUESTION 1

What attracts you to another person?

TYPICAL RESPONSES   Their smile
Their physical appearance
Common interests
A nice body
Whether they are attracted to me
If they treat me well
I watch how they treat others

How do you determine whether someone is sexually attracted to you?

TYPICAL RESPONSES   The way they look at me or respond to me
If they speak to me or try to get my attention
If they try to flirt with me
If they ask me out

> If they compliment me
> If they whistle at me on the street
> If they brush up against me
> If they give me a gift

For women who have not felt in control of many of their relationships, defining what they like in another person can feel quite empowering. However, you should be aware that sexual response and desire often are confused for women who were raped or abused at an age when they were able to be sexually responsive. These women feel their bodies betrayed them if they felt aroused while they were being raped or abused. Consequently, they now feel extremely guilty and confused talking about sexual attraction since sexual response has been linked to abuse.

QUESTION 2

How do you and your partner communicate about sex?

TYPICAL RESPONSES   My partner tells me what she or he likes.
My partner shows me what she or he likes.
We make lists and trade them.
We watch videos and talk about what we like.
We pay attention to each other's responses.
We read sexy books to each other.
My partner tells me what to do and if I refuse he tells me he'll find someone else.
My partner teases me and I have to guess what she wants.

You need to suspend judgments initially about what may sound like dysfunctional or abusive communications (e.g., threats, orders, saying the opposite of what you really want). After women have generated a long list of communication styles and techniques, leaders can ask about the effectiveness and the secondary impact (intimidation, confusion, etc.) of particular styles. Remember that couples generally do not communicate well about sexual needs and preferences.

QUESTION 3

Do you know what gives you sexual pleasure? What gives your partner sexual pleasure?

TYPICAL RESPONSES

Self
A massage
Raw passion
Being held
Having someone touch me
Making love with the lights on
Holding hands
Loving words

Partner
When I pay attention to her responses
My body
Oral sex
Seeing me get excited
When I dress in sexy clothing

Be attentive to members who express that the only time they experience pleasure is when their partner is aroused or satisfied. Because they have felt themselves to be sex objects, women trauma survivors often begin to read their responses from their partners and believe that the only pleasurable sexual experience is when the partner indicates satisfaction with sex. Assist members to understand that they too can experience sexual pleasure by tuning into their own bodies.

Some members may feel that this question asks for information that is too personal. Reassure them that the goal is not to obtain intimate details but rather to help women become cognizant of how aware or unaware they might be about their sexual responses. Members should be reminded that the group *always* will respect a woman's decision not to respond to a particular question.

QUESTION 4

What happens when one of you does not want sex?

TYPICAL RESPONSES   We argue.
I get called frigid.
I give in.
She cheats on me.
He forces me.
We cuddle and massage each other.
He asks me to help him masturbate.
I feel guilty.

This question may introduce the topic of spousal abuse. Some women will want to tell their stories of domestic violence. You will want to allow for some disclosure at this time. Also, be ready to point out that there are other ways to interpret and handle differences in sexual desire that do not cause one partner to feel guilty, inadequate, or frightened.

QUESTION 5

Are there things that might interfere with having an intimate partner?

TYPICAL RESPONSES   Feeling used.
Being afraid the person will leave or beat me after we have sex.
Being afraid of abuse memories from the past.
Feeling guilty.
Being hurt.
Not wanting to risk trusting someone else.
I don't want a permanent relationship.
Fear of getting diseases.
Being criticized for my performance.
Being called a slut.
Being afraid of becoming too vulnerable.
I do things that make me feel ashamed.
I cheat on my partner and then I feel bad.
Once I get started I can't stop.

Help members to organize these responses into categories (e.g., things I do, things the other person does, things from the past, etc.). Also, ask members what, if anything, it would take for members to overcome these barriers to intimacy.

ADDITIONAL QUESTIONS

1. How important is it for you to feel emotionally close before you have sex?
2. How are emotional and sexual closeness related?

EXERCISE 1

Open up this discussion by asking group members whether they have specific criteria that others must meet before they engage in sex with them. If members do not have such criteria, leaders can prompt members to examine what information they would want from the other person before agreeing to have sex, for example:

- How long have you known this person?
- Do you feel safe with them?
- What have they disclosed to you about themselves?
- Do you know anything about their sexual history?
- Do they listen to you about your needs?

Ask members what they would want their partners to know about them before agreeing to have sex. Do the same criteria apply as noted above? You can assist members to develop the list by posing questions and writing answers on a flip chart.

MARIA'S STORY

I am always meeting these real smooth guys. They seem to have it all together. We start having sex and they take me places and buy me things and treat me special. We spend lots of time together. Everything is great. Then the guy moves in. He's still smooth, but all of a sudden he doesn't have any money and I'm paying for everything and taking care of everything. And if I complain, he gets angry and threatens me. He forces me to have sex. He doesn't think twice about hurting me. One day he gets real angry and leaves me. And it starts all over again with someone new. I think I have found true love, but then the same things happen.

I've gotten to the point where I don't want to get involved with anyone. I still go out and party and meet guys. But even if they seem nice, I know that once I let my guard down and we start having sex, they will start taking advantage of me and hurting me. It's better to keep to myself. I hate to say it, but I'm beginning to think that there aren't any good guys out there.

TOPIC 11 Transition Session from Empowerment to Trauma Recovery

SESSION RATIONALE

This session serves as a bridge between the skills focus of the empowerment modules and the psychoeducational emphasis of the trauma recovery sessions. Women are given a chance to consolidate their impressions of themselves before moving forward. This kind of self-monitoring often has been absent in the lives of trauma survivors.

GOAL: Members will review what they have learned about themselves in the group.

QUESTIONS

1. What have you learned from the trauma group during the past several months?
2. What has been difficult for you during this group?
3. What do you hope to learn and/or talk about during the next part of the trauma group?

EXERCISE

Members will complete a road map of their lives (see Appendix Item G).

LEADERS' NOTES

QUESTION 1

What have you gained from the trauma group during the past several months?

TYPICAL RESPONSES   Discovering a new sense of openness with the group
by way of trust and taking that ability to be open
outside of the group.

Being around others who care.

Finding out I'm not the only one who has been
abused.

Learning that if others judge me, that's their problem.

Becoming better at setting boundaries.

Feeling more empowered.

Becoming better able to listen to others.

I realize that there is a road to recovery.

I have more respect for my own intuitions.

I realize that I'm not crazy.

I make my needs known.

I know I can trust other women.

I can now set limits with my friends.

It's often useful to catagorize the responses into four or five subheadings (i.e., self-esteem, group cohesiveness, issues of trust, skill development, etc.). This will assist group members to organize and integrate their responses more effectively.

QUESTION 2

What has been difficult for you during this group?

TYPICAL RESPONSES   Learning to accept the reality of what has happened
to me in the past.

Feeling emotional pain.

Opening up to others and sharing my story.

Talking about sex and the secrets I was taught not to
talk about.

Feeling vulnerable.

Talking to other women.

It has changed my relationship to my family.

> Realizing that it may get harder before it gets better.
> It has been hard to hear some of the other stories.

During this group, some women find that they have reached a new and perhaps deeper level of acceptance about their abuse experiences. They also may report that they have reconnected with some of the feelings associated with the abuse. This deeper understanding goes hand in hand with acknowledging the full truth about the abuse (feelings about bystanders, etc.) and gaining an appreciation of just how many of their experiences fell outside the normal range.

QUESTION 3

What do you hope to learn and/or talk about during the next part of the trauma group?

TYPICAL RESPONSES   How to cope better.
How to be in better control of myself.
How to accept myself.
How to get along with others.
How not to feel so bad.
How not to blame myself.
How to handle the flashbacks.
How to understand myself better.
I want to learn why the abuse happened.
How not to have it happen again.

Members will usually respond to this question by naming the skills they hope to develop. You should explain to the group that although there will be a discussion of skills, there also will be a focus on the impact trauma has had on relationships, lifestyle, and emotional well-being.

ADDITIONAL QUESTIONS

1. Has your behavior changed in any way as a result of the group?
2. Are you afraid of making changes in the process of recovery?
3. How do you think other people will respond to the changes you might make?

EXERCISE

Supply a road map for each member (see Appendix Item G). Members can complete the road map in approximately 10 minutes. Members should include successes, barriers, and important choices made in one's life (i.e., abuse, school, death of a loved one, marriage, pregnancies, employment, education, or illnesses). Members will present and explain their road maps to the group. A discussion should cover the following questions:

1. Where are they on the road now?
2. What obstacles might stop them from going forward?
3. Where would they like to be on the road a year from now?
4. What role has trauma played in the appearance of this road map?

REBECCA'S STORY

As much as anything else, this group has helped me see that I am not alone, and that has given me a sense of hope and possibility. Hope has been absent in my life for a very, very long time. I'm still afraid about what the recovery group sessions will bring up for me. It's just that I'm learning that I can begin to take control of my life and my emotions to a far greater extent than I had imagined possible. I don't want to become so upset that I go back to feeling the way I did, confused and anxious all the time. I no longer want to dignify the abuser by letting the abuse run my life. I hope it's possible for me to truly move on.

PART II

Trauma Recovery

TOPIC 12 Gaining an Understanding of Trauma

SESSION RATIONALE

Women who were abused as children may know that something bad happened to them but they may not have words to describe their experience. Abuse became the secret that no one talked about. This session begins the process of developing a shared vocabulary for discussing and understanding the impact of trauma.

GOAL 1: Each member will gain an understanding of what is meant by trauma and the role that trauma has played in her life.

GOAL 2: Each member will gain insight into the coping strategies that have helped her deal with the feelings associated with trauma.

QUESTIONS

1. Define trauma.
2. What are the feelings associated with trauma?
3. What events have caused intense fear for you?
4. When have you felt totally helpless?
5. When have you felt a loss of control?
6. When have you ever felt in danger of complete destruction?
7. How have you handled these feelings? List the strategies you have used to cope with the feelings of trauma. Now rank those strategies in order of effectiveness.

EXERCISE

Draw the feelings of trauma. Use shapes and colors. You may choose to make your drawing abstract or representational.

LEADERS' NOTES

QUESTION 1

Define trauma.

TYPICAL RESPONSES The destruction of self
Being attacked on your most basic beliefs
Having nightmares
Being overpowered
Being raped
Being beaten time and time again
Being called crazy for speaking out about trauma
Having mind games played on you

Women often confuse symptoms and the personal and interpersonal consequences of trauma with an actual definition of what trauma is. You will need to assist group members to distinguish between a definition of trauma and its resulting symptoms. You can focus the discussion by asking each member to remember a specific traumatic event.

DSM-IV defines trauma as the exposure to an extreme stressor involving direct personal experience of an event that involves actual or threatened death or serious injury, or threat to one's physical integrity; or witnessing an event that involves death, injury, or a threat to the physical integrity of another person; or learning about unexpected or violent death, serious harm, or threat of death or injury experienced by a family member or other close associate. The person's response to the event must involve intense fear, helplessness, or horror (or in children, the response must involve disorganized or agitated behavior).

The traumatic event can be experienced in various ways; recurrent and intrusive recollections of the event; recurrent and distressing dreams during which the event is replayed; dissociative states; intense physiological distress and reactivity; deliberate efforts to avoid thoughts, feelings, or conversations about the traumatic event; diminished interest or participation in previously enjoyed activities; feeling detached or estranged from others; reduced ability to feel emotions; a sense of a foreshortened future; difficulty falling or staying asleep; hypervigilance; exaggerated startle response; irritability or outbursts of anger; and difficulty concentrating or completing tasks. American

Psychiatric Association: *Diagnostic and Statistical Manual of Mental Disorders,* 4th ed. (Washington, D.C., American Psychiatric Association, 1994), p. 424.

You may wish to consult *DSM-IV* as a guide for defining Post-Traumatic Stress Disorder (PTSD) and its characteristic symptomatology.

QUESTION 2

What are the feelings associated with trauma?

TYPICAL RESPONSES

Devastation
Feeling ripped apart
Terror
Disgust
Being on edge
Helplessness
Loss of control
Feeling like I'm in a trance
Wandering through a fog
Being overwhelmed
Feeling like garbage
Guilt
Rage
Feeling dirty

Pain
Numbness
Intimidation
Suffering
Fearfulness
Wanting to die
Feeling trapped
Feeling like I'm
    gasping for air
Loss of self-respect
Shame
Voices telling me that
    I am bad

After compiling the above list, organize these responses under the following headings:

Intense fear
Helplessness
Loss of control
Threat of total destruction

Often, group members are much clearer about how trauma feels than about what trauma is. Members should be supported and, where appropriate, thanked for articulating their feelings.

QUESTION 3

What events have caused intense fear for you?

TYPICAL RESPONSES

Being left alone
Being raped
Being physically
    abused
Being abandoned
Being approached at a
    bus stop by a
    strange man
Hearing sounds in the
    night

Watching others get
    hurt
Holding a dangerous
    secret
Being yelled at
Being in a dark room
Being leered at by my
    minister. . . . I
    wasn't sure what
    he wanted

If members are ready to share memories, encourage them to do so. Ask group members, "Is there something specific you remember that scared you a great deal either as a child or during the recent past? Is there something of which you are currently scared or fearful?" Encourage members to be as specific as possible. Bear in mind that some of the responses may seem quite benign to women who do not have a history of abuse. Trauma predisposes women to be frightened easily and often.

QUESTION 4

When have you felt totally helpless?

TYPICAL RESPONSES

While I was being raped
When I was unfairly treated
When I was being abused by my parents
When I was abandoned
When my father beat me
When I was falsely accused of something
When I was threatened
When I watched my father beat my mother

When I became pregnant after a rape
When both my parents died
When my mother told me that I was evil
When I realized that my son was an abuser and I
was powerless to do anything

As mentioned under Question 3, encourage group members to be as specific as possible.

QUESTION 5

When have you ever felt a loss of control?

TYPICAL RESPONSES   When I was taken to a hospital against my will
When my mother allowed someone to abuse me
When I was beaten
Whenever I feel very angry or agitated about something
When I was forced to take medication
When I had to give up my baby
When my brother's friend would come over and rape me
When my mother would lock me in a room by myself every day
When I got so drunk I couldn't stand up
When I couldn't stop dieting
When I couldn't stop shaking my child
When I thought I would kill my lover for staying out late

Once again, assist group members to articulate specifics about when they have felt a loss of control. This question, more than the others, will elicit accounts of institutional abuse or abuse by caregivers outside the family. The question will also allow women to talk about their rage and their fears or experiences of being abusive toward others.

QUESTION 6

When have you felt in danger of complete destruction?

TYPICAL RESPONSES   When I was being beaten up
                      During those times when I felt so angry that I
                           wasn't sure what I was capable of doing
                      When I was put in a hospital against my will
                      When I was raped and I was not sure whether or not
                           I'd survive
                      When my sister died of AIDS and I was still shoot-
                           ing drugs
                      When I was suicidal

This question is most relevant for women who have felt overwhelmed by multiple sources of abuse.

Where appropriate, ask members if there are distinctions among those situations (as discussed during Questions 3, 4, 5, and 6) that made them feel helpless and out of control as opposed to fearful and in danger of destruction. The purpose of asking such a question is to discover whether members' responses are category specific. For example, you may ask "What aspect of being beaten, being raped, or being threatened made you feel helpless as opposed to feeling afraid?" By making the responses more differentiated and more specific, you can begin to suggest interventions that might lessen a woman's fear or her sense of powerlessness.

In some groups, members may not distinguish among feelings of fear, loss of control, helplessness, and personal destruction. Rather, they may lump these together as part of the constellation of despair and dysphoria left behind by trauma. When this happens, try not to push members to make what feels to them like artificial distinctions; instead adopt the language used by members to describe the feelings of trauma.

QUESTION 7

How have you handled these feelings? List the strategies you have used to cope with the feelings of trauma. Now rank them in order of effectiveness.

TYPICAL RESPONSES

Put the blame on myself	Pray
Try to be perfect	Go crazy
Accept my life circumstances	Fantasize
Drink or use drugs	Avoid sex
Engage in reckless behaviors	Mutilate myself
Shut people out and withdraw	Forget the past
Try to make sense of what has happened	Become promiscuous
Exercise	Keep a journal
Stop eating	Develop another personality
Got married so I could leave home	Space out
Gain weight to feel bigger and less vulnerable	Distract myself with other people, things, or activities
Try to guess what people want and then give it to them	

Make sure that members' responses represent a balance between positive and dysfunctional coping styles and behaviors. If members' responses are heavily slanted in one direction, prompt the discussion by contributing coping mechanisms that balance the list. For example, if members express only healthy ways to cope, balance the list by contributing examples that are dysfunctional in nature (e.g., use of drugs or alcohol, engaging in unsafe sex, overeating, etc.). When leaders contribute the negative strategies, members feel less shame in acknowledging the dysfunctional strategies on which they have relied.

Assist members in ranking the effectiveness of particular strategies. Group members may need some criteria for ranking (e.g., amount of time required, extent of risk, etc.).

ADDITIONAL QUESTIONS

1. Have you heard stories of trauma from other women in your family? How do you think those stories influenced your own experience?
2. How does trauma differ from other painful events in your life?

EXERCISE 1

Prepare for the Draw the Feelings of Trauma exercise by supplying paper, Magic Markers, and adequate table space for group members to draw. Members will be given approximately 10 minutes to complete their drawings. Explain to group members that they can use various shapes and colors to reflect their feelings about trauma. The picture can, but does not have to be, representational of their abuse experience. Members should be reminded that this is not a measure of artistic skill.

After group members complete their drawings, each woman will discuss her drawing with the group. Ask members to name the feeling they were trying to draw.

TYPICAL FEELINGS INCLUDE		
Isolation	Confusion
Uncertainty	Incompetence
Shame	Determination
Anger	Disappointment
Destructiveness	Pain
Sadness	Rage
Guilt	Panic
Feeling trapped	Disintegration
Voicelessness	

Sometimes, drawings are not focused specifically on feelings but rather they represent a response to certain feelings about past abuse experiences.

TYPICAL RESPONSES TO FEELINGS INCLUDE		
Reaching out to others	Spirituality
Character assassination	Manipulation
Oppression	Survival
Deception	Danger
Evil	Escape
Hopefulness	Gain a new identity

This exercise permits group members who have difficulty verbalizing their feelings to express themselves in an alternative manner. The following discussion assists women in relabeling feelings that may have been mislabeled in the past. This exercise allows women an opportunity to have their feelings about abuse heard and understood. Often a woman will reveal some deep and long-buried feeling during this exercise.

MAGGIE'S STORY

There was one woman in particular in the group I led, I'll call her Bobbie, who was confused and filled with rage. Bobbie had a long history of sexual, physical, emotional, and institutional abuse. When our group talked about what abuse was, Bobbie talked a lot. Bobbie said that when she was a kid, her chore was to wash the family dishes. The kitchen was in the back of a ramshackle house. As she stood washing the dishes, she could hear rats gnawing under the sink. Sometimes, one would actually run across her feet. She was frightened, but when she begged her father to do something about the rats, he refused. He told her he would beat the living daylights out of her if she did not finish the dishes. On the nights when she could not stand it and fled the kitchen, her father would tell her to go upstairs, undress, sit on her bed, and wait for her beating. One night, fed up with what he saw as Bobbie's defiance, her father told her he would beat her until she cried. The beating went on and on until her little sister could stand it no longer and called the police. Bobbie never did cry that night, not even in the ambulance on the way to the emergency room.

I sat there and listened to this story in a sunlit room with two other clinicians and a group of connected and caring women. Intellectually I could deal with this; it explained so much about Bobbie, but an interesting thing was happening. I could feel the muscles in my body tense. My body was telling me to lean over in my chair, to put my head between my knees to protect myself from fainting, to protect myself.

TOPIC 13   The Body Remembers What the Mind Forgets

SESSION RATIONALE

Survivors of trauma often feel very uncomfortable about their bodies and unable to read body cues; yet the body stores feelings and memories from the past. The session is designed to help women begin to appreciate how experiences of trauma have alienated them from their own bodies.

GOAL 1: Each member will begin to identify how her feelings toward her body are connected to her experiences of abuse.

GOAL 2: Each member will gain an understanding of how current physical pain and bodily distress may be connected to prior abuse.

QUESTIONS

1. Where do you feel stress in your body?
2. Have your trauma experiences affected the way you feel toward your body? Do you get angry at your body? Do you disconnect from your body?
3. Is there a connection between your trauma experiences and the way you feel in your body? If so, how do you understand it?
4. How do you carry (hold) your body?

EXERCISES

1. Leaders will show group members The Body Before Abuse, an outline of the female body. Leaders will ask members, "How is the body distorted after abuse?" In response to this question, members will draw an image of their own bodies after their abuse experiences. Group members will discuss their distorted body images.

2. Each group member is given a lump of clay and asked to mold it into a shape representing her body.

3. Leaders will begin the exercise by asking members to visualize a tree in winter. Leaders can assist by suggesting such adjectives as brittle, gnarled, closed down, and so on. Leaders ask members to imagine how the same tree looks in spring and summer as its leaves and buds burst forth and as its branches reach for the sun. Members will use their bodies to re-create the transformation of the tree. They will begin the exercise seated with their bodies in a constricted position; they will slowly rise and stretch out their arms in a gesture of expansion and openness. When they return to a normal posture, leaders will have the members discuss how they felt during the transformation.

LEADERS' NOTES

QUESTION 1

Where do you feel stress in your body?

TYPICAL RESPONSES		
	Tension in my shoulders	Vaginal pain
	My leg and feet muscles get tight	Chest pains
		Heart palpitations
	My neck	My throat gets tight
	Stomachaches and I get diarrhea	My back and shoulders
		Headaches
	In my mouth, I get cold sores	Physical ailments
		My skin starts to crawl
	In my breathing, I get short of breath	I'm always hungry
		On my scalp and then
	Voices in my head	my hair falls out

Almost everyone in the group will be able to readily identify the sore parts of her body. Keep the discussion focused so that it does not become merely a listing of somatic complaints.

QUESTION 2

Have your trauma experiences affected the way you feel toward your body? Do you get angry at your body? Do you disconnect from your body?

TYPICAL RESPONSES   I wish I didn't have a female body.
I feel betrayed by my body.
I think I have a weak body.
I hate my body.
I have no mirrors so I don't have to look at myself.
I never feel that I am thin enough.
I hate my body for always being sick and hurting.
I think I am anorexic because I want to look tough and mean.
I cut myself so that I will feel something.
I cut myself off from my body so I don't feel anything; I use drugs and alcohol to do it sometimes.
I think my body is unclean.

This discussion requires that members have the capacity to step back and think about their bodies. For a few moments, members must talk about their bodies as being separate from themselves. Members who are more concrete and literal in their thinking may have difficulty with this question. Leaders may assist members by giving examples of what it means to be angry with your own body. A woman who is mad at her body may fail to bathe or nurture herself properly. Her behavior serves as a way to punish her body.

QUESTION 3

Is there a connection between your trauma experiences and the way you feel in your body? If so, how do you understand it?

TYPICAL RESPONSES   I never made any connection.
Whenever I have an urgency to urinate, I flashback to when I was a child and how I would suffer in

terrible pain holding my urine through the entire
night because I wasn't allowed to get out of bed.

My father threatened me that if I woke him during
the night he would beat me.

I feel like I must always keep pain stuffed inside my
body and not tell anyone, just like when I was a
child and could not tell anyone about the abuse.

I feel I have to be perfect and can never be sick. . . .
When I was young, my mother told me that I'd
better not get sick because I was the one who
had to care for my family and the household.

As a child, I would get stomachaches anticipating
my father's arrival home from work knowing
that he would want sex from me. . . . Now as an
adult, I get stomachaches whenever I'm getting
ready to have sex with my partner.

My vagina hurts whenever I have (or think about
having) sex.

I think I have a worse period because the cramping
reminds me of being raped.

Once again, you may need to help members make the connection between current pain and past abuse. For some members making this connection produces a
genuine "aha" response. All of a sudden certain physical ailments make sense.
When this happens, a member may become flooded with feelings that have been
buried for many years. Be prepared to provide extra support as necessary.

QUESTION 4

How do you carry (hold) your body?

TYPICAL RESPONSES　　Hunched over.

I like to be covered up so others will not see my
body.

I wear oversize clothes to cover me.

I carry myself in a way that I wish I were invisible.

> Sunken in, then there is less of me to see.
> Defiantly.
> I restrict my movements.
> I flaunt my body.
> I try to be sexy.
> With lots of fat to protect me.

Because women experience so much discomfort both with and from their bodies, they often do not have difficulty recognizing that much of their body posture and language says stay away or I don't like myself. Women may begin speculating about why they hold themselves in such ways.

ADDITIONAL QUESTIONS

1. What kind of behaviors (rituals) do you use to help you cope with negative feelings about your body?
2. Was there any secret part of your body that was kept safe from the abuse?
3. Is there anyway your body helped you survive the abuse?

EXERCISE 1

Show group members an outline of the female form. Ask members, "How is the body distorted after abuse?" In response to this question, members will draw images of their own bodies after their abuse experiences. Supply members with paper and Magic Markers to complete this exercise. Group members will be given approximately 10 minutes to complete their drawings. Group members will explain their drawings to the group and should incorporate material they talked about earlier during Questions 1–4. Most often, a member's drawing of her body will reflect the following:

Powerlessness—a very small figure on the paper or other distortions in size

Destruction—a tattered body or a body lying down in a prone position

Nonexistence—various body parts missing

Shame—a shrouded body or body parts disproportionate in size

EXERCISE 2

Prepare for this exercise by purchasing art clay, commonly found in art stores or drugstores. Each group member will be given a large handful of clay. She will have approximately 10 to 15 minutes to mold a shape symbolizing her own body. Once each member has completed molding the clay, she will explain why that particular shape represents her body. You may need to prompt group members to discuss their feelings about the body sculptures.

EXERCISE 3

As women imagine themselves being a tree in transformation, they will experience their bodies and a range of bodily sensations. This exercise provides a nice complement to the rest of the session which is both more sedentary and intellectual in content. The exercise also allows women to have a more positive experience of their bodies and to acknowledge that their bodies can indeed change and blossom.

Leaders will want to choose either Exercise 1 or Exercise 2 and then follow with Exercise 3. Exercise 3 helps women to counter the feeling of being constricted and closed down.

NORA'S STORY

I always read this session over a few times before doing it with a new group of women. As I read it, I let images of the women in the group come up before my eyes; I visualize their posture from previous sessions. As I do this, I often notice something about a woman that I have missed. Then I can think about what I have just noticed in relation to the session. It is vital for me to have these images in my mind because most of the women have their trauma written all over their bodies.

No one tried to hide more than Sue, with so little success. Sue came hobbling into each session, moving slowly and leaning on her cane. The main picture Sue conveyed to the world was pain—intense, extreme, overburdening pain. I remember how she fumbled with items in her purse: dropping keys, cane, and glasses; fishing out a piece of paper; dropping that while reaching for the glasses she needed to read the paper. Her elbow jutted into another client, she pushed her cane with her foot while reaching for something and the cane fell over on another client's leg. It seemed as though Sue's pain was spreading, infecting everyone.

When I asked the group members where in their bodies they experienced stress, I hoped Sue would be quiet, but she was the first to speak. "I don't feel stress," she loudly announced, "I am not stressed out, but every part of my body hurts."

TOPIC 14 What Is Physical Abuse?

SESSION RATIONALE

Often women experience more than one type of abuse. Sexual and physical abuse, for example, are almost always accompanied by emotional abuse. Survivors often find it easier to begin their disclosure by talking about physical trauma, which although painful, carries less stigma than sexual abuse and is more immediately identifiable than emotional abuse.

GOAL 1: Each member will be able to define what constitutes physical abuse.

GOAL 2: Each member will gain an understanding of the impact that physical abuse has had on her life.

QUESTIONS

1. What do you think constitutes physical abuse?
2. What dynamics between the abuser and the victim tend to make it more likely that abuse will occur?
3. What role do threats and intimidation play in physical abuse?
4. What impact has physical abuse had on your life? On your relationships?

EXERCISE

Imagine that you could invent a magical recipe for healing the scars of abuse. What would you put in your prescription? Love? Revenge? Forgetfulness?

LEADERS' NOTES

QUESTION 1

What do you think constitutes physical abuse?

103

TYPICAL RESPONSES   Being beaten by my mother
                     Being hit over and over again
                     Getting hit by my partner
                     Getting disciplined with an electrical cord
                     Being hit with a bat or a belt
                     Getting hit until I bled
                     My brother being thrown across the room
                     Being burned
                     Being shaken as a small child
                     Being shot or stabbed
                     Being choked
                     Having my mouth washed out with soap
                     Being held down
                     Being locked in a closet
                     Being starved

Use the following as prompts if members have difficulty answering this question:

    Nature of the injury—What was done?
    Severity of the injury—How bad was the abuse?
    Public versus private—Did anyone other than the abuser and the victim
        know?
    Frequency of the abuse—How often did it occur?

This question often allows members to tell their own stories of physical abuse. Members also will combine stories of childhood abuse with more recent accounts of domestic violence.

QUESTION 2

What dynamics between the abuser and the victim tend to make it more likely that abuse will occur?

TYPICAL RESPONSES   The abuser has power over you.
                     The abuser is older or bigger.

The abuser is around a lot and has multiple opportunities to take advantage of you.

You feel very dependent on the abuser.

The abuser has power in the family (even if younger).

The abuser has control over money and resources.

The abuser drinks.

The abuser is more likely to be believed because of his position in the community.

Once again, if members have difficulty answering this question, you can use the following prompts to foster discussion:

Are the abuser and the victim intimates?

Family members?

Known to one another?

Are they hostile to one another?

Do they have equal power?

If members continue to cover the same material as in Question 1, feel free to move on to Question 3.

QUESTION 3

What role do threats and intimidation play in physical abuse?

TYPICAL RESPONSES   My abuser constantly put pressure on me or threatened me.

My mother always told me I was bad so I came to believe I deserved to be hit.

My husband would wear me down with his threats; that is when he beat me most.

I was told I was stupid and was punished until I felt worthless.

I was afraid someone else would be hurt if I told.

Threats made me afraid to tell anyone.

Help members to see that living in constant fear of being hit is a form of violence. Members may report that they actually felt relieved when the beating finally occurred, ending the tension associated with waiting.

Members will also begin to see that physical abuse rarely exists in isolation. It is frequently accompanied by emotional abuse in the form of threats and criticism. An abuser maintains power by keeping the victim in a state of constant fear.

QUESTION 4

What impact has physical abuse had on your life? On your relationships?

TYPICAL RESPONSES   I'm fearful about getting into a relationship. . . . I'm afraid I'll get hurt.

I am unable to trust another person.

I never believe those who say they care.

It's hard for me to express my anger because I'm afraid I'll be beaten for it.

When I hear a loud noise my body becomes rigid.

I have made a vow to myself never to spank my children.

I turn my anger and rage inward.

I feel like I need to take care of the other person to keep him happy.

I don't know what a good relationship is like.

I am afraid I will hit someone.

I feel numb.

I am determined to come out on top always.

I have come to expect to be hit; I don't even try to avoid it anymore.

I never thought I was being beaten; I always thought I was giving as good as I got. . . . I think hitting is part of every relationship.

I get depressed easily.

I don't take good care of myself.

I would kill someone who tried to hurt me.

The most apparent impact of physical abuse on survivors is their lack of trust and ongoing sense of fearfulness. You may want to help members see how low self-esteem, paranoia, and their own ragefulness also may be connected to a history of physical abuse.

Members often are able to be quite articulate about how abuse has affected their current functioning. They may feel stuck, however, when they try to think of how to change that impact. Make sure that members have some hope that their scars may eventually heal.

ADDITIONAL QUESTIONS

1. Have you had relationships in which there was no physical abuse? What was that like for you?
2. Do you know people who use physical abuse as a sexual turn on? Have you ever thought about that yourself?

EXERCISE 1

Ask members to develop a recipe for healing the scars of abuse. You can prompt members for this exercise by asking, "What ingredients would you put in the recipe?" As members develop the recipe, write the recipe on the flip chart. Often, members request that leaders make copies of this recipe for distribution during the next group.

TYPICAL RESPONSES   Tell the abuser how much they hurt you
Letting out the pain and anger with a good cry
Keeping physical distance from the abuser or abusive situation
The passage of time
Keeping emotional distance
Fantasizing about getting revenge
Taking care of myself
Talking and thinking about myself in a positive manner
Getting involved in a caring relationship
Acknowledging the abuse

Believing my version of the story
Knowing that I'm important, too
Spirituality
Creating my own family the way I want it to be
Self-assertiveness

Members generally find it easy to participate in this exercise. Even though they may have been unable to heal themselves, most women know what a healing formula might look like.

DARLENE'S STORY

When the leaders of the group asked us what we thought physical abuse was, I could almost feel myself shrinking. I never will forget the hitting when I was a child, but I wanted to deal with talking about it just like I dealt with it when I was little. I wanted to disappear, to get small, to not make a sound, to not be noticed.

So when the other women began talking about what physical abuse had been like for them I just folded into myself. It was a shock to hear my name; one of the group leaders had called on me. She asked me what the beatings had been like for me. It was strange—for once I didn't think I could just totally shut up, so I talked. My father beat me all the time. Every day someone in the house was beaten by my father. My mother too—he broke her bones and gave her lots of bruises. Sometimes when she thought he was going to go after her, she would meet him at the door of the house after work and immediately tell him how bad we had been that day. Then he would most likely start in on us and leave her alone. He broke my bones, I had bruises all up and down my arms and on my back—I wore long-sleeved clothes all the time, even on the hottest days. I learned to cover my face with my arms right away, as soon as I heard that tone in his voice—I didn't want anyone to see me with bruises on my face.

I learned to stay out of the way. I learned not to cry or make noise when he beat me because that made him madder—if I made noise. I learned silence.

TOPIC 15 What Is Sexual Abuse?

SESSION RATIONALE

Although they have experienced abuse personally, many survivors know little about the facts surrounding sexual abuse. Survivors sometimes tune out what information is available in the popular media, allowing themselves to remain naive and uninformed. Survivors need information to be able to label their experiences correctly. They also need to be able to place their personal experiences in a broader context, acknowledging the prevalence of abuse in the general population.

GOAL 1: Each member will be able to define what constitutes sexual abuse.

GOAL 2: Each member will gain an understanding of the emotional impact of abuse.

QUESTIONS

1. What acts constitute sexual abuse?
2. What are some of the tactics used by abusers?
3. What are the long-term emotional aftereffects of sexual abuse?
4. What are the emotional repercussions if sexual abuse is ongoing in a current relationship?

EXERCISE

Leaders will read a selection about sexual abuse from modern literature. Women will then discuss their responses.

LEADERS' NOTES

QUESTION 1

What acts constitute sexual abuse?

TYPICAL RESPONSES   Forced sex
Threatened, attempted forced sex
Unwanted oral, anal, vaginal penetration
Rape
Someone touching my body without my consent
Someone exposing his sexual body parts to me
Someone looking in my bedroom window
A parent having sex with her child
My mother giving me enemas every night
Being forced to watch sex
Being forced to masturbate while others watched
Being examined by my father so he could check to
see if my breasts were developing

How often does an act have to occur for it to be considered sexual abuse?

TYPICAL RESPONSES   Only once!
Usually ongoing.
Intermittent.
It happens and then you think you are safe and then
it happens again.

Members usually have no trouble naming the most extreme forms of abuse involving acts of penetration. They may be surprised, however, to learn that fondling and voyeurism also constitute abuse. You will need to help women draw accurate boundaries around the word *abuse*. It can be confusing either to draw the boundary too tightly and reserve the term *abuse* only for acts of rape or to draw it too loosely and include nuisance harassment and gender discrimination in the category of sexual abuse.

QUESTION 2

What are some of the tactics used by abusers? Make sure that force, violence, coercion, and intimidation are included. The discussion can be facilitated by asking questions such as:

- Must you be forced?
- What kinds of threats are there? Discuss how spoken and unspoken threats can be used.

TYPICAL RESPONSES

Force	Physical force
Intimidation	Manipulation
The abuser gave me no choice	Attacking my self-esteem
Isolation	Threats of violence or death
Bribes	
Educating me about life and sex	Giving me drugs and alcohol
Threat of losing something valuable to me if I don't submit	The abuser telling me that I don't have a right to say no
Psychological pressure	

This discussion of tactics often leads to women's recounting their actual abuse experiences. Some women may become angry or overwhelmed as they remember how they were forced or threatened to have sex. Women who felt that they complied with the abuser too willingly may feel guilty and ashamed as other women talk about brutal forms of coercion. Be sure to point out that some of the more subtle and manipulative tactics also are destructive.

QUESTION 3

What are the long-term emotional aftereffects of sexual abuse?

TYPICAL RESPONSES

Loss of trust

Feeling trapped

Feeling that no one will believe me

Thinking that no one likes me

Feeling disgusting and dirty

Feeling the need to protect others

Feeling that I need protection

Feeling different

Feeling nothing at all

Being scared to be close to anyone mentally or physically

Feeling uncomfortable with my sexuality

Feeling depressed

Feeling ashamed

Feeling suicidal

Feeling disrespected

Feeling angry and rageful

Having low self-esteem

Feeling alone and adrift

Losing hope

Feeling disconnected from others

Feeling like I don't have an identity

Feeling guilty about everything

Feeling unclear about my sexual identity

Women should not merely make a list of consequences but should think about the connection between past abuses and current feelings and behaviors. In a few cases, it might be useful to diagram behavior chains, specifying the steps that led from abuse to current dynamics. Help members distinguish between immediate effects, such as fear, and longer-term effects, such as difficulty forming relations, which may only become evident many years after the abuse occurred.

QUESTION 4

What are the emotional repercussions if sexual abuse is ongoing in a current relationship?

TYPICAL RESPONSES

I am unable to trust my abuser.

I am scared and fearful of my partner.

I am constantly bowing to the abuser's demands, trying to buy a little peace.

I am scared to leave him.

I start lying more to keep the secrets.

I am scared to stand up for myself.

I can't get perspective on what's going on.

I hate myself for staying in the relationship.

I become isolated because I'm so ashamed of the abuse and I don't want anyone to ask me questions.

I feel like I don't exist; I wish she didn't exist either.

I am always covering up for my abuser.

I feel guilty that I made him do it.

I want to kill her.

I even hate the good times because I know I'll have to pay for them later.

I pray for his death.

For many women, abuse is not merely a past event. They are currently involved in abusive relationships with romantic partners or family members. Any action to end those relationships must be preceded by an awareness of the emotional stresses caused by living with ongoing abuse. Leaders may be surprised at how many of the responses involve escape via a denial of one's very existence.

ADDITIONAL QUESTIONS

1. Did your feelings about the abuser vary over time? How did you reconcile conflicting feelings?
2. What was the most troubling or confusing aspect of the sexual abuse? Having a sexual response? Liking the abuser?
3. How might some of the painful feelings be transformed into positive coping strategies?

EXERCISE

Prepare for this exercise by choosing an abuse scene from modern literature. One suggestion is the rape scene from *I Know Why the Caged Bird Sings* by Maya Angelou, pp. 64–69.

Begin by reading the selected prose out loud to the group. The reading should take approximately 5 minutes but no longer than 10 minutes. Upon completion of the reading, group members will discuss their reactions to the story. Often, members are silent immediately after the reading as it reminds them of their own abuse experiences.

This reading enables members to get in touch with their own feelings and memories of their abuse experiences. Ask members, "How did it make you feel to hear this story? Does this cause you to remember things in your own life? Can you share your reaction to the story with the group?" Members may discuss common themes or feelings about their own experiences that parallel the story such as:

Not being believed about the abuse
A parent not protecting her or his child
The abuser making threats against people or possessions valued by the child
Feeling a need to protect other siblings
Being overwhelmed by feelings of fear, sadness, powerlessness, and shame

CARMEN'S STORY

My first suicide attempt was when I was 12 years old. I found a bottle of pills that belonged to my grandmother and took all of them. I didn't really want to die, but I was so down. Twelve years old and so very depressed! You see, I was carrying this burning secret inside of me.

My parents moved to Washington from Kentucky when I was four years old. They separated when I was nine. I would go to my father's house to visit and that's when it started. He touched me, fondled me, and raped me. He told me it was our little secret and I believed him. I never told my mother about what he did until many years later. She never protected me from his beatings, so I knew she wouldn't do anything about the sexual stuff.

I have such mixed feelings toward my father. I still love him even though he touched me like no father should ever touch his daughter. Am I twisted for still caring about him? On the other hand, I hate him for the craziness he brought into my life and my head. How could he have done those things to me? I was just a child! I didn'   t lose only my virginity to my father. I lost my sanity, too.

I feel especially crazy when my partner wants to have sex. I've never enjoyed sex and don't understand how other people can. When it's happening I find a crack on the wall to stare at until it's over. It makes me feel hollow and very, very alone.

TOPIC 16 Physical Safety

SESSION RATIONALE

To avoid the repeated victimization that characterizes the adult lives of many survivors of severe childhood abuse, women need practical assistance in learning how to keep themselves safe. Early in the recovery skills program, women often are unrealistic about how to live safely in the city. Denial, false bravado, or passive acceptance characterize their views of the possibility of future injury. After several months of group work, women are better able to learn how to take care of themselves. Self-esteem has been enhanced and women believe that they have the right to be safe. It is also important for women to see how the same bodies that they believed once betrayed them can now be transformed to help keep them safe.

Leaders should remember, however, that even with the best precautions, no one is ever totally immune from random violence. Women need to be clear with themselves about how safe they can realistically expect to be.

GOAL 1: Each member will begin to understand that an element of physical safety is being aware of one's self in one's environment.

GOAL 2: Each member will begin to develop some strategies for self-protection.

QUESTIONS

1. What constitutes a physically dangerous situation?
2. Have you ever felt in danger when you were alone? What were you afraid of?
3. How do you protect yourself from danger?

EXERCISE

Group leaders will either direct or bring in assistants who can lead basic self-defense exercises. This experience should be both practical—focusing on how to walk, how to respond, and so forth—and symbolically healing, allowing women to use their bodies as agents of self-defense.

LEADERS' NOTES

QUESTION 1

What constitutes a physically dangerous situation?

TYPICAL RESPONSES   Going out alone at night.
Going out to a dangerous area.
Waiting for the bus and encountering a stranger.
Keeping your doors and windows unlocked.
A stray dog snarling at you.
Being alone in an isolated area.
Being around an abusive person.
Witnessing an abuser attack someone or something else.
Being at a family gathering with an ex-abuser.
Being too high to know what's going on.
Getting cash from the bank machine after dark, I'm afraid I'll be followed and robbed.

Women often get into a discussion of how to balance their safety concerns with a desire not to live a life dominated by fear.

QUESTION 2

Have you ever felt in danger when you were alone? What were you afraid of?

TYPICAL RESPONSES   I'm afraid to walk into my apartment without the lights on.
When I walk home from the grocery store carrying my grocery bags, I feel more vulnerable.
When I am alone and waiting for the bus, I am afraid someone will attack me.

When I'm at home alone and I hear noises, I'm
afraid someone has broken in.
When I sleep in a totally dark room.

You may need to help women distinguish between realistic and irrational fears.
Members also may become aware of how certain present dangers are reminiscent of past situations in which abuse occurred. Members are helped by being
able to distinguish how past and present situations are similar and more importantly, how they are different.

QUESTION 3

How do you protect yourself from danger?

TYPICAL RESPONSES   Keep a light on in your apartment so you don't enter
in the dark.
Have your keys ready when you need to use them.
Avoid deserted locations.
Walk with confidence and know where you're
going.
Carry pepper spray or an alarm.
Either carry your purse under your coat or don't
carry a purse.
Walk in the street rather than on an isolated side-
walk, especially if it is bordered by bushes.
Don't engage someone trying to provoke you.
Increase your visibility.
Don't take shortcuts in isolated areas.
Don't look like an easy target.
Plan ahead.
Keep a heightened sense of awareness around you.
Don't lie to yourself; see the situation for what it
is—be realistic.
Don't interact with known abusers or dangerous
people.

Trust your instincts.
Exercise caution and go slowly in new relationships.
Pay more rent to live in a better neighborhood.
Carry a weapon.
Own a big dog.
Have a tough companion.
Take a self-defense class.

You will want to assist members in distinguishing between practical techniques for self-defense, (e.g., pepper spray) and more intrapsychic skills (e.g., don't lie to yourself about what you feel or see). The latter are internal changes that help women to become more self-aware and self-confident in general.

ADDITIONAL QUESTIONS

1. Can some self-defense strategies backfire? How might this happen?
2. How do you deal with ongoing vulnerability even after you have done everything in your power to stay safe?

EXERCISE 1

In the absence of a self-defense expert, leaders can have members practice how they might carry their bodies in a less vulnerable way. Members also can share other recommended safety precautions with each other. Just the act of walking across a room with her head held up can feel empowering for a woman who has been looking down most of her life. As women practice carrying their bodies in more assertive ways, they can share how they feel with one another.

CLAUDIA'S STORY

When the group leaders announced that we were going to discuss physical safety, I thought why should I think about physical safety? I live my life on my own terms. If I want to go out in the middle of the night, I do it. If I want to walk alone in the dark, I do it. Why should I be afraid of anyone? As a kid, I lived my life always being afraid and having to fend for myself. Back then, I was never safe. I decided that after I left home, nobody would ever make me feel afraid or unsafe again.

This session was really hard for me. If I admit that I need to be safe, it must mean that I am vulnerable, not in control, and that someone might hurt me. No one will ever hurt me again. I am too tough to get hurt again. Some of the other group members said that no one ever can be 100 percent in control. It was difficult for me to hear that from other group members. If they feel that way, should I?

Some of the other group members mentioned ways they try to keep themselves safe, such as avoiding dangerous places or never going out alone after dark. I guess the question for me is, "Why don't I feel like I need to worry about safety when others do?" Am I fooling myself?

TOPIC 17 What Is Emotional Abuse?

SESSION RATIONALE

Survivors of physical and sexual abuse inevitably also suffer the scars of emotional abuse. However, emotional traumas are so much a part of everyday life that they often go unnoticed. These emotional abuses contribute to a damaged and distorted sense of self in adulthood.

GOAL 1: Women will recognize and accurately label emotional abuse.

GOAL 2: Women will begin to appreciate that emotional abuse may have a lifelong impact.

QUESTIONS

1. What is emotional abuse?
2. What strategies did you use to escape the abuse?
3. What impact do you think this abuse has had on your adult functioning?

EXERCISE

Women are asked to think about words or phrases used by abusers that were emotionally abusive. Leaders will ask members to write down a phrase that they would like erased from the English language. Members will discuss their choices and will symbolically destroy the phrases by shredding the paper.

LEADERS' NOTES

QUESTION 1

What is emotional abuse?

TYPICAL RESPONSES
Being neglected by my parents.
Never being given any attention by my mother.
Having parents who didn't interact or talk with me.
Being criticized all the time.
Being constantly compared to my siblings and never measuring up.
Having mind games played on me.
Constantly being given mixed messages by someone.
My mother's telling me "You'd be better off dead."
My dad's always wanting to control me.
My boyfriend's threatening me all the time.
Family members always telling me that I'm dumb or crazy.
Being given too much responsibility: I was raising my siblings when I was 12 years old.
Being called names.
Never being allowed to have a childhood.
Being made to feel ashamed all the time.
Being told I was not wanted.

Make sure that the following areas are included in members' responses:

Neglect
Abandonment
Deprivation
Dysfunctional parents
    due to alcoholism,
    depression, or mental illness

Isolation
Role reversals—parentified child
Severe criticism
Shaming
Manipulation
Extreme control
Witnessing the abuse of others

Several conditions are necessary but not sufficient for emotional abuse to occur: (1) a woman depends on the abuser for affection or practical support; (2) a woman feels trapped in the relationship; and (3) the abuser wields power, authority, and control. A discussion of the dynamics of emotional abuse can be aided by asking members about specific relationships (e.g., with parents, with adult children, with domestic partners, or with bosses).

QUESTION 2

What strategies did you use to escape the abuse?

TYPICAL RESPONSES I was always trying to please.
I tried to be perfect.
I withdrew from everyone.
I started using drugs.
I tried to get attention from other people.
I fantasized a lot of the time.
I ran away from home.
I got into a lot of fights with my family because I
    was so angry.
I ignored it.
I was very good and obedient.
I started having boyfriends when I was very young
    so I could be out all the time.
I joined a cult.
I did not try to escape and now I hate myself for it.
I went to my neighbor's house all the time.
I stayed late at school.
I stuffed the feelings down by eating all the time.

The term *escape* may suggest unhealthy ways of coping with the abuse. If members only mention negative strategies, you can ask members if they know of any more positive ways of handling emotional abuse.

QUESTION 3

What impact do you think this abuse has had on your adult functioning?

TYPICAL RESPONSES I have very poor self-esteem.
I feel out of control.
I'm hopeless.
I don't trust anyone so it's hard to have a relation-
    ship.
I don't trust myself.

I'm always angry.
I usually assume the worst.
I withdraw.
I know I have a pretty poor attitude about my life.
I'm depressed.
I have a weight problem.
I still try to please everyone.
I am never satisfied with myself.
I'm afraid to speak my mind or disagree with any-
one.
I'm more critical than I would like to be.

Prompt members by asking about the impact of emotional abuse on self-esteem, relationships, success, ability to experience pleasure, and day-to-day functioning.

ADDITIONAL QUESTIONS

1. Do you think you were forced to grow up ahead of your time? Describe what that was like.
2. How can you recognize emotional abuse in current relationships? Think about current relationships. Are there some about which you feel uneasy? What is happening in those relationships?
3. How do you respond to criticism as an adult?

EXERCISE

Ask members to think of abusive comments directed toward them as children. Anything that made them feel bad, inferior, or threatened can be included. Members should write the phrase on a piece of paper and discuss the comment with the group. Members will shred the piece of paper to symbolically eliminate the phrase from the English language.

TYPICAL RESPONSES　　You should never have been born.
You're just like your father, the rotten SOB.
You'll never amount to anything.

> If you do that one more time, you can go live out on
>   the streets.
> Keep that up and you'll never go to college.
> You are ugly and stupid.
> You are evil because you're so black.

It is useful for members to see that many of the abusive comments were either irrational criticisms or things over which they could not possibly have had any control.

FELICIA'S STORY

For me emotional abuse meant losing my childhood. I had to act like an adult even when I was a child.

I was the oldest in the family. I always had to do a lot for my mom. There were so many chores around the house. And then there were the younger kids. Mom was busy so I did most of the feeding and diapering and washing all of their dirty clothes. Lots of the time I had to miss school or stay up late to get everything done. Mom always said what a great little helper I was. I didn't feel like a helper, I felt like a mom. I can't remember a time when I wasn't taking care of somebody. My mom put so much pressure on me to be grown-up.

I never got taken care of when I was little; I always had to be the one taking care of others. Even when the family did something fun like go to the carnival, I had to be in charge; I had to be sure no one got lost. It wasn't any fun feeling responsible for everything.

When I left home, I started taking up with guys who I thought would watch out for me, but it never worked out. I always ended up with someone to take care of, someone who needed help more than I did. I got fed up with it and decided to stay away from people. Now I won't ask for help from anybody. I feel like I always have to be on my own. It makes my recovery really hard. You can't see the scars from the emotional abuse, but I feel them all the time.

TOPIC 18 Institutional Abuse

SESSION RATIONALE

Members who have been abused by service providers feel a sense of betrayal and powerlessness. Abuses on the part of helpers or people in authority become the little secrets that haunt the relationship between client and clinician. If openness and honesty are indeed to mark recovery from trauma, clinicians must be willing to own their role in revictimization. Clients must be permitted to name *all* the abusers and to feel safe in doing so.

GOAL 1: Women will recognize that even would-be helpers can be abusers.

GOAL 2: Women will be given support for making what often are judged by others to be unbelievable accusations.

QUESTIONS

1. What helpers or people in authority in your life have abused you?
2. Did you try to tell someone about the abuse? What happened? If you did not tell, why not?
3. What are the specific abuses of the mental health system?

EXERCISE

Group members will design their own emergency protocol. Members will be asked to imagine that they are feeling out of control, and they ask a friend to help. Each woman is asked to design her own protocol, detailing how she would like to be treated. What techniques will help calm her down? What will she find soothing? What should friends or outside helpers not attempt? What will feel abusive?

LEADERS' NOTES

QUESTION 1

What helpers or people in authority have turned into abusers?

TYPICAL RESPONSES

Minister	Prison guard
Police officer	Psychologist
Hospital staff person	Church officials
Social worker	My boss
Apartment manager	Nurse
Doctor	Psychiatrist
Baby-sitter	School bus driver
Teacher	Substance abuse
Halfway house director	counselor

Encourage members to think beyond some of the obvious answers. This question does not merely generate a list of abusers; women often use this as an occasion to tell their stories of abuse. Some women may relabel past experiences as actually being traumatic and abusive when in the past those same events were merely thought to be annoying or mildly upsetting.

QUESTION 2

Did you try to tell someone about the abuse? What happened?

TYPICAL RESPONSES   I tried to report it but school officials thought I was hysterical and wouldn't take me seriously.
The police would not believe me and wanted to arrest me instead of the abuser.
I tried to tell my doctor but he just gave me medication.
My peers got angry because after I reported the abuse our shop teacher was transferred.
When I tried to tell, they changed the rules.
When I told, I lost my job.

If you did not tell, why not?

TYPICAL RESPONSES   I believed I would need a lot of proof and that no
                    one would believe me.

I didn't think anyone would think I was credible.

I didn't tell my mother that the teacher hit me
because I was afraid my mother would hit me
even more.

Everyone loved our minister and I thought they
would think I was lying to get attention.

Because my coach was a woman, I thought people
would think she couldn't molest me.

This question often generates much discussion about stigma and a lack of empowerment. Women who have limited resources, emotional problems, or substance addictions, and/or women members of a minority group, may feel that their reports of abuse carry less weight than those made by other women. Consequently, they may be especially reluctant to report even gross misconduct on the part of caregivers and authority figures. This question may lead to a more general discussion of empowerment. The question also may raise the issue of client credibility for the group leaders. If leaders believe that abuse by a caregiver is ongoing they should be prepared with a plan for reporting the abuse.

QUESTION 3

What are the specific abuses of the mental health system?

TYPICAL RESPONSES   Having my confidentiality violated
Being overmedicated
Being put in restraints
Being hit by a staff person
Having no part in decisions affecting my treatment
Being treated like a child
Having staff make sexual advances toward me
Being controlled and criticized
Being treated like an object, not an individual
Being threatened by staff

Being ridiculed and put down
Having my privacy violated
Having my visits denied for minor violations
Having helpers suggest that I was to blame for the
    abuse

This question may pose special problems for group leaders as they find themselves becoming part of the problem. Help members to distinguish between genuinely abusive behaviors by service providers and the inevitable annoyances of being on the receiving end of services (e.g., waiting in line). A distinction also needs to be made between abusive behaviors and nontherapeutic but not necessarily abusive actions. You should not be in the position of deciding what is genuine abuse and what is not. The purpose of this question is to acknowledge that abuse by caregivers *does* occur and sometimes the behavior may fall into a gray area.

ADDITIONAL QUESTIONS

1. What are some of the different tactics used by various groups of abusers?
2. How has the abuse changed your pattern of service use?
3. What factors influence whether the victim of institutional abuse is believed?
4. How is institutional abuse similar to or different from family abuse?

EXERCISE 1

You should be clear that this exercise is designed to help women think about what works to calm them down. Women will feel empowered by thinking about and designing their own protocols; yet this exercise will not necessarily produce protocols that can be used by treating

CATHY'S STORY

Institutional abuse. This session causes me more anxiety than any other and requires a different kind of preparation. I have to prepare to hear stories of abuse at the hands of care providers. I will be seen as the villain by some of the women in the group because of my association in the mental health system; I have to prepare to listen without judgment or defensiveness. This session is for the women, so they can feel validated. To those in the group who have experienced abuse within the mental health system, I must apologize. I cannot defend colleagues who have used their positions to perpetrate abuse. It is important for the group members to know that at least one person in that system believes them and believes that what was done to them was in fact wrong and abusive.

TOPIC 19 Abuse and Psychological or Emotional Symptoms

SESSION RATIONALE

To understand fully the impact trauma has had on their lives, women need to see the possible link between current problematic feelings and behaviors and early or ongoing adult experiences of abuse. In many cases, what are now labeled as symptoms were either responses to trauma or else a child's strategy for coping with trauma. The session is appropriate even for women who have never been formally diagnosed as having psychological or emotional problems because of the prevalence of subacute emotional and psychological distress among trauma survivors.

GOAL 1: Each member will begin to explore the possible link between past abuses and intense feelings or dysfunctional behaviors.

GOAL 2: Members will consider that currently labeled symptoms may have developed originally as responses to trauma.

QUESTIONS

1. Name some emotional or psychological symptoms you have experienced.
2. What abuse do you think caused or continues to cause these symptoms?
3. How could these same symptoms have been reasonable or coping responses to the abuse?

EXERCISE

Leaders will use the list generated at the beginning of the session to create a set of Symptom Cards. Each card will list one of the symptoms. Leaders will place all the cards in a container and pass the container around the group asking each woman to select a card. If the woman has experienced the symptom, she will keep the card, otherwise she will select another card. Women will continue passing the container until all cards are selected. Women may choose to discuss their selections.

At the end, women are asked to select either those symptoms they *feel ready* to get rid of or those symptoms they would *like* to discard but do not yet feel ready to relinquish. The cards bearing those words are then destroyed in a ritual ceremony. Once again, women will have the opportunity to discuss the choice to save or discard particular symptoms.

LEADERS' NOTES

Select five behaviors or feelings from the list generated in Question 1. Then ask Questions 2 and 3 in order and fill in the Understanding Abuse chart as you go along. When completed, the chart illustrates a possible connection linking abuse, the attempt to cope, and eventual symptom formation.

QUESTION 1

Name the emotional or psychological symptoms you have experienced.

The discussion will begin with members' generating a list of emotional and psychological problems they have experienced. Make sure the list includes *some* of the following:

TYPICAL RESPONSES		
	Excessive crying	Uncontrollable rage
	Anxiety	Hypervigilance
	Dissociation	Memory loss
	Panic attacks	Isolation
	Eating disorders	Agoraphobia
	Self-mutilation	Mania
	Sleep disturbances	Abandonment issues
	Low self-esteem	Mistrust or paranoia
	Substance abuse	Flashbacks
	Delusions	All or nothing thinking
	Hallucinations	Depression
	Suicidality	Perfectionism

QUESTION 2

What abuse do you think caused or continues to cause these symptoms?

QUESTION 3

How could these same symptoms have been reasonable or coping responses to the abuse?

The answers to these questions are used to help complete the Understanding Abuse chart. The chart helps group members understand the connection between trauma and coping strategies previously labeled as emotional or psychological symptoms. Leaders should return to the member who gave a particular symptom to obtain the corresponding answers to Questions 2 and 3.

UNDERSTANDING ABUSE
TYPICAL RESPONSES

SYMPTOMS (From Question 1)	ABUSE (From Question 2)	HOW THIS DEVELOPED AS A COPING STRATEGY OR AS A REASONABLE RESPONSE (From Question 3)
Dissociation	My father having sex with me	To escape and survive the abuse
Perfectionism and the need to please	Being sent to a youth facility because my mother thought I was out of control and she could "throw me away"	To survive and to stay with my family
Paranoia	My family always protecting and covering up for the abuser	To look out and protect myself because I couldn't trust anyone else to help me

UNDERSTANDING ABUSE: TYPICAL RESPONSES *(continued)*

SYMPTOMS (From Question 1)	ABUSE (From Question 2)	HOW THIS DEVELOPED AS A COPING STRATEGY OR AS A REASONABLE RESPONSE (From Question 3)
Anxiety	Waiting for my father to get home and beat me	To be alert so I could run
		To brace myself for the inevitable
Depression	Being told I was evil again and again	I felt so hopeless and desperate

Group members may need some assistance to see how these behaviors or feelings might have begun as coping strategies. Once a member sees the connection, however, it is a true aha experience. All of a sudden behaviors make sense. Symptoms that are understood as coping strategies feel less alien and out of the member's control. When a woman feels that she controls her emotions and behaviors rather than being controlled by them, she is in a better position to dispense with unwanted behaviors and reactions.

ADDITIONAL QUESTIONS

1. What might be the consequences of relinquishing a particular symptom?
2. Are there additional coping strategies that might be less painful or destructive?

EXERCISE

Make sure that enough symptom cards are generated so that each member can choose two or three cards. If two members both want the same card, be prepared to make a duplicate. The cards may be destroyed by tearing, burning, or crumpling.

SUSAN'S STORY

When I was 13, I told my mother that my father was having sex with me. She did not appear distressed with this but sat me down and fixed me some kind of tea. When I asked her what it was, she said it would make me forget what my father was doing to me. It didn't, and my father, and then my brother, continued to abuse me. I thought I was crazy because it bothered me and no one else seemed to think it was a problem. I began having scary dreams—even in the daytime, when I was awake. I dropped out of school because I couldn't concentrate or control my temper.

When I was 14, I really lost control. Finally, I was admitted to a mental hospital. I began to hallucinate, I was paranoid and trusted no one; I alternated between being deeply depressed and bouncing off the walls. My mother continued to say that she was worried about me and couldn't understand why I was behaving the way I was.

Now this group is telling me that I'm not crazy and probably never have been. You're saying that my hallucinations and nerves were because I was abused by my family? On one hand, I'm relieved; I have a reason for what has happened to me. It also makes me very angry and sad. I have lost 20 years of my life because my family would rather have had me crazy then to admit that my father and brother raped me. I feel betrayed by all the doctors and therapists who kept finding more and more things wrong with me. All those symptoms felt like so many accusations. It's going to take me awhile to really believe that I'm not some crazy lady.

TOPIC 20 Trauma and Addictive
or Compulsive Behavior

SESSION RATIONALE

Frequently, compulsive behaviors, emotional distress, and trauma recovery are seen as separate issues and women receive treatment from separate systems for each of these problems. An integrated approach to recovery and skill development demands that survivors be helped to see addictions as dysfunctional coping mechanisms tied directly to past, current, and future trauma.

GOAL 1: Group members will begin to see connections between their own compulsive behaviors and their histories of sexual and physical abuse.

GOAL 2: Group members will begin to see how their excessive dependence on drugs, alcohol, food, sex, and so on may be a form of self-abuse.

QUESTIONS

1. Do you have behaviors that could be considered compulsive or addictive? What are they?
2. When did you first engage in these compulsive or addictive behaviors? What purpose have these behaviors served?
3. What kind of relationship do you have with your compulsion? Adversarial? Friendly? Loving?
4. How has your addiction or compulsion been a form of self-abuse? What has it cost you?

EXERCISE

Leaders will ask members to follow them in a quiet, relaxing exercise. The exercise should be one that members can use in their private lives as a soothing gesture or as a means to center oneself against compulsive habits.

LEADERS' NOTES

QUESTION 1

Do you have behaviors that could be considered compulsive or addictive? What are they?

TYPICAL RESPONSES

Hypersexuality	Cutting myself
Overeating	Exercising
Hoarding	Lying
Shopping	Stealing
Masturbating	Praying
Cleaning	Playing video games
List making	Hand washing
Drinking or drugging	Hair pulling
Gambling	Checking and recheck-
Smoking	ing the appliances

You may need to begin by defining compulsive behaviors. A compulsion is not merely a habit; it is a behavior that seems out of one's control—a behavior so powerful it seems to rule one's life. A woman may engage in more than one compulsive behavior at a time and even women who have used drugs and alcohol may recognize that they also engage in other compulsive behaviors. It is useful for members to see that all compulsions serve similar purposes and have similar characteristics.

QUESTION 2

When did you first engage in these compulsive or addictive behaviors? What purpose have these behaviors served?

TYPICAL RESPONSES My father taught me to keep everything . . . he wouldn't allow me to waste anything or else I suffered the consequences; that's how I started hoarding.
I scratch myself so I can feel alive.

> I thought that as long as I was skinny no one would see me as a sex object.
>
> When I cleaned my room at home, I felt in control.
>
> My father injected me with heroin while he was abusing me; that was the beginning of my addiction.
>
> I started shopping in high school because it made me feel clean and pretty again.
>
> When I cried as a baby, my parents gave me alcohol to quiet me.
>
> Watching the TV was a way to escape.
>
> I shop to keep busy so I won't have to think.
>
> Whenever I felt bad about myself I would gorge on sweets and then force myself to throw up.

You may want to use this discussion to allow women to retell their trauma stories. Some women may be able to make creative connections between their trauma experiences and their addictions. You will want to steer women away from connections that seem too facile or superficial.

QUESTION 3

What kind of relationship do you have with your compulsion? Adversarial? Friendly? Loving?

TYPICAL RESPONSES
> When everyone else let me down, I could turn to my drugs and beer.
>
> Cleaning felt like the only thing I had control of in my life. Now I know that wasn't true.
>
> I never felt lonely when I was shopping.
>
> Drugs were the only friend that never let me down.
>
> The gambling became a trap I couldn't escape.
>
> I felt good when I was eating but my problems were still there when I was done.
>
> The drug let me down; it gave me false hope.

> I felt secure when I had a lot of things.
> I felt the exercising would save me.
> I hated the cigarettes even though I craved them.
> I felt like I was married to cocaine.

Women may be surprised to realize just how important their compulsions have been to their survival. In many cases these behaviors have become more than just a way to block out pain; they can be a way to feel normal or even become a woman's best companion.

QUESTION 4

How has your addiction or compulsion been a form of self-abuse? What has it cost you?

TYPICAL RESPONSES
> Using drugs cost me my kids . . . CPS took them away from me.
> I'm HIV positive from having so many sex partners.
> I lost my home.
> I went to jail for possession of cocaine.
> I lost my self-respect.
> I've spent so much money on shopping I have nothing to show for myself.
> My boyfriend dumped me because I was using.
> My family won't let me come in the house.
> I actually dropped out of school because I was too busy cleaning.
> I gained so much weight that I couldn't even go out anymore.
> My family lost respect for me.
> My self-esteem went way down.
> I can't have friends over because of the clutter.
> I lost my car due to a gambling debt.
> I have never really had a serious relationship.
> I got lung cancer from smoking.

> I'm ashamed to wear a bathing suit because of the
> cuts on my body.

As women recall what they have lost, they may begin to feel emotions that have been suppressed for years. Some will feel great sadness. Others will feel enraged at perpetrators, at circumstances, or at themselves. You should allow women to feel their feelings and then direct the conversation toward how one can move beyond the pain toward genuine recovery.

Additional Questions

1. How do family and friends respond to your compulsive behavior?
2. Did you ever try to stop the behavior? How did you feel?

Exercise

Ask members to focus on their bodies and to assess how they feel in their chairs. Then begin to guide group members verbally through a body awareness exercise by asking the following questions:

- Can you feel the weight of your thighs and hips against the chair?
- Are your feet flat and relaxed against the floor or tucked under your chair? Is there a different sensation in each position?
- Do you feel the weight of your arms as they hang down by the side of your body or when they are resting in your lap?
- Do your shoulders feel relaxed? Imagine the weight of your arms relaxing your shoulders.
- Now, focus on your head, does it feel heavy? Does it float effortlessly on your spine? Imagine your spine like a flower growing, reaching toward the sun and your head like the bud of the flower blooming and responding.
- Now, focus your attention deeper within yourself. With eyes lowered or closed, take time to listen and to tune in to your body. Focus on your breathing. We are always breathing and it changes depending on our activity. How does your breathing feel now? Breathe in until the count of three then breathe out to the count of three. Inhale then exhale. How does your breathing feel to you? Is it short or long, jagged or smooth, shallow or deep, easy or hard? Does your breath feel nourishing?

You can choose to fall silent while the group breathes on its own. Women may react by yawning or needing to shift or stretch. Continue the breathing exercise by asking the following questions:

- Which areas of your body do you feel as you inhale and as you exhale?
- Are you aware of your nose, neck, chest? Is your chest rising and falling? Does your stomach extend? How does your breath and breathing spread through your body?

Complete the exercise by leading the women in several deep inhales and exhales. Members will inhale holding their breath to a count of three, then release their breath through an exhale at which time they will stand and stretch their bodies.

LINDA'S STORY

I left home when I was 13 to get away from my mother's boyfriend who was sexually abusing me. I lived on the street for awhile until I met a man who took me in. He was 15 years older than me, and he took care of me. He made money dealing drugs, and he turned me on. I guess he got tired of me because after a few years he made me start prostituting for him. I stayed with him because I needed him, he took care of me, and he gave me drugs when I needed them. Yeah, he would beat me sometimes, but he took care of me. Eventually, he got someone new and kicked me out. Then I was on my own with no place to live, and no drugs. So, I kept prostituting for drugs and money. Sure I got abused sometimes, but that goes with the territory.

The worse things got, the more I would do drugs, so the more I had to prostitute. I was stuck in this cycle until I got arrested. I was court ordered into a long-term drug treatment center, and I got the chance to turn my life around. I've been clean for three years now, and I'm getting to know myself. I even like myself most days.

TOPIC 21   Abuse and Relationships

SESSION RATIONALE

Women often have difficulty balancing the need for love and connection with a healthy sense of self-love and self-care. Often women believe that any relationship, regardless of how abusive, is better than no relationship at all. If women are to avoid revictimization, they must seriously question what price they are willing to pay for a relationship. Some women who have decided that the cost is too great opt for no relationship as a way to stay safe.

GOAL 1: Group members will identify those interpersonal patterns that are hurtful and abusive and those that are healthy and supportive.

GOAL 2: Group members will begin to see how past abuses might be related to their current ability to form and maintain relationships.

QUESTIONS

1. What constitutes a healthy relationship? What constitutes an unhealthy relationship?
2. What part do manipulation, intimidation, aggression, and domination play in your current relationships? Give an example of the following in a current relationship: *(a)* Manipulation *(b)* Intimidation *(c)* Aggression *(d)* Domination.
3. What are the normal ups and downs that characterize any healthy relationship? How can you tell if you are settling for more strife and heartache than you need to?
4. What has your relationship pattern been and how is it related to your abuse history?
5. Have there been times when you were abusive or destructive in a relationship? Do you know why you behaved the way you did?

EXERCISE

Women are asked to imagine that they want to influence the behavior of another.
The only strategy they are prohibited from using is direct communication. Each
woman should tell what methods she would use to influence the other. Women
should discuss the advantages and potential disadvantages of each strategy.

LEADERS' NOTES

QUESTION 1

What constitutes a healthy relationship? What constitutes an unhealthy relationship?

TYPICAL RESPONSES

Healthy Relationship

Trust	Self-respect
Comfort with the other person	Acceptance
	Reliability
Closeness	Communication
Respect	Mutual admiration
Openness	Mutuality
You feel good about yourself	Security
	Having fun together
Shared goals or interest	Mutual attraction
Getting something good or valuable out of it	
Emotional support	

Unhealthy Relationship

Intrusiveness	Violence
No boundaries	Controlling behavior
Disrespect	Lack of trust
Too much criticism	Too judgmental

Overdependence	No communication
Suffocating closeness	Overly jealous
Both too immature	Fear of partner
Too much drinking	Unfaithfulness

Despite their often unsatisfying relationships, women trauma survivors remain both invested in or intrigued by relationships. Most women have a lot to say about what constitutes both a healthy and an unhealthy relationship even though their experience may have been only with the latter.

QUESTION 2

What part do manipulation, intimidation, aggression, and domination play in your current relationships? Give an example of the following in a current relationship: *(a)* Manipulation *(b)* Intimidation *(c)* Aggression *(d)* Domination

TYPICAL RESPONSES

Manipulation

Playing emotional blackmail

Being sneaky to get something I want

Using me for her own gain

Playing guilt trips on me

Doing or saying things to keep my partner hooked in the relationship

A date buying dinner for me and then expecting sex later

Lying

Giving me drugs so I'll do what he wants

Silence

Withholding sex

Intimidation

Threatening to leave if she won't agree with me or do what I want

Being a bully

Threatening to tell my secrets if I don't do what he wants

Threatening to hurt me or my children
Stalking
Being forced to watch the abuse of others
Screaming
Threatening my family
Threatening that he will:

- throw me out of the house
- hospitalize me
- commit suicide
- cut me off financially

Aggression

Being physically violent to me
Threatening to be violent with me or someone I
    love
Hitting the walls and furniture or kicking things
    around
Yelling and being verbally abusive to me or others
Grabbing me by the arm
Raping me

Domination

Always telling me that he knows what is best for me.
Never asking permission to borrow something.
Withholding information.
Controlling my life by restricting my use of the
    phone and not allowing visitors or family to
    come over to my house.
Lying and distorting the truth.
Telling me that her decision is for my own good.
Never consulting me about something that per-
    tains to me.
Everything is in my partner's name; I have no
    personal identity.
Not allowing me to go to therapy.
Controlling all the money.

Women will use this question to share their personal experiences with abusive relationships. Often women will have graphic and chilling details of how they have been mistreated. Allow women to tell their stories, without encouraging a series of sequential monologues. Women should be prompted to respond to one another's stories.

QUESTION 3

What are the normal ups and downs that characterize any healthy relationship?

TYPICAL RESPONSES   Some disappointment

Shifting dependency on both sides of the relation-
    ship

Being out of sync with one another

Sometimes one person can be preoccupied and
    unavailable to the other person

Getting on each other's nerves

Variability in the amount of affection given or the
    desire for sex

Feeling moody and less accommodating

Responding to external demands rather than spend-
    ing time with my partner

Some downtime, quiet time, or even boredom

Disagreements over priorities with time and money

Disagreements over child rearing

How can you tell if you are settling for more strife and heartache than you need to?

TYPICAL RESPONSES   When I'm not getting anything out of the relation-
    ship

When I start feeling constantly resentful and bitter
    toward the other person

When I feel like I'm giving more than I'm getting to
    a point that I feel drained

When I start feeling too much pressure

> When I start feeling physical symptoms like
>   headaches or stomachaches
> When I begin to feel afraid or in danger
> When I am taking care of the other person more
>   than I am taking care of myself
> When I feel unhappy most of the time
> When I am feeling worthless

Women who primarily have experienced abusive relationships often have little familiarity with the normal rhythm of nonabusive relationships. They know what terrible relationships are like and they fantasize about what perfect relationships might be like, but they have limited experience with average relationships. Leaders may need to begin the discussion by offering concrete examples of ups and downs.

QUESTION 4

What has your relationship pattern been and how is it related to your abuse history?

TYPICAL RESPONSES   Being used—I've been used my entire life in one
                     way or another.
                     Acting as a caretaker—I took care of my mother
                     and siblings since I was very young.
                     Being an outsider—I've always felt odd or strange
                     and never fit in.
                     Being in relationships that I'm not pleased with but
                     settle for because I feel needed and valued. I've
                     felt discarded since I was a child and I want to
                     mean something to someone.
                     I get myself into relationships with people who need
                     me to fix them or take care of them. I think that
                     is because I always felt of value by taking care
                     of my screwed-up family.
                     I withdraw from relationships so I won't get hurt.

> I've been burned too many times and it's too
> painful.
> I seek out relationships where I have all the power.
> If I don't have power I end up getting abused.
> I scream at them. They make me feel bad and I
> don't want to take it.

The question invites members to focus on their relationship histories. You may need to prompt members to make the discussion current with comments such as, "Do you still get into those kinds of relationships? How has your style changed in recent years?" Leaders will want to have members acknowledge a range of styles. Categories such as clingy, submissive, avoidant, and hostile should be mentioned as a way to stimulate discussion.

QUESTION 5

Have there been times when you were abusive or destructive in a relationship? Do you know why you behaved the way you did?

TYPICAL RESPONSES

> I know I'm too needy—I feel like a victim and I
> want someone to care about me.
> I can be very passive and submissive—I don't want
> to start any trouble in the relationship because
> relationships are hard to come by.
> I can be too self-sufficient—I don't want anyone to
> do anything for me that they might later use
> against me. I feel like I must protect myself.
> Sometimes I lose myself in the relationship and for-
> get my own needs.
> I can be an enabler and overlook the bad stuff no
> matter what it costs.
> I like to be in charge. Either I get them or they'll
> get me.
> I tried to ruin the relationship—I didn't feel I
> deserved to be loved.

I threaten suicide when I don't get my way.
I call her names and put her down.
I know I'm much too critical.
I embarrass him in front of our friends.
I flirt a lot and then I flaunt it.

Women generally have an easier time acknowledging their role in bad relationships when they have been too passive, too loving, or too needy. They have more difficulty admitting the problem when they have been abusive or overcontrolling. Leaders will need to help women feel safe enough to begin to acknowledge their own dark sides.

ADDITIONAL QUESTIONS

1. How do you feel about being alone? Do you think that has anything to do with your relationship style?
2. If you could change one thing in your current relationship, what would it be?

EXERCISE

Women should be encouraged to name as many strategies to influence another as they can.

TYPICAL RESPONSES   Sex.
I would try to be really cute and charming.
I would withdraw.
I would pout or start to cry.
I would tell him that someone else wanted him to do
    something.
I would get really mean and threatening.
I would do favors for her.
I would ignore him.
I would give attention to someone else.
I would cook a nice dinner.
I would leave and go to my friend's or mother's
    house.

Women may be surprised to recognize how many of their communication styles are indirect and circuitous. They also may be embarrassed to acknowledge how often they use sex to get what they want.

MARY'S STORY

It's hard for me to admit that I've carried on an imaginary relationship for almost ten years with a priest I met briefly a long time ago. In my mind, Father Paul is the perfect man. He is kind, gentle, and always listens. We never fight or mistreat each other. In my mind, we never even disagree. When I am feeling lonely or confused, I write him long letters, telling him all about myself. I never send them; I don't even know his address anymore. It may sound bizarre, but I prefer a relationship with Father Paul—one that I can control and that is always good—to a relationship with someone who might try to manipulate or intimidate me. I don't want to deal with a relationship that's good one day and bad the next. I want a relationship that never changes.

Advanced Trauma Recovery Issues

PART III

Advanced Trauma
Recovery Issues

TOPIC 22 Family—Myths and Distortions

SESSION RATIONALE

Part of the trauma of growing up in a home where abuse occurs comes from the systematic denial of reality required to maintain even a semblance of normal family life. Family members lie not only about the abuse itself but also about the nature of their relationships to one another. Frequently, families construct myths designed to paint a more pleasant picture of family life for themselves as well as for outsiders. These myths become so powerful that they eventually obscure the truth; family members may no longer be able to distinguish reality from fantasy. If women are to begin to see themselves and current relationships more honestly, they must begin by deconstructing some of the myths of childhood.

GOAL 1: Members will understand the ways in which particular family myths were used to deny the realities or abuses of family life.

GOAL 2: Members will understand how those myths continue to interfere with current functioning.

GOAL 3: Members will begin to consider alternative ways to understand family dynamics.

QUESTIONS

1. What stories did your family invent to justify or obscure its dysfunction?
2. What were the implicit roles and functions assigned to different family members?
3. How did outsiders view your family?
4. How have you been helped or hindered by these family myths and distortions?

153

EXERCISES

1. Remember an event or a story about your family that captures how you feel about the family.
2. Try to fit your family into a folk tale or popular story. Which one would you choose and who would play the different parts?

LEADERS' NOTES

QUESTION 1

What stories did your family invent to justify or obscure its dysfunction?

TYPICAL RESPONSES
Dad works hard and he deserves to relax (have a drink) when he comes home.

God never gives you anything you can't handle.

What doesn't kill you will make you strong.

Family problems belong in the family.

I only do this because I love you.

This hurts me more than it hurts you.

Your mother can't handle the stress because you kids won't listen.

Your family are the only ones who *really* love you.

We've earned the right to make our own rules.

If it was good enough for me, it's good enough for you.

You may find that you need to help members understand what you mean by the word *stories*. Members should be encouraged to explore how the family rationalized some of its behavior. By remembering some specific events that were confusing or did not seem to make sense at the time, members may be able to discover underlying family stories. This question can lead to a discussion of family ethics or philosophy.

QUESTION 2

What were the implicit roles and functions assigned to different family members?

Choose the following prompts to facilitate the group discussion:

What roles did your parents and siblings play?
What role did you play?
Were you ever uneasy with your role?

TYPICAL RESPONSES I was the oldest child and the message given to me was that I would always be the responsible one to care for everyone else in my family.

I was the middle child and the one identified as having problems.

My sister was the star of the family and I was the bad seed.

My father was totally in charge and my mother seemed like his lackey.

I was considered Miss Suzy Sunshine.

My father expected me to accompany him to events.

My mother put me in charge of my younger brother and told me that if anything happened to him she would never forgive me.

My sister played the clown whenever Dad was drunk.

My mother seemed incompetent and I felt responsible for everything.

I was the punching bag and got blamed for everything.

My brother was the mediator and tried to make things right between me and Mom.

As members recall the often damaging roles they were asked to play, they may be overwhelmed by painful feelings from the past. Many will become angry as they realize, perhaps for the first time, just how inappropriate the forced roles were.

QUESTION 3

How did outsiders view your family?

TYPICAL RESPONSES   They were pillars of the community—PTA president and church elder.

My father was known to be able to fix or repair anything.

They were known to be helpful, busy, and intelligent.

My mother was seen as the witch of the block . . . she yelled at neighborhood kids and in turn they would play pranks on her. . . . I was always embarrassed and got harassed by the neighborhood kids.

When my mother was widowed everyone commended her for her independence . . . but I think she played the martyr.

My mother never allowed anyone to know her . . . she was a very private person.

People in the community thought my mother was a saint for raising seven kids on her own.

When my father died, no one even knew I didn't have a father who lived at home.

My family went to extremes to look like the normal family. What happened in the family *stayed* in the family.

My brother was retarded which made others view my family as different.

This question helps members to address appearance versus reality issues. In families where abuse occurs, parents often try to mask what goes on inside the family by presenting a false face to friends and neighbors. This leaves a child feeling not only alone and isolated but also in doubt about what is real. When the family is viewed as being upstanding and ethical, a child may feel even more reluctant to tell the truth about what goes on inside the family.

QUESTION 4

How have you been helped or hindered by these family myths and distortions?

TYPICAL RESPONSES   I learned that you could keep secrets no matter what
the cost.

It took me a very long time to realize that the rest of
the world was not like my family.

I grew up thinking no one cared about me. . . . Now
as an adult I can't understand why anyone would
care about me.

I learned that appearances don't necessarily tell the
whole story.

I learned that I couldn't trust my family and now I
find it difficult to trust anyone.

I learned to distrust anyone in authority.

I turned to alcohol whenever I got tense.

I second guess myself all the time.

I became more independent and self-reliant.

I got good at hiding how I feel.

I try to do everything perfectly and never take any
risks.

I'm very secretive and don't give out much information.

Generally, women focus on how they have been hindered rather than helped. In
some cases, leaders will want to help members see how what began as an
impediment has been transformed into a strength.

ADDITIONAL QUESTIONS

1. How did family life shape your behavior?
2. Are there myths that you see being passed to the next generation?

The following exercises can be interspersed throughout the session.

EXERCISE 1

Remember an event or a story about your family that captures how you feel
about the family.

TYPICAL RESPONSES I was trying to care for our bird; the bird died and my family blamed me.

I was sexually abused by men in the neighborhood when I was only six years old.

They all knew that I was on my own and that no one in my family took care of me. . . . They knew they could take advantage of me.

My dad would wake us up in the middle of the night. He would throw things all over our room and then demand that we clean the house immediately while he played loud music to keep us awake.

I would have a disagreement with my sister and she would hit me. Then my father would blame me for what my sister did and he would beat me all over again.

Once we were too noisy on Christmas Eve and my father threw all of our presents in the trash.

When I told my mother I was being abused, she gave me something to drink and told me it would make me forget.

My mother locked me outside in the snow because I was crying too much.

Women have no trouble remembering these incidents. The stories are filled with great personal pain and members need to give one another psychological space and respect as these stories are recounted. Leaders may find themselves wanting to condemn caregivers or to offer excessive support. These responses are often more helpful to the leaders than to the members who may just need to have others listen and bear witness to the pain they experienced.

EXERCISE 2

Try to fit your family into a folk tale or popular story. Which one would you choose and who would play the different parts?

TYPICAL RESPONSES

Cinderella—I was the scapegoat who was always mistreated, but I never got to the end of the story.

I was the Ugly Duckling who never grew up and I never found my real family.

Cinderella, because my sister was the wicked stepsister.

The Road Runner and the Coyote—I felt like I was constantly being beaten down.

I felt like the Three Little Pigs and the wolf was always at the door.

I desperately wanted to have a father like the Cosbys or the Brady Bunch.

Beauty and the Beast, but I felt like the Beast.

I felt like Sleeping Beauty but the Prince never came.

I imagined I could turn into a spirit and just disappear.

Most members have no trouble with this exercise. Ask members, however, how the fairy tale related specifically to their family. In some cases, the story describes family dynamics. In other cases, a particular character captures how the member felt about herself although the story itself is unrelated to how the family functioned. In still other instances, the story suggests the family life a member would have wanted to have.

LOIS'S STORY

We lived a lie. Outsiders thought we had the perfect family. We were all helpful and intelligent people. No one outside the family would have guessed that my dad and sister were physically and verbally abusive to me. They mistreated me until I was an adult, but I was too ashamed to tell anyone. After awhile it became easier if I just pretended that I had the perfect family, too. Pretending helped me cope. At least part of the time I could believe I was normal, maybe even better than normal.

This fantasy has caused me real trouble as an adult. The problems begin when I imagine that things are OK when they are not. Then I start making plans and promises I can't keep and getting in over my head in all kinds of situations. I can't get the help I need because I have become so good at acting like nothing is wrong. At some point, however, my life ends up in crisis, and I can't pretend anymore.

TOPIC 23 Family Life: Current

SESSION RATIONALE

Abuse (even when it occurs outside the family) soon becomes a family affair and influences the way in which future family dynamics develop. A past or current history of abuse within the family only makes the problem of clarifying current relationships more difficult.

Because of their often impoverished social networks, women who are multiply victimized and stigmatized often feel that they have no choice but to continue some relationship with family members—even with the abuser. Being honest about what type of relationship is currently possible with family members helps to avoid future disappointments and abuses. Women also realize what emotional and practical precautions they must take if they are to have ongoing family contact.

GOAL 1: Members will explore current relationships with family members and identify sources of tension.

GOAL 2: Members will begin to decide both what kinds of relationships they want with family members and what kinds of relationships are possible.

QUESTIONS

1. What kind and how much contact do you have with your family of origin and any abusers within the family?
2. What are the current tensions and pressures in your family?
3. Are there regrets or old grievances that currently get in the way of your relationship to family members?
4. Are there dysfunctional patterns or roles that still seem to dominate your interactions with your family?
5. How would you like family dynamics to change? Are there changes you alone can make?

EXERCISE

Leaders will read the poem entitled, "Autobiography in Five Chapters" from *The Tibetan Book of Living and Dying* (see Appendix Item I). Members will discuss their reactions to the poem and will assess where they are on the path of letting go of old patterns.

LEADERS' NOTES

QUESTION 1

What kind and how much contact do you have with your family of origin and any abusers within the family?

TYPICAL RESPONSES	We keep the conversation very superficial.
	I still live at home and I can't seem to break away.
	I only see them with my husband present.
	I haven't been home in 14 years.
	I never leave my children alone with my father.
	I never stay overnight at my parents' house.
	I refuse to be present if my brother is going to be there.
	I only want to talk to them on the phone.
	I never go to family reunions.
	I'll only meet them in public places.

Women often experience pain and anger as they acknowledge how much accommodation they must make to remain safe from past abusers. Abuse in the past often results in the loss of happy family life in the present.

QUESTION 2

What are the current tensions and pressures in your family?

TYPICAL RESPONSES	My father does a guilt trip on me every time I go to my parents' house.

> I am afraid of being pulled back into the craziness if
> I go home to visit my mom.
> I'm always afraid of hurting my mother.
> My sister tries to control everything.
> They treat me differently based on whether they
> need me or not.
> I have to put up with my abusive brother if I want to
> maintain a connection with my parents.
> My family keeps asking me for money.
> My sister only wants me when she needs a baby-
> sitter or a maid.
> My mother relies on me for all her emotional needs.
> My family prefers I stay sick so they don't have to
> look at or do anything about their own problems.
> I always feel the pressure from my family not to blow
> the whistle on them or tell any family secrets.
> My parents still want to control me even though I
> am an adult.

Current pressures may or may not be related to past abuses. Sometimes there is pressure to revert to old patterns. At other times, the tensions exist because a member will not comply with new demands.

QUESTION 3

Are there regrets or old grievances that currently get in the way of your relationship to family members?

TYPICAL RESPONSES Because of the way they treated me in the past, I try not to put myself in a position where I ask for their help.

I wish I had not allowed my family to blame me for all their sick stuff.

I still believe that my parents favor my siblings over me and that still gets in the way when we are all together.

> I wish I had confronted my father before he got so
> old and sick.
> I can't forgive my mother for letting the abuse go
> on; I'm sure she knew.
> My father always ignored me growing up; now I
> don't want his attention.
> Whenever I am with my parents I feel guilty that I
> didn't live up to their expectations.

If possible, encourage members to be as specific as possible. General objections, such as "They treated me unfairly," do not suggest obvious ways a member might change the situation.

QUESTION 4

Are there dysfunctional patterns or roles that still seem to dominate your interactions with your family?

TYPICAL RESPONSES
> I still cater to my mother's needs.
> I'm scared of my sister; I can't stand up to her.
> My mom starts criticizing me the moment I walk in
> the door.
> We don't know how to be together unless we're
> drunk.
> I hate to go home because when I do I become
> hypervigilant again.
> I just say "Yes ma'am" and stuff my feelings.
> I always feel like I should not rock the boat or cause
> any problems.
> I'm constantly isolating myself—just as I did when
> I was young.

This question focuses members' attention on their own behavior. Often members need to be prodded to see how old patterns of relating contribute to their being abused and mistreated in the present. Some interactions are so embedded in the family routine that they go unnoticed even though they are destructive.

QUESTION 5

How would you like family dynamics to change? Are there changes that you alone can make?

TYPICAL RESPONSES   No, I wish my mother would stop trying to manipulate me.

I wish my family respected me.

I would like to be treated as a human being.

No, I would like for my father to stop playing me against my siblings.

I believe my sister should go into therapy.

I wish my parents could show me affection.

I need to find a different family . . . a family of choice rather than a family of origin.

I need to work on my self-esteem and learn to feel more empowered.

I want to learn not to isolate myself.

I have to separate myself from the unhealthy people in my life.

I want to set clear limits about what I'm willing to do.

Members may have an easier time articulating how they would like others to change than focusing on how they themselves might behave differently. You will want to guide the discussion so that members do not lapse into a litany of unsolvable complaints. Frequently, families are so dysfunctional that only by completely severing contact can members end the pattern of abuse and revictimization. Leaders should be sensitive that some changes group members desire may in fact be beyond their immediate control.

ADDITIONAL QUESTIONS

1. What consequences have resulted, or do you imagine will result, from changes you make in relation to your family?

2. How might your needs be met by sources outside the family?
3. Are there extended family members who can hear your story of abuse and assist your recovery?

EXERCISE

Read the poem entitled "Autobiography in Five Chapters" from *The Tibetan Book of Living and Dying* (see Appendix Item I). Members will discuss their reactions to the poem and will assess where they are on the path of letting go of old patterns.

Be careful to avoid leaving members with the feeling that they have failed if they are not yet ready to let go. Most members will feel pleased if they are able to identify dysfunctional patterns successfully and then consider what they might need to do to *begin* the process of altering old patterns.

DENISE'S STORY

I've always wanted my mother to say she loved me. I raised my younger siblings while my mom was out drinking, and my father had disappeared. I did the best I could for a 12 year old, but my mom never gave me any credit or praise. I have the darkest skin in my family and my mother used to call me the black sheep. She never showed me any affection either.

Even though I'm the most functional of her daughters, she still insults me, and for some reason I still want her approval. I want her to see how well I'm doing and say, "Denise, I'm proud of you!" So I keep showing up at her doorstep and trying to please her. I'm still waiting to hear those magic words.

People have said that she is abusive and that I should stay away from her. They ask how I can still love someone who hurts me so much. Well, it's because she's my mother, and I just can't walk out of her life.

TOPIC 24 Decision Making:
Trusting Your Judgment

SESSION RATIONALE

Abusers frequently demand that victims keep the secrets of abuse if they are to survive. In the maze of secrets and untruths, a child learns to ignore her own responses and perceptions and to relinquish authority for making decisions to others. All of these safety maneuvers need to be unlearned in the process of recovery.

GOAL 1: Members will begin to assess and understand the process by which they make decisions.

GOAL 2: Members will identify those factors that caused them to cede decision-making authority in the past.

QUESTIONS

1. What factors do you consider when making decisions?
2. What factors lead you to make bad decisions?
3. What factors have caused you to stop trusting your own judgments?
4. What are some negative consequences experienced as a result of a decision you made?

EXERCISE

Members will discuss areas in which they trust themselves versus areas in which they distrust themselves.

LEADERS' NOTES

QUESTION 1

What factors do you consider when making decisions?

TYPICAL RESPONSES
I try to make sure I take care of myself.
I try to know what I can handle at the time.
I consider what the consequences of my decision will be.
I talk with someone I trust about a decision I need to make.
I think about what my favorite grandmother would say.
I recognize that I have a choice.
I consider how much time I have.
I think about who will be affected by the decision.
I think about what I have done in the past.
I weigh the pros and cons.
I think about how this will affect me.

You will want to help members to identify their decision-making strategies. Members may want to distinguish among how they made decisions, how they make decisions now, and how they would like to make decisions in the future. Many members may be surprised to learn that they are actually following a clear strategy when making decisions.

QUESTION 2

What factors lead you to make bad decisions?

TYPICAL RESPONSES
Wanting to be accepted by others.
Being scared of others.
Being afraid of losing control.
Being worried that I will miss out on something.
Wanting to please others.
Not having considered how the decision will impact me.

Being addicted to drugs or alcohol.
Needing instant gratification.
Hanging around with a bad crowd.
Not wanting to be alone.
Needing money.
I am afraid of getting caught in a conflict with
    others.

This question gives members a chance to tell their stories of past bad decisions. Encourage members to remember examples of bad decision making.

QUESTION 3

What factors have caused you to stop trusting your own judgments?

TYPICAL RESPONSES   Having a psychiatric diagnosis.
Listening to others and their doubts about me and
    my ability to make a decision.
Being compared to others who are not credible or
    use poor judgment.
Being compared to someone I could never measure
    up to.
Believing that I could never make a decision even if
    I wanted to.
Having my parents invalidate or alter my reality.
Having threats of violence made against me.
Not believing in myself.
Being accustomed to having others control my life.
My history of making bad choices.
I'm afraid of making a mistake.

As women remember how they have relinquished or lost their capacity to make decisions, they may experience significant pain. Some women will mourn the loss of a self that was more confident and decisive. Others will feel angry as they recall how parents, friends, or partners assaulted their self-confidence and left them feeling incapable of making even the simplest of decisions.

QUESTION 4

What are some negative consequences experienced as a result of a decision you made?

TYPICAL RESPONSES   I lost all contact with my loved ones.

I became homeless.

I decided to leave my abusive husband and he set the house on fire.

My family ostracized me.

I earned a bad reputation.

My family told me that I shamed them and they no longer were supportive of me.

My family became so angry with me that I felt they no longer loved me.

My children were taken away from me.

My credit rating was ruined and I had to start all over again.

I got arrested for DWI.

Help members differentiate between good decisions that had negative secondary outcomes (e.g., saying no to abuse and having family members ostracize you) versus bad decisions that predictably led to bad consequences (e.g., seeking drugs late at night and getting mugged).

For many women, the loss of the ability to speak out is not reflective of poor cognitive skills or an inability to see the truth. Instead, it grows from a fear of the consequences if they choose to speak out. Women are thus forced to commit what has been called "soul murder" whereby they deny their own accurate perceptions to avoid alienating others.

ADDITIONAL QUESTIONS

1. From whom or where did you learn to make decisions?
2. What role do ambivalent feelings play in your decision-making process?
3. What will help you make better decisions in the future?
4. When should you defer to others to make decisions?

EXERCISE

Members will discuss areas in which they trust themselves versus areas in which they distrust themselves.

TYPICAL RESPONSES

Areas in which I trust my decision making	**Areas in which I distrust my decision making**
My sobriety	Drug use
Parenting	My weight
My ability to do my job well	Driving safely
My commitment to life	Parenting
My boundaries	My boundaries
My motives and intent	My relationships
My care and concern for others	Spending money
Issues about my physical health	Food and eating habits
	I don't trust what looks good on me

Begin by discussing the areas in which women feel confident about their decision-making skills. Many women will express great pride as they take credit for their struggles to trust themselves. After a discussion of these positive accomplishments, women will have an easier time revealing those areas where they still have difficulty trusting their own judgment.

JILL'S STORY

Decision making is very difficult for me. One of the things that being abused did was to teach me to downplay or ignore my own perceptions and feelings. No one in my family, particularly my father, cared much about how I felt or what I thought, so why should I take myself seriously? My feelings seemed irrelevant; my perceptions seemed wrong. I thought of myself as stupid and confused. As I got older, I proved to myself just how bad my judgment was. I've had five jobs in six years; I've been divorced twice, and I'm only 28 years old. I don't feel able to make good choices. Sometimes I feel that I'd be more successful if I did the opposite of what I thought I should do. I'm not sure how I'll ever learn to trust myself.

TOPIC 25 Communication: Making Yourself Understood

SESSION RATIONALE

Clear and direct communication is compromised and thwarted in a home in which abuse occurs. Family members create elaborate and often circuitous schemes to communicate with one another. When these indirect strategies are transported out of the home, they often fail miserably. Trauma survivors need both permission to speak their minds and practice in using forms of direct communication.

GOAL 1: Group members will begin to identify faulty and unsuccessful communication patterns.

GOAL 2: Group members will consider alternative styles that might allow them to speak more clearly.

QUESTIONS

1. Do you ever find that others misunderstand or do not pick up on the message you are trying to communicate? Why do you think this happens?
2. Are there times when your words say one thing and your actions or body language say another?
3. Are you ever provocative in your communication style? If so, how do you behave?
4. When do you ever choose to avoid communication altogether?

EXERCISE

Group members will divide into pairs and participate in an Active Listening Exercise. One member of the pair will play the role of the speaker and the other member will act as the listener. The speaker is instructed to express her feelings about a topic to the listener. The listener is instructed to listen carefully to what the speaker is saying, and not to try to develop her own response. When the speaker is done, the listener is to say back what she heard the speaker say. Group members will provide feedback about how well ideas were expressed by the speaker and the listener. The group should look for areas in which the listener projects her own ideas/perspectives into what she says she heard the speaker say. The pairs will take turns doing this one at a time.

LEADERS' NOTES

QUESTION 1

Do you ever find that others misunderstand or do not pick up on the message you are trying to communicate? Why do you think this happens?

> **TYPICAL RESPONSES** I rarely say what I really mean.
> I rely on people to read between the lines.
> I'm not sure what I want to say, so I don't say it clearly.
> I am so focused on the other person's response that I monitor myself too much.
> People can't tell when I'm joking.
> I talk so aggressively that people get defensive.
> Other people refuse to listen.

You may need to provide concrete examples of blocked or distorted communication. At first members may become defensive, arguing that misunderstood communication is usually, or even always, the other person's fault. Once one member acknowledges her role in poor communication, other members quickly follow.

QUESTION 2

Are there times when your words say one thing and your actions or body language say another?

TYPICAL RESPONSES   I say I want sex and then I tense up.

I say I'm fine, but I sigh a lot.

I say I agree with his idea and then I roll my eyes.

I say I want to be left alone, but I'm really angry and I want to hurt the other person.

I say I'll do something and then I get so busy I forget.

I tell him to stop but I'm laughing while I say it.

I say I'm not angry but I know I sound mad.

It may be helpful to observe the communication styles that members use during the group. If members are comfortable with comments that focus on process, you can point out examples of mixed communication as it occurs in the group. If members are overly sensitive or defensive, you might want to draw examples from past groups.

QUESTION 3

Are you ever provocative in your communication style? If so, how do you behave?

TYPICAL RESPONSES   I exaggerate.

I get passive aggressive.

I use humor.

I distort information.

I grandstand.

I minimize.

I try to go someone one better by topping the last story.

I lie.

I try to control the conversation.

I taunt.

I flirt.

I behave outrageously.

I talk very softly and make people work to hear me.

I start to cry.

I deliberately push buttons.
I refuse to drop the argument.
I give the silent treatment.
I become sarcastic.

You may need to define or operationalize what you mean by *provocative*. Provocative communication is often indirect, having an emotional intent other than merely transmitting information. It may be intended to shock, seduce, challenge, or punish the listener. Members should discuss not only *how* they behave provocatively but *why* they do and *what* they hope to accomplish.

QUESTION 4

When do you ever choose to avoid communication altogether?

TYPICAL RESPONSES When I fear confrontation
To avoid stress and pain
To get out of a difficult situation
When I feel inadequate
To avoid hurting someone else
When I fear losing control
To avoid punishment
When I don't know how to repair a situation or a rift
    in the relationship
When I don't want to feel vulnerable
When I fear rejection

Most women have ample experience in avoiding communication and group members are well aware of why they choose to opt out of a problematic dialogue. Make sure that the reasons go beyond self-protection and include control and manipulation.

ADDITIONAL QUESTIONS

1. Are there times when you communicate indirectly?
2. What works best when people want to communicate with you?

3. How do you communicate directly to another person so that you are clearly understood?

EXERCISE

The group will divide into pairs and sit facing one another. One member will play the role of the speaker and the other will act as the listener. The speaker is instructed to express her feelings about a topic to the listener. The listener is instructed to listen to what the speaker is saying, and not to try to develop her own response. When the speaker is done, the listener is to say back what she heard the speaker say. Then the speaker and the rest of the group will give the listener feedback about how well she captured the ideas expressed by the speaker. The group should look for areas in which the listener projects her own ideas/perspectives into what she says she heard the speaker say. The listener and the rest of the group will also give the speaker feedback about how well she articulated her feelings as she spoke, with possible suggestions for how the speaker could have been clearer. The pairs will take turns doing this one at a time.

Possible topics the women could speak about:

- What she would like to say to someone that she has been unable to say previously to that person
- How she feels about a particular friend, relative, or significant other
- How she feels about her favorite leisure activity

JEAN'S STORY

I ask for what I want in a relationship; I just don't do it directly. Like, if I'm with a man and I want to go out to eat and to the movies, I'll ask him what he wants to do or what he wants to eat. Then, he can feel like he decided what to do, but I know that I really got to do what I wanted. It doesn't always work, and sometimes I get angry and frustrated when they don't figure it out. But, I don't believe I can get what I want by asking for it directly. Then the person can say no just to be mean or have their way. I guess this came from when I was growing up. My stepmother would never let us have or do what we asked. I learned to make it look like she came up with the idea.

To me, it sounds pretty risky to just say what you want or how you feel. It's hard even to notice what I do because it's so automatic. Besides, when people figure out what I want, I feel that's really special because they read me so well. If they really care about me, they will be able to know what I want without my saying it.

TOPIC 26   Self-Destructive Behaviors

SESSION RATIONALE

Women who have been repeatedly abused often come to feel that they deserve to be abused. In the absence of an external abuser, the woman becomes both victim and perpetrator. Understanding and breaking the pattern of self-abuse often is difficult; yet it is essential if recovery is to occur.

GOAL 1: Members will explore precipitants of self-abuse.

GOAL 2: Members will share experiences of self-abuse in a nonshaming, nonjudgmental atmosphere.

QUESTIONS

1. What do you do that is self-destructive?
2. Why do people engage in self-destructive behavior?
3. What situations or behaviors stimulate feelings of self-hate?

EXERCISE

Each woman will develop a list of alternative strategies for strengthening self-worth. Women will also devise a specific behavior that can compete with the self-destructive behavior.

LEADERS' NOTES

QUESTION 1

What do you do that is self-destructive? Make sure the list includes:

Excessive use of drugs or alcohol   Self-mutilation
Starvation or binge eating   Suicide attempts

TYPICAL RESPONSES   Being reckless and impulsive
Sabotaging good relationships
Playing chicken with semitrucks while I'm driving
Trying to kill myself
Using alcohol and drugs
Cutting myself with a knife or razor
Having unsafe sex
Smoking cigarettes
Letting my anger get out of control
Choosing an abusive partner
Eating only candy bars
Having a series of one-night stands
Refusing to eat
Getting fired from jobs again and again
Never backing down from someone even when I
      know I'm overpowered or outnumbered

Members may find it difficult to acknowledge the ways they have hurt themselves. Often it is easier to see how others have been abusive than to admit to abusing oneself. Leaders will need to monitor members' disclosures to prevent women from feeling overwhelmed by shame and pain. For some women this will be a new topic and they may be surprised to consider how they have caused or contributed to some of the hurt in their lives. You will also want to help women distinguish risky behavior (which might lead to growth and new opportunities) from reckless behavior (which may lead to a self-destructive outcome).

QUESTION 2

Why do people engage in self-destructive behavior? Make sure the list includes:

Atonement or punishment for some transgression
Avoidance of some greater pain
Calming or self-soothing
An attempt to gain or regain control

TYPICAL RESPONSES   Because they feel a need to be punished
Because they do not care about life anymore
Because they feel inadequate
Because they do not know any better
Because they hate themselves
Because they are too passive
Because they are trying to avoid anxiety
Because they feel despair
Because they feel isolated and have no one to count on
Because they always come up too short or fail to meet standards
Because they want a visible scar
Because they want some sense of control
Because they feel they deserve it
Because they get a high from it
Because they want to avoid feelings of shame
Because they want to forget the abuse
Because they want to feel something
Because they feel unlovable and abandoned
Because they are trying to find a way to stop the pain

You should pay attention to the categories of responses represented. Women who are prone to depression will have an overrepresentation of responses that suggest failure or inadequacy. In contrast, women with addictive disorders who are stimulus seeking will emphasize wanting to feel something even if it involves pain. Make sure that all the responses do not fall in only one category. When possible, leaders should attempt to connect self-destructive behavior to past abuses. At times, women abuse themselves because that is how they were treated as children. At other times, they become self-destructive to punish themselves for being abused in the first place.

QUESTION 3

What situations or behaviors stimulate feelings of self-hate?

TYPICAL RESPONSES   Feeling unworthy and not up to the task
Trying to be a perfectionist at any cost
Feeling paralyzed and powerless
Hating my body size
Showing too much emotion or feeling that I've over-
    exposed myself
Disappointing myself or others
Not feeling good enough for anyone
Feeling like I should have done this or could have
    done that
Feeling out of control with drugs, sex, and alcohol
Knowing that I've hurt someone else
Becoming something or someone I don't want to be
Not managing or coping with my life very well
Growing up with the message from my parents that
    I'm not valued or that I'm hated and beginning
    to believe it myself
Doing something wrong
Feeling ashamed

Women will include both sins of omission and commission in their list of situations that stimulate self-hate. The omissions include all types of personal failure, while the commissions often focus on impulsivity and lack of control (hypersexuality, drug relapse, and psychiatric decompensation).

ADDITIONAL QUESTIONS

1. What have you done in the past that might be an alternative to self-destructive behavior?
2. How do you forgive yourself when you have been unkind to yourself?

EXERCISE

Each woman will develop a list of alternative strategies for strengthening self-worth. Women will also devise a specific behavior that can compete with the self-destructive behavior.

TYPICAL RESPONSES

ALTERNATIVE STRATEGIES

Reading inspirational literature or listening to motivational recordings

Putting things in perspective

Giving myself a pep talk

Putting my energy toward my spiritual beliefs

Recognizing what I'm here for and what I'm good at

Trying not to be so hard on myself and giving myself a break

Keeping a sense of humor about life

Getting involved in altruistic activities

Keeping in touch with nature and experiencing it

Doing something that brings order to my life such as cleaning my apartment

Trying not to overwhelm myself so that I don't set myself up for failure

SELF-DESTRUCTIVE BEHAVIOR	COMPETING BEHAVIOR
1. Smoking	Sucking lollipops
	Chewing gum
	Wearing a nicotine patch
2. Self-cutting	Using an ice cube or a red marker
3. Overeating	Meditating
	Exercising
	Eating an apple instead of a cookie
	Dancing to some music

NANCY'S STORY

I was 13 when I started drinking beer, getting high, and having sex with older boys in high school. It gave me the feeling of being attractive, in control and part of the "cool" group. At least for a while. But then the self-hate and depression would return. The drugs and sex no longer helped and I turned to food for solace. But no matter how much I ate, I could not fill the emptiness within.

I don't remember the first time I took a razor to my arm. It wasn't suicide I wanted. I just longed to feel something else other than hate and shame and guilt. The pain felt strangely comforting and soothing. I am somehow proud of the scars on my body. They are an outward sign of the emotional scars I have within.

TOPIC 27 Blame, Acceptance, and Forgiveness

SESSION RATIONALE

Issues of blame, responsibility, and power often become confused for women who have been abused in childhood. Women find themselves blaming themselves for situations over which they have no power. They also fail to assume responsibility accurately for circumstances they can control. A realistic assessment of personal power and responsibility is necessary if women are to feel confident in making decisions about their lives.

GOAL 1: Members will explore the concepts of blame and responsibility.

GOAL 2: Members will begin to think about the roles of acceptance and forgiveness in recovery.

QUESTIONS

1. What criteria do you use to hold someone responsible or not responsible for a harmful event?
2. What are the consequences of holding someone responsible?
3. What would it take for you to come to terms with what has happened to you?
4. What role does forgiveness play, if any, in coming to terms with what has happened to you?

EXERCISE

Think of someone who has hurt you. What would it take to forgive that person? Are there some offenses you cannot forgive? Describe them.

LEADERS' NOTES

QUESTION 1

What criteria do you use to hold someone responsible or not responsible for a harmful event?

TYPICAL RESPONSES   If they meant to do it
How they felt afterward
If they were drunk at the time
If they knew what they were doing
If they could control their behavior
If they themselves had been abused as children
If I provoked them
How much harm was actually done
How old or responsible the person was
Who the person is
If they knew how much it hurt me and kept doing it anyway

You might begin by helping members distinguish legitimate criteria for assessing responsibility from rationalizations excusing the abuse. Often members are quite adept at excusing the abuser and need to develop standards that ascribe legitimate blame.

QUESTION 2

What are the consequences of holding someone responsible?

TYPICAL RESPONSES   It's pointless because there's nothing I can do now.
It takes the blame off of me.
It makes me want to find some way to retaliate.
It makes me feel guilty.
I don't want the responsibility of holding someone responsible.
I'm so angry and it's eating me up.
It gives me some place to direct my anger.
I feel pressure to confront.
Now I feel I can move on . . . I know who the problem was.
I really want the other person to suffer.
I feel a real sense of loss . . . my image of my ideal father is gone forever.
It makes me more fearful.

This question may take some women by surprise because people often assume that finally holding abusers accountable is a positive act. Yet, for many, assigning responsibility may usher in a wave of painful feelings that now must be addressed.

QUESTION 3

What would it take for you to come to terms with what has happened to you?

TYPICAL RESPONSES
Time
Confrontation with the abuser
Acknowledgment of complicity on the part of other family members
An honest conversation with the abuser or writing a letter
Being able to understand why it happened
Falling in love
Having good things happen in my life
Nothing
God's love
Being able to grieve
Knowing the perpetrator was dead

You want to be clear that this question is not necessarily a call to action. Women may know what needs to happen but it may well be an action that remains out of their immediate control.

QUESTION 4

What role does forgiveness play, if any, in coming to terms with what has happened to you?

TYPICAL RESPONSES
None, I will never be able to forgive and don't want to.
It's not my role to forgive—that's God's province.
I have to forgive to be forgiven myself.

I have to forgive to move on.
If I don't forgive, I'm just like the abuser.
I'm a Christian woman, I should be able to forgive.
The only person I want to forgive is myself.
I won't be at peace until I forgive.

Women use this question to think about the range of behaviors—not just for-giveness—that are part of healing and recovery. Make sure that members do not make excuses for the abuser and confuse this with forgiveness. Genuine forgiveness requires that one admit that a real injury was committed.

ADDITIONAL QUESTIONS

1. How do you think your life would change if you could come to terms with the past?
2. How has not coming to terms with the past impeded your personal progress?

EXERCISE

Think of someone who has hurt you. What would it take to forgive that person?

TYPICAL RESPONSES   To hear "I'm sorry" from the person who hurt me.
For my son to take responsibility for his actions.
For the person really to have changed.
To have my mother tell me that she wished she'd been a better mother to me.
For my parents to accept responsibility for their actions and to admit to me that they hurt me.
For the abuser to admit that he caused me pain.
For my mother to own up to what she did.

Are there some offenses you cannot forgive? Describe them.

TYPICAL RESPONSES   I'm not yet able to forgive my son for raping and killing another woman.
I don't think I can forgive someone who doesn't really believe they should be forgiven.

> Maybe my mother did the best she could do
> but I'm still hurt and angry.

Be careful not to imply that forgiveness is a necessary part of recovery. Many women move on with their lives without ever having to forgive or even confront the abuser. Women who do not choose to forgive should not be made to feel guilty or deficient.

EMILY'S STORY

My husband was a mean drunk. In fact, he was mean even when he wasn't drunk. Each and every day of our 10-year marriage I would start to get anxious late in the afternoon. Getting his dinner on the table at 6:00 P.M. sharp was crucial. But, even though I tried to do everything right, and have everything clean and in its place, something was always wrong.

So each evening we went through the same horrible routine. With each drink his voice got louder. He would start to pace around. He would holler, "You're worthless, you're nothing." And the slaps or shoves or punches would come. The stinging and soreness became constant companions.

After 10 years of this I finally just left. I got on a bus and headed north, putting over 600 miles between us. I stayed in a shelter in D.C. for awhile, and then got into a program to help women like me.

My husband was a mean, mean man. I will never trust another man because of him. Just because he was drunk all the time doesn't mean he wasn't responsible. He went to work every day—he was responsible enough for that. And he treated me worse than trash! He's responsible for his horrible behavior. I used to think I must have done something really wrong to deserve that treatment. But I don't think that anymore. I've built a new life, but I'll never forgive him. I'm sure he is not sorry for what he has done. And, even if he were, sorry is not good enough.

TOPIC 28 Feeling Out of Control

SESSION RATIONALE

Early experiences of abuse flood the survivor with powerful feelings. Now, survivors find themselves emotionally volatile and brittle with even minor provocation. Survivors need to develop a new, more differentiated continuum of emotional reactivity. They also need a model for understanding what happens to them when they feel flooded by feelings, so they don't think they are going crazy.

A woman who has been repeatedly abused has every right to feel rageful. Yet, when a woman feels controlled by her anger, she is unable to get her needs met or feel good about herself. Trauma survivors need to acknowledge the legitimacy of their anger while working to find ways to express that anger in a manner that others can bear to hear.

GOAL 1: Members will learn to put words to their responses during an emotional storm.

GOAL 2: Members will begin to understand the triggers and consequences of feeling out of control.

GOAL 3: Members will begin to consider ways in which they might be able to modulate their emotions.

QUESTIONS

1. What does being out of control feel like for you?
2. How do you behave when you feel out of control?
3. What triggers feelings of being out of control?
4. After an episode in which you feel you have been out of control, how do you respond?
5. What are some positive ways to bring an emotional storm to an end?

EXERCISE

The group will make a list of things that each member can use the next time she feels out of control or rageful. Each member will then make copies of the list and hang them in visible spots in her apartment to use the next time she needs them.

LEADERS' NOTES

QUESTION 1

What does being out of control feel like for you?

TYPICAL RESPONSES

BODILY SENSATIONS

Tingly	Hot	Energy rush
Rigid	Numb	Dizzy
Suffocating	Flushed	Out of breath
Dry mouth	Paralyzed	Frozen

EMOTIONAL STATES

Scared	Panicky	Overwhelmed
Violent	Frustrated	Frightened
Explosive	Reckless	Irrational
Rageful	Withdrawn	Stubborn
Mad	Distant	

BELIEFS AND COGNITIONS

I think I am going to die.
I want to give up.
My thoughts are spinning.
I think I am going crazy.
My brain won't work.
I think I am spinning out of control.
No one understands me.

Begin by helping members make the distinction among bodily sensations, emotional states, and beliefs and cognitions. Be clear that there is no one way in which feelings of being out of control manifest themselves. For some women out of control feelings are explosive, for others they manifest more like paralysis.

QUESTION 2

How do you behave when you feel out of control?

TYPICAL RESPONSES	Laugh hysterically	Scream	Get high
	Punch the wall	Leave the room	Sleep
	Curse	Refuse to speak	Cut myself
	Clean my house	Pick fights	Lash out at
	Cry	Binge eat	others

You should focus specifically on behaviors, not on the out of control feelings themselves because they were covered in the previous question.

QUESTION 3

What triggers feelings of being out of control?

TYPICAL RESPONSES   When people ignore me

When someone does not acknowledge me or say hello to me

When I'm treated disrespectfully

When others don't understand me

When someone interrupts me while I'm talking

When I have to wait for someone or something

When others hurt me

When someone takes advantage of me

When things don't go my way

When I feel overwhelmed

When I am confused and can't think

When I become highly anxious and I can't make a decision

When I'm completely broke and have no money

When I feel jealous

When I see others treated unfairly
When I am bored
When I'm left alone
When I am abused
When I have flashbacks
When I drink too much
When I am criticized

Help members distinguish between those causes that arise from narcissistic injury (feeling slighted and misunderstood) and those that arise from an internal state of disease or discomfort. Are there differences in how these two are handled or how they eventually resolve?

QUESTION 4

After an episode in which you feel you are out of control, how do you respond?

TYPICAL RESPONSES

I withdraw.
I feel guilty.
I deny it.
I feel stupid.
I try to make amends.

I feel ashamed.
I try to minimize it.
I drink and drug.
I feel foolish.
I think I have let people down.

I get upset because I don't know how to fix it.
I do something to draw attention away from myself.
I become scared of repercussions.
I believe I have done something unforgivable.
I try to find someone else to blame.
I start to think I am worthless.
I try to put on a false front.

Once again, you will want to distinguish actions from thoughts and feelings. Members may find it useful to speculate on why they behave the way they do. Are these reactions different from the original feelings of being out of control? How much is related to past trauma and learning associated with that trauma?

QUESTION 5

What are some positive ways to bring an emotional storm to an end?

TYPICAL RESPONSES
Do something soothing for myself.
Say affirming things to myself.
Take medication.
Isolate myself and have some downtime or peace and quiet.
Avoid what is making me feel rageful.
Have positive contact with others.
Allow time to pass.
Be good to myself by eating something.
Go somewhere that is peaceful.
Apologize or make reparations to someone I became rageful at.
I let it run its course.
Exercise.
Pray.
Listen to music.
Write in my journal.
Do some mindless repetitive task such as cleaning or knitting.

Leaders may want to help members focus on the consequences of the behaviors. At what point in the storm, if at all, are consequences considered? Does this ever help bring the outburst to an end? If all of the behaviors are negative or destructive, leaders can help members consider more benign responses.

This discussion should lead naturally into the exercise and does not arbitrarily need to be kept separate.

ADDITIONAL QUESTIONS

1. How have past abuses left you vulnerable to feeling out of control?
2. Are you sometimes just mad at the whole world?

EXERCISE

Be sure that the list of things a member can do or say to have control includes some of the following:

1. Self-talk
   I have been through this before and survived.
   This will not last forever.
   I can get through this.
   Count to ten and take some deep breaths.
2. Being held by another person
3. Listening to soothing music
4. Eating a soothing food
5. Being assured by someone in charge that the problem precipitating the storm will be cared for or that everything will be okay.
6. Writing in my journal
7. Taking a bath or shower
8. Taking a walk or exercising

This exercise may remind many members of the Comfort Cards made in the early part of the Trauma Recovery and Empowerment intervention. Members may find it useful to share which strategies on the Comfort Cards have proven to be effective. If some strategies do not work, members should say why they failed and brainstorm how they might be improved.

JANE'S STORY

My memories have started coming back to me and with them has come rage. For weeks at a time, I feel rage churning inside me. That out of control feeling starts inside my body, but quickly overflows and taints everything around me. I berate my therapist, my parents, and my friends. I get angry about stupid small things that happened years ago. I don't feel in charge of this feeling; it's in charge of me. I feel anxious and desperate. I want to talk about what is going on, but I can't. I get sarcastic and volatile. I pick fights. So I distance myself from the people who care, and I drop out of my usual activities. This only makes me feel worse, but it's all I can do. I starve myself, and I sleep. Some days I am too tired to feel all the rage, and that is a relief.

I need time to get myself back in control; time and someone understanding who will stick with me, even when I don't make any sense. Sometimes I need tranquilizers to help me calm down, when the anxiety is too much. My therapist gave me a book about trauma and that really helped me understand the recovery process. I want to believe that I'm neither crazy nor alone.

TOPIC 29 Relationships

SESSION RATIONALE

Relationships remain an important and difficult challenge for trauma survivors. Many women consider forming a successful relationship to be the final
stage in their recovery. Yet, most women continue to need assistance in avoiding abusive interpersonal patterns.

GOAL 1: Members will gain a more sophisticated understanding of the
stages of relationship development.

GOAL 2: Members will understand current impediments to forming healthy
relationships.

QUESTIONS

1. What are the key elements of a relationship?
2. What characterizes the stages of a relationship?
3. What ideas or fantasies about relationships interfere with your having a real
   relationship with someone?
4. What behaviors, attitudes, or circumstances ruin or prohibit relationships?

EXERCISES

1. Leaders will draw a relationship continuum as shown below. Members will
   discuss where their own relationships fit on the continuum.

   Casual   Closest
   Acquaintance _____   Friend

   Leaders will ask members where lovers, family members, roommates,
   and so forth fit on the continuum.

2. Make a list of the things you absolutely will not tolerate in a relationship. Is this list different from a year ago? Ten years ago?

LEADERS' NOTES

QUESTION 1

What are the key elements of a relationship?

TYPICAL RESPONSES   Coming together
Having something in common
Feeling attached to another person
Bonding
Feeling reciprocity
Feeling trust
Feeling mutuality toward one another
Participating in good communication
Feeling empathic toward the other person

Many members have such limited experience with relationships that they need some time to step back and define just what constitutes a relationship. The beginning step often involves members' recognition that a relationship includes more than sexual or romantic intimacy. Members come to see that the term *relationship* applies to the connections they have with family members, friends, and even therapists. For many, this question will be a review of material discussed in past sessions.

QUESTION 2

What characterizes the stages of a relationship?

TYPICAL RESPONSES

INITIAL PHASE   Thinking about first impressions
Being cautious
Finding out about the other person's interests

	Looking at physical appearance and body language Being curious about the other person Feeling attracted Feeling comfortable
MIDDLE PHASE	Doing things together Taking the initiative and investing more time with each other Beginning to idealize the other person Disclosing more about myself Building respect for the other person and the relationship Becoming more sexually intimate Building trust
SUBSEQUENT PHASES	Feeling a strong connection to the specific individual Experiencing disappointment Humanizing the person and accepting imperfections Making future plans together Being able to sustain the relationship through ups and downs

By breaking the process of engaging in a relationship into quasi-developmental stages, members come to see relationships as dynamic and changing rather than as static and lifeless. The concept of stages in a relationship also helps members to key their expectations of others to the specific phase of the relationship.

QUESTION 3

What ideas or fantasies about relationships interfere with your having a real relationship with someone?

TYPICAL RESPONSES	I should never make the first move. The other person has to be perfect. The other person should be serious, hard working, and successful.

If I open up or become vulnerable, I will lose
   control.
Relationships are too much trouble and are like full-
   time jobs.
Happy couples never argue.
When they really know me, they will reject me.
The intensity will last forever.
The other person will rescue me from my life.

You may need to assist members by giving an example of how certain cognitions may influence how we behave in a relationship and what we expect from others. Leaders can use one or two of the typical responses as examples.

QUESTION 4

What behaviors, attitudes, or circumstances ruin or prohibit relationships?

TYPICAL RESPONSES   Only meeting people who are different from me
Being controlled by someone
Being exploited or abused
Being rejected
Fearing that I will lose control
Worrying that I might have to change my behavior
People who are cynical and sarcastic
People who are unkind and critical
Someone who is defensive
Someone who is easily distracted by others and
   doesn't pay attention to me
Someone who has a hidden agenda
Someone who wants physical intimacy too quickly
Someone who is insensitive to my needs
Someone who always needs to be in charge
Feeling pessimistic about relationships
Doubting that I can even have a relationship
Someone abusing drugs

Members may begin by trashing potential partners, operating on the assumption that relationships fail because of the faults of others. You may need to redirect members to consider what they do to sabotage new relationships.

ADDITIONAL QUESTIONS

1. How do you handle disappointment in a relationship?
2. What is emotional safety in a relationship and how can you achieve it?

EXERCISE 1

CONTINUUM Most members have more experience with casual acquaintances than they do with intimates. Be careful that members do not feel shamed because they have so few close relationships.

EXERCISE 2

TYPICAL RESPONSES **I WILL NOT TOLERATE:**
Lying
Deceptiveness
Being used
Being put down
A lack of communication
Being ridiculed
Physical or sexual abuse, but I can tolerate some
   emotional abuse
Being abandoned after someone promised me she
   would be there for me
Being treated unfairly or unjustly
Someone who doesn't have any ambition
Someone who is still involved in another
   relationship

Members often have no difficulty naming what they will not tolerate. They have much more trouble addressing how they can actually keep these negative elements out of their relationships.

NOREEN'S STORY

I'm feeling so much more confident and comfortable with myself, but sometimes I have such a hard time with other people. My boyfriend says that he loves me, but sometimes I feel like he doesn't know the real me, and if he did, he couldn't possibly care for me any more. It's like there's this ugly monster within me that I have to keep hidden so that others will like me.

I'm afraid to take the next step in our relationship—afraid to open up and let him know me. I realize that I do things to keep distance. I make small talk, keep things light and breezy. I withdraw when he tries to get too close. Sometimes I tell him I have to work late, just so I can get the space I need.

TOPIC 30 Personal Healing

SESSION RATIONALE

As women come to the end of the Trauma Recovery and Empowerment intervention, many express a desire to move beyond the pain of abuse. This session shifts the focus from the past to the present and from the work done inside the group to the world outside. Women appreciate the chance to assess their strengths and at the same time to plan for the recovery work that remains to be done.

GOAL 1: Members will gain an understanding of the personal process of recovery and will take inventory of their own progress.

GOAL 2: Members will look beyond the group to the next steps in their healing.

QUESTIONS

1. What more would need to change for you to feel you had recovered?
2. What has been your greatest strength in the process of healing?
3. What has been the biggest obstacle to overcoming the effects of abuse?
4. What role does reaching out to others play in your recovery?

EXERCISE

Each member will design a Resource Treasure Chest. Leaders will ask each member, "If you were to collect all the things you need for your recovery, what would they be?" The Resource Treasure Chest may include a list of names, supportive activities and networks, phone numbers, quotes and readings, and personal characteristics.

LEADERS' NOTES

QUESTION 1

What more would need to change for you to feel you had recovered?

TYPICAL RESPONSES The flashbacks would stop.
I would stop thinking about the abuse all the time.
I would feel joyful and lighthearted again.
I would see the abuse as only one part of my past.
I would be able to relax.
I would be more forgiving of myself.
I would finally forgive the abuser.
I would be able to fall in love and sustain the relationship.
I would no longer drink to feel comfortable.
I would enjoy sex.

Be careful that members identify realistic goals. Impossible changes, such as making the past different, should be discouraged. You may want to help members plan how a particular recovery goal might be accomplished.

QUESTION 2

What has been your greatest strength in the process of healing?

TYPICAL RESPONSES My determination
My optimism
My belief in God
My sense of humor
My own fantasies
My hopes and dreams
My ability to think things through
My ability to find good friends to talk with
My belief in myself
My ability to focus beyond my own story
My courage to go through the process of therapy

Once again, help women focus on specific and personal strengths. Women who identify external sources of support should be encouraged to focus on internal resources as well.

QUESTION 3

What has been the biggest obstacle to overcoming the effects of abuse?

TYPICAL RESPONSES Fear
Dealing with my anger
Having ongoing contact with the abuser
Substance use
Being unable to stop blaming myself
Being unable to understand or explain what happened
Being impatient for recovery to begin
Being angry because I can't change the past
Not taking the abuse seriously
Getting too caught up in other people's problems
Feeling depressed saps my energy
Feeling defeated and powerless

This question may repeat some of the material generated in question 1. Leaders should distinguish those obstacles that can be removed and those that must be accepted.

QUESTION 4

What role does reaching out to others play in your recovery?

TYPICAL RESPONSES So far I haven't been able to.
It helps me to gain perspective.
I feel less alone.
By helping others I feel more worthwhile.
I feel strong when I help someone else.
Talking to others has validated my experience and
confirmed that I wasn't crazy.

> Helps me focus on the positive aspects of healing
>   rather than just the negative.
> It allows me to make a contribution.
> It gives meaning to what I've gone through.
> It means I have really learned something and can
>   move on.
> It allows me to see that other people accept me for
>   who I am.
> It helps me get to the next stage of my healing.

Begin by helping members to distinguish between reaching out because they need help and reaching out because they are ready to help someone else.

ADDITIONAL QUESTIONS

1. What is the next step for you in your process of integration?
2. What are the negative aspects of acknowledging and sharing your trauma history?

EXERCISE

Ask members, "If you were to collect all the things you need for your recovery into a Resource Treasure Chest, what would you include?"

> **TYPICAL RESPONSES** A phone list of people to call for support
>   My comfort card from this group
>   Pictures of happy events and safe places
>   A list of my strengths
>   My Bible
>   My journal
>   A list of activities I enjoy
>   My favorite quote
>   My sense of humor
>   A stuffed animal

Members should include both tangible (My Bible) and intangible (My sense of humor) treasures.

MAXINE'S STORY

The group was almost over, only three more sessions left. At this point, I always assume that the women have gotten whatever they are going to get from the group. There will be no new revelations, just a gradual winding down and saying good-bye.

For almost 12 months, Ruth had talked about her history of spousal abuse. Her husband had beaten her regularly for over 10 years. Often she would ask questions about incest. Can you ever recover? Isn't that the worst kind of abuse? Doesn't incest ruin your life? Just questions mind you; yet I knew that somewhere deep inside Ruth had buried a story of incest.

As we talked about personal healing and the things that helped, women mentioned many things: self-acceptance, forgiveness, and over and over again the ability to share your story with someone, trusting someone enough to say the dreaded words out loud.

I was sitting next to Ruth. She turned to me with tears in her eyes and said, "My stepfather raped me when I was nine years old. My whole life changed; I had plans. I was going to go to college. Nothing was ever the same. How do you tell your mother that her husband just had sex with you? I couldn't; so I blocked it out—blocked everything out. I lost my whole childhood, lost so many years. What a waste."

I looked at her, tears in my eyes too, held her hand for a minute. The group fell silent. There it was, the moment of personal healing.

PART IV

Closing Rituals

TOPIC 31   Truths and Myths About Abuse

SESSION RATIONALE

Coming at the end of the module, this topic helps women to evaluate how they have changed and to assess what further work they need to do to continue their recovery. Distorted assumptions about male and female behavior and about abuse contribute to the injurious and long-lasting impact of childhood trauma. As those assumptions change, women are better able to relabel past events and to move forward.

GOAL 1: Group members will review how their understanding of abuse has evolved.

GOAL 2: Group members will solidify a more reality-based perception of what abuse is and is not.

QUESTIONS

1. What is a myth?
2. What are some commonly held myths about abuse?
3. What role have societal or familial myths about men and women in general played in your own ideas about abuse?
4. Have any of your beliefs about abuse changed since you began attending this group? If so, give examples of your current beliefs.
5. Why do the various myths about abuse have so much influence over how we think?

EXERCISE

Women should generate a list of items under the heading, "What I know to be true about abuse." This exercise should help women develop an inventory of what they have learned as a result of the Trauma Recovery Skills Program.

Women should focus on how their ideas and feelings have changed as well as highlighting what beliefs about trauma remain unchanged.

LEADERS' NOTES

QUESTION 1

What is a myth?

TYPICAL RESPONSES   A story that explains some phenomenon
A fable
A story that is not completely true
False beliefs
An explanation handed down from one generation
to the next
A story used to explain something that really has no
explanation
A way to justify behaviors and beliefs
An old wives' tale

The purpose of this question is to help members begin to see that unproven and often erroneous assumptions and myths underlie much of our behavior. Once members have gained that core insight, you can move on to the next question. The discussion should not focus on myth as literature or on the relative merits of particular myths.

QUESTION 2

What are some commonly held myths about abuse?

TYPICAL RESPONSES   Women who get abused must ask for it in some way.
If a woman really wants to, she can resist attempts
to abuse her.
Physical abuse is just a good, old-fashioned form of
discipline.
If abuse occurs only one time then it is not really
damaging or upsetting.

Abusers are just being playful or masculine—some
version of "boys will be boys."

There is something wrong with you if you cannot
just forget the abuse.

You were mistreated because you were really bad.

Memories that come to you later in life are false.

The husband has the right to do what he wants.

A woman would never abuse me.

If you get pregnant or have an orgasm, it's not rape.

Incest is how you learn about sex.

If they love you, it's not really abuse.

Women who dress seductively are asking to be
raped.

If you love someone enough, you can get them to
change.

If you have been abused, you become abusive.

After several months of group participation members should be able to generate a list of false beliefs about abuse. Members may also feel comfortable
admitting which of these myths they did, or still do, believe.

QUESTION 3

What role have societal or familial myths about men and women in general
played in your own ideas about abuse?

TYPICAL RESPONSES   **Common Myths**
Women are weak and need men to survive.

I need a baby to feel good about myself.

Men are superior to women.

Men are supposed to dominate.

Women are too emotional.

A woman should stand by her man.

A woman is nothing without a man.

No means yes.

What role have these myths played?
Caused me to blame myself when anything went
    wrong
Made me feel passive and helpless
Made me feel guilty
Caused me to be easily intimidated
Made me ashamed of being abused
Made me feel I should stay with the abuser
Made me feel the abuse was okay

Some of the myths suggest reasons why women remain in abusive relationships or why certain symptoms and dysfunctional behaviors develop. Women
may begin to see how personal and cultural attitudes contributed to the destructive impact of the abuse itself.

Question 4

Have any of your beliefs about abuse changed since you began attending this
group? If so, give examples of your current beliefs.

TYPICAL RESPONSES   Abuse is not only sexual or physical but can be
                          emotional, too.
                      Emotional abuse can be as damaging as other forms
                          of abuse.
                      The abuse did not happen because I allowed it . . . it
                          happened because the abuser had power over
                          me.
                      I am not the only one who has been abused.
                      Physical abuse is *not* an old-fashioned form of dis-
                          cipline.
                      My being abused is no excuse for abusing others.
                      It is always rape when I don't give my consent.
                      I don't think it was my fault anymore.
                      I can be abusive, too.
                      I realize the abuse affected my life.

Encourage members to do a serious and honest inventory of their beliefs. Women who still hold on to certain myths should not be made to feel ashamed for admitting what they believe. Rather, the discussion can focus on why these unfounded assumptions hold so much power. Make sure that members do not just pay lip service to what they believe leaders want to hear.

QUESTION 5

Why do the various myths about abuse have so much influence over how we think?

TYPICAL RESPONSES   Myths allow the abuser to avoid taking responsibility for his or her actions.

Myths permit people to deny the truth about abuse.

People believe myths because they don't understand how anyone could be an abuser or do such horrible things to another human being.

People would rather believe the abuser than the survivor.

Myths justify the power imbalance between women and men.

Religion gives validity to the myths.

They are passed within our families by mothers and grandmothers.

The truth would destroy my family.

Women may feel more comfortable discussing why others believe these myths than why they themselves still hold to beliefs that are unsubstantiated by any data. You will want to balance the discussion between personal motives and social/political agendas.

ADDITIONAL QUESTIONS

1. Are there some myths that are particularly difficult to give up?
2. Are there some beliefs that you have used to combat these myths?

EXERCISE

TYPICAL RESPONSES

Truths About Abuse

It destroys self-esteem.

I feel very passive because of my abuse experiences.

I have poor boundaries.

It is hurtful.

I'm learning that the responsibility rests with the abuser.

It takes a lot of work and pain to understand my abuse experiences and how they have affected my life.

Abuse can continue into adulthood and sometimes it can get worse.

It has distorted my reality and makes me doubt my own judgment.

Ignoring abuse doesn't make it go away.

It can cause physical symptoms.

It can ruin my sex life.

It can make me distrust people.

This exercise may be painful for some women as they realize how much abuse has cost them in their lives. The exercise helps women not only to review their progress but also to give testimony about the progress they have made.

ROSETTA'S STORY

My father was a mean drunk. He used to come home and beat my brother most nights. Then my brother would turn around and hit me. My mother told us that all the hitting was OK because we were a "close family." For a long time I believed that was true.

In recovery, I have been able to understand that closeness is not about being hit. I am accepting that my older, bigger brother was actually hurting me. I no longer believe that I gave as good as I got in those fights or that I'm so tough it doesn't matter.

TOPIC 32   What It Means to Be a Woman

SESSION RATIONALE

A woman's self-esteem is closely tied to her views about womanhood. If she has only negative feelings about being a woman, it is difficult for her to feel very good about herself. If the trauma intervention has helped women to feel better about themselves, then it also will have changed the way they feel about being women.

GOAL: Each member will revisit her feelings about womanhood as a way of summarizing and integrating her group experience.

QUESTIONS

1. What does being a woman mean to you?
2. What are your feelings about being a woman?
3. How have your feelings about yourself and about being a woman changed during this group?

EXERCISE

Leaders and members will review the responses given during the original discussion of what it means to be a woman (Topic 2). Members should discuss whether their responses differ since participating in the group. The exercise is done at the same time as members answer questions 1 and 2.

LEADERS' NOTES

QUESTION 1

What does being a woman mean to you?

ORIGINAL TYPICAL RESPONSES	CURRENT TYPICAL RESPONSES
Being the strong one	Being an individual
Being a good girl	Not being vulnerable
Being a caretaker	No longer staying behind the scenes
Being a doormat	No longer listening to "You can't"
Being a sex object	Doing what I want to do
Being assertive = Bitch	Feeling strong
Being dumb	Making my own decisions
Being a baby machine	Being a mother
Being vulnerable with the	Not living through a man opposite sex
	Not doing things because of others' expectations
	Being in control of my body
	Being able to be responsible for myself even when it's difficult

In general, women's views change to reflect more individuality, greater strength, and increased independence. Women often express surprise that they actually held their earlier views. Some may even have trouble remembering the statements they made at the beginning of the group. Some women may still hold negative views and they too should be given a chance to express their opinions.

QUESTION 2

What are your feelings about being a woman?

ORIGINAL TYPICAL RESPONSES	CURRENT TYPICAL RESPONSES
Sad	Pleased.
Disgusted	I'm feeling more worthy.
Lonely	I feel more accepting of myself.
Unable to trust	I'm no longer sad about being a woman.
Feeling unworthy	
Hostile	I'm feeling more powerful.
Tired	I'm feeling glad that I'm a woman.
Wished I'd been a man	I'm still working on my ability to trust.

Angry	I'm feeling less dependent on others.
Frustrated	I'm feeling stronger.
Strange	Sometimes I still feel sad.
Guilty	I'm feeling more connected to other
Powerless	women.
	I am more appreciative of my body.
	I'm better able to trust other women.

Generally women's feelings become more positive. There is often a striking absence of anger and hostility. As women feel more empowered, more competent, and more hopeful about their lives, they have less reason to be angry. Women also report a greater acceptance of themselves and a newly found appreciation for their strengths and skills.

QUESTION 3

How have your feelings about yourself and about being a woman changed during this group?

TYPICAL RESPONSES I have started listening to my own voice.

I'm getting to know myself better and to realize what I want in my life.

I feel less need for validation from others.

I realize that I have a choice about whom I involve myself with in relationships.

I've started asking myself, "What do I expect *from* myself and *for* myself?"

I realize that I am important.

I now understand that many of my behaviors were just a way to cope with the abuse.

Be careful that members do not feel obliged solely to praise the group experience. Women who feel profoundly moved by the group will predictably be the most vocal. You want to ensure that women whose feelings have not changed also feel entitled to speak out.

SONDRA'S STORY

I've learned so much about myself from this group. I now realize that being a woman doesn't mean that you have to be submissive and always be the victim. I'm clearer about who is responsible for things. I realize that my husband was responsible for beating me, but I need to accept responsibility for not leaving him. My sense of who I am comes from inside me now. I don't rely on my current boyfriend to tell me who I am. I know I have a ways to go, but I feel happy about who I am for the first time in my life, and I am excited about the person I am becoming.

I never thought I could get out of the hole I was in. It seemed so hopeless with no solutions. Now I see that I have a voice and that I can be responsible for my own life and not be controlled by others. Being a woman can mean that you're strong and in control of your life.

TOPIC 33 Closing Ritual

SESSION RATIONALE

So often, women do not have good experiences with saying good-bye. Endings are aborted or painful. This last session gives women a chance to say good-bye in a meaningful and caring way.

GOAL: Women will have a chance to process their group experiences and say good-bye.

EXERCISES

CLOSING RITUAL

1. *Ritual Cleansing* Members will sit in a circle around a large bowl placed on a small table. In turn, each member will be given a smooth rock to hold while another member pours warm water over her hands. Each member will wash away something in her life that she does not want. It may be a memory, a feeling, an attitude, or a belief. After each member washes the rock, the entire group will join in tossing out the water.
2. *Medicine Bag* Leaders will buy or collect small semiprecious stones, beads, natural objects, or anything that can serve as a totem (5 or 6 per person) and small bags to be used as Native American medicine bags. Leaders will place the totems on a table with a written statement about what each object represents (health, strength, happiness, etc.). Each member will take a medicine bag and choose which objects she wishes to take to symbolize her new life goals. Women can place the objects in the medicine bags that they can then wear around their necks as a remembrance of the group experience.
3. *Parting Meal* The leaders will bring supplies (e.g., cider, juice, soda, and some sweet bread) for a bread breaking ritual. Members and leaders can then sit around the circle sharing food and discussing the group experience, their individual progress, and their future plans.

LEADERS' NOTES

You will need the following supplies in preparation for the Ritual Cleansing, Medicine Bag, and Parting Meal exercises:

Ritual Cleansing	One smooth rock the size of a potato One or two pitchers of warm water One large bowl Paper towels
Medicine Bag	Enough semiprecious stones, beads, or symbols to allow every group member and leader to select five or six totems each One medicine bag for each member and leader Definitions of totems typed onto labels
Parting Meal	Cider, juice, or soda Sweet bread Napkins and cups

EXERCISE 1

RITUAL CLEANSING

TYPICAL RESPONSES   I would like to wash away some of the physical pain I carry around.

I want to give up being so concerned about other people's feelings that I do not take care of myself.

I would like to give up thinking that others always have the wrong impression of me.

I want to give up the feeling of not being loved and not loving myself.

I want to wash away my habit of trying to control other people and what they do.

I would like to give away some of the things in the past that I have been holding onto.

> I would like to give up the way I have disregarded
> my own inner voice.

Women are quite thoughtful about what they want to give up. Some consider two or three things before deciding. Occasionally women realize that there are some things they are not yet ready to relinquish.

EXERCISE 2

MEDICINE BAG The semiprecious stones, beads, symbols, and so on, may have the following meanings:

Emerald	This soft green gem contains the energy of the Goddess Venus. It brings love, good luck, and richness to its owner.
Cowrie shell	Remembrance of one's heritage and connection to one's roots and is regarded as a female symbol.
Rose quartz	This stone brings healing to the inner child and promotes increased self-esteem.
Cat	Signifies wisdom and the ability always to land on one's feet.
Feather	Carries to its owner energy to endure, gentle strength, and the trust to bend with the changes of life.
Azulite	This stone helps its owner to receive and share messages from spiritual guides.
Garnet	According to Native American legend, this stone heals and protects its owner.
White quartz	Promotes healing and works as an energizer.
Jade	Brings peace and calm and intensifies expressive ability.
Seashell	Like a walk alone beside the ocean, a shell can

remind its owner of her power, her ability to go on, and her beauty.

Green pine cone   Each new cone carries to her owner the capability to create herself anew.

Brown pine cone   This mature cone offers security for reflection, and the ability to learn from past mistakes and to see one's successes.

Fish   A female symbol.

Green tourmaline   This stone brings healing to the heart of its owner; it inspires balance and promotes joy and creativity.

Smoky quartz   The clarity of this stone carries with it positive energy to be fully in the here-and-now; its depth brings strength for reaching one's goals.

Orange calcite   This stone reminds one to keep a sense of humor and facilitates change with a sense of joy and anticipation.

Most of the above stones, beads, symbols, and medicine bags can be purchased at do-it-yourself bead shops or New Age gem stores. You should take the above list merely as suggestions and should feel free to substitute any comparable and readily available items. If you are unable to find actual items, substitute pictures cut from magazines.

Women usually choose their totems carefully. Often, after sharing the group experience, women know which member needs which totem and members join in making sure each women gets what she needs. Make sure that there are enough objects so that each woman feels she has been cared for. You may also want to remind members that the bags are symbolic and if a woman's bag is lost or stolen, she still retains the valuable lessons she has learned in the group.

EXERCISE 3

PARTING MEAL During the meal, women share conversation and reminisce about the group.

SOPHIE'S STORY

I wasn't going to come today, just make up some excuse that I was sick or something. I hate good-byes. They sound so final. This group has been so important, just to know that I'm not the only one who has had terrible things happen to me. I have found new supports and an energy to move on that gets me excited.

I'm sitting here, and I'm supposed to think of some feeling or memory that I want to wash away or get rid of. It's hard to decide on one thing. If I had to make a choice, I guess it would be my anger. This anger has overwhelmed me and poisoned all my relationships. I've never thought about it before, but it's exhausting to be angry all the time.

This ceremony is making me sad because the group is over, but I'm also understanding that it's helping me review my experiences. I don't think I've ever had a good ending before. I have always gotten angry in the past, leaving people before they could hurt and leave me. Maybe there is another way to do it.

PART V

Modifications or Supplements for Special Populations

WOMEN DIAGNOSED WITH SERIOUS MENTAL ILLNESS

Margaret D. Hobbs, M.S.W.

Rebecca M. Wolfson, M.S.W.

INTRODUCTION

Women diagnosed with a psychotic spectrum disorder experience significant impairment in both their quality of life and their functioning in the world. These women share many of the problems of women in other special populations, such as homelessness, substance addiction, and single motherhood. In addition, they have unique difficulties, such as disordered thinking, hallucinations, cognitive impairments, and experiences of institutionalization. These women also have an increased vulnerability to stress, a tendency to decompensate periodically, and the need for occasional hospitalization. Therefore, leaders must make some special alterations in treatment protocols to facilitate trauma recovery work.

Clinicians may be concerned that the material in *Trauma Recovery and Empowerment* is too threatening and/or difficult for women with severe emotional or mental disorders to address. It is important to remember, however, that this manual was initially developed in an agency that serves this very population. This chapter suggests adaptations to the core manual that take into account the special needs of women with serious mental illness (SMI).

GENERAL PRINCIPLES OF WORKING WITH SMI WOMEN

Women with serious mental illness may be withdrawn and unsure of themselves. They may be frightened of new and unfamiliar people and settings. They are accustomed to being overlooked and excluded. Connecting with clinicians is difficult; groups are particularly troubling as members must interact with leaders as well as with other participants. As groups are forming, women with serious mental illness need special outreach and frequent contacts with leaders. To encourage attendance, these women need repeated invitations that let them know that their participation is valued and that they are welcome. All contacts should be respectful and as nonintrusive as possible.

Disorganized thinking and somewhat chaotic presentation are often additional identifying markers of chronic mental illness. Women may present with tangential and confused thinking. They may be slow to grasp information and to connect discrete fragments of data into usable material. They generally have little experience of being challenged to think for themselves or to make their own decisions. The social skills model of the group works well for these women. It provides structure and safety while encouraging focus and order. Concepts are easier to grasp in a psychoeducational format. Experiential and artistic exercises hopefully present the work in an enjoyable way and allow clients to be successful group members.

Women with chronic mental illness are likely to have great difficulty in managing practical issues required by group attendance. They may have difficulties with transportation and time and money management. It can be difficult for group leaders to address these problems without crossing boundaries. Active practical support from the referring clinician may be needed to deal with these issues.

Sadly, most women with chronic mental illness have a great deal of experience with the uglier aspects of life. They may have histories of street drug use and prostitution. Leaders need to deal with these issues carefully. These women do not need to be judged any more; they have dealt with criticism much of their lives. Leaders do, however, need to give women genuine feedback, pointing out destructive behaviors and suggesting new options where possible.

Finally, women with emotional problems severe enough to have a major impact on their lives often are seen as being much more vulnerable to stress with resulting decompensation than other women. Special care should be given to individuals who appear vulnerable. These women are allowed to remain silent during discussion of certain issues or topics. Checking in with the women at the end of each session is also a good idea. It is important, however, that leaders be aware of boundary issues and that they rely on the referring clinicians to help deal with an individual woman's distress.

Specific Issues Pertaining to Women with SMI

Engaging withdrawn and socially insecure women is the initial step in forming the group. These women respond well to personal invitation, expressed interest in their stories and problems, and repeated encouragement to attend from leaders. Because there are many practical and psychological obstacles to a woman's attendance at the group, leaders need to take some steps to facilitate each woman's participation. Leaders should call each member the night before the group to remind her of the time and place of the group and to reiterate to her that her participation is important to the group. Although attendance and participation in the group is important, rules about missing sessions, leaving sessions early, or remaining quiet in the session should be flexible as some women may need to absent themselves from material they are not yet ready to discuss. This show of respect from leaders promotes a sense of safety and facilitates engagement and relationship building.

Structure is another important aspect of these groups. The safety and effectiveness of the group will be strengthened by following the social skills format of the manual. Leaders will find that keeping both the sessions' goals and questions in mind will move group members through the material in an organized and focused way. It is important to spend as much time as needed on the primary questions rather than to try to cover the additional questions. When time allows, the additional questions provide enrichment opportunities that supplement the core material. The exercises are an important part of each session because they allow women to express their feelings nonverbally. Some women may feel more comfortable participating in artistic/movement activities.

Typically, one to two leaders facilitate group work. For this population, however, three leaders are recommended. The addition of a third leader allows for individual attention for women who may be struggling or upset during and/or after the group. It also increases the chances that each group member will form a connection with a leader. With the intensity of the group and the highly emotional content of the women's stories, more than one clinician is needed to manage the group effectively. Two or more leaders can process the group better afterward and provide support to one another.

Another factor that affects attendance and the ultimate success of the group is the involvement of the member's primary case manager or therapist. A client should be able to have contact with her primary case manager or therapist after the group if she feels the need for additional support before leaving the clinic. Within the context of the host agency, the leaders should assess how much support they can expect to receive from the referring clinician. The referring clinician can be helpful in assisting the client with both logistical and clinical issues. And while the support and potentially active assistance from the referring clinician may be valuable, this involvement needs to be tempered with respect for confidentiality. The leader should not assume that the referring clinician knows the specific details of the client's story. For clinical and ethical reasons, the client should control the sharing of her trauma history. The only exception to this rule is the exchange of information about dangerousness, as information about suicidality and homicidality must be shared with the larger system and dealt with quickly.

While most women with psychotic disorders can effectively participate in this group, not all women with psychotic disorders can. A woman whose thinking is always confused and/or whose speech is very tangential is not a good referral to this group. The group can handle a few quiet, withdrawn, and somewhat tangential members if there are enough verbal members participating at the same time. Severe paranoia should be evaluated carefully. The group may exacerbate paranoia as the women talk of very private issues and feelings. Moreover, a woman's paranoid concerns may be compounded when she has contact with other members in more than one setting. Group members may share housing, psychiatrists, and even a case manager. In many cases, a woman's paranoia can be tempered by leaders' stating the rules about confidentiality very clearly and often. If this is not enough to reassure the woman, she may not feel comfortable participating in the group.

Another consideration in the group makeup is the variety of symptoms exhibited by the women. Some women are symptom free, others are depressed and withdrawn, and others may make bizarre statements or act out. So that the more bizarre statements are not ridiculed or do not distract from the group discussion, leaders can take a variety of approaches to handle the less organized client. A leader may validate an individual woman's experience while pointing out that it may not be a common or shared experience. If possible, the leader should extract the relevant idea and restate the comment for the group. There will be times when a client is so disruptive to the group process that one leader will need to escort the client out of the group and speak with her individually. The member is welcome back in the group when she is again able to participate. The consistency of the same leaders, same group location, and the social skills format of the group help to stabilize the group and keep members on target.

Leaders experienced in group work with higher functioning women will be familiar with the ability of participants to connect one topic logically to the next. Women with psychotic thinking, however, will struggle much more with concepts and will need to have connections made for them. They tend to be less spontaneous in discussion and more reactive to ideas articulated by other group members and the leaders. This means that leaders need to be prepared to do a good deal of focusing, keeping the group on topic, and even prompting responses. Leaders also will need to provide links and transitions as they guide the group to deeper levels of understanding. Leaders should be aware of their own vocabulary as some members may not be as sophisticated as others.

Leaders should be prepared to state ideas, questions, and concepts in several ways. It is a good idea for leaders to take nothing for granted, and to monitor reactions to ensure that members understand and follow the material. The abilities of individual members will vary greatly. It is better to recruit women who vary in their level of functioning to a single group rather than to track groups by cognitive ability. The slower women often learn effectively from their higher-functioning peers. In turn, their questions and comments may help the higher-functioning women look more closely at some issues. Group members may range in educational experience from illiteracy to advanced degrees. For this reason it is important that a variety of activities be offered. Drawing, making collages, and movement exercises, as well as discussion, allow all members to express their strengths.

Leaders will have to work actively to keep discussion lively and relevant. Leaders should expect to help women articulate their ideas and feelings through interaction and prompting. Modeling by leaders will help facilitate discussion as many of these women will be withdrawn and timid about revealing their opinions and emotions in front of others. Leaders should be prepared to participate in the exercises both by helping members and by doing the exercises themselves. The more disorganized women in the group may need some individual attention from a leader during the exercise portion of the session.

Women with SMI are particularly vulnerable to stress and have difficulty managing anxiety. Both client and clinician may fear that participation in the group will stimulate flashbacks and upsetting memories that will overwhelm the client and lead to increased psychiatric symptomatology and to a hospitalization. Therefore, it is the leaders' responsibility to monitor carefully the women's responses to group material, noting any difficulty they have in managing stress. As each session comes to a close, leaders should sum up the content of the session to help participants gain control over issues and anxieties raised during the group until those issues can be safely addressed again in the next meeting. In a member's efforts to manage her own stress, she may choose to sit out for certain sessions or to take a break from all of the material. In many cases leaders need only to support the client's decision, but in a few cases the leader or referring clinician may need to encourage the client to take a break or to discontinue her participation in the group altogether. When a client decides to discontinue her participation in the group, she should retain the option to start again in another group at a later date.

Flexibility around participation will allow this population to reap the greatest benefits from the psychoeducational model. Some clients who complete the group will want to repeat it because they were unable to absorb much of the material the first time around. Others who missed a number of sessions or needed to drop out because of either external circumstances such as transportation difficulties or medical problems, or simply because they were not yet ready to deal with trauma issues, may be ready for a group in the future. Leaders should remain positive with clients and referring clinicians about the option of participating in a future group.

Ultimately, leaders need to attend to the balance of providing the group with structure and also allowing individuals flexibility and granting them understanding.

ISSUES OF DIAGNOSIS

Generally, women with psychotic symptoms are grouped together under the diagnosis of schizophrenia. Some psychotic symptoms, however, may have originated out of the need to organize and cope with extreme anxiety and pain. Such coping can result from severe abuse, major depression, or a single traumatic experience. Initially, leaders may not be able to distinguish this type of psychosis from true biological schizophrenia. As the group progresses, however, leaders should consider the origins of each woman's symptoms to help develop realistic goals for each client. Women who do not suffer from true biological schizophrenia will make the most significant change in behavior and symptoms. The combination of antipsychotic medications and a structured trauma intervention is likely to lessen psychotic symptoms and increase a woman's level of functioning. Truly schizophrenic women can benefit from the group intervention, but do not show such a marked shift in level of functioning. They benefit in such ways as increasing self-esteem, gaining comfort in relating to others, and expanding their ability to self-soothe. Although there may be a decrease in psychotic symptoms and some improvement in level of functioning, it is unlikely to be as great as that achieved by nonschizophrenic women.

The following sessions have been modified to address the special needs and issues of women with serious mental illness.

TOPIC 18 Institutional Abuse

The questions, session rationale, and leaders' notes remain the same as the session in the main manual. Leaders, however, will need to direct the session toward the specific abuses of the mental health system. While these women will have experienced other types of institutional abuse, their experiences of abuses in the mental health system may be of more immediate concern to them. Following are the questions and typical responses leaders are likely to hear from women with diagnoses of serious mental illness.

LEADERS' NOTES

QUESTION 1

What helpers or people in authority in your life have abused you?

TYPICAL RESPONSES

Psych techs	Social workers
Group home staff person	My psychiatrist
Nurses	Teachers
Doctors	Case managers
Receptionist in doctor's offices or hospitals	Lawyers
	Ministers

QUESTION 2

Did you try to tell someone about the abuse? What happened?

TYPICAL RESPONSES I tried to tell my doctor but he just gave me more medication.

I told the patient advocate that the nurses were mistreating me but nothing ever changed.

I asked to leave the hospital and they put me in restraints.

> I told the nurse that the psych techs had been too rough when they were bathing me, but I don't know if they ever did anything about it.
>
> I told my mom that my doctor was giving me breast exams even when he saw me for a head cold, and she said just to put up with it . . . there wasn't anything I could do.
>
> I tried to get the police to protect me from my abusive boyfriend. But when I shouted and screamed my boyfriend told them I was a mental patient, and the police took me away to a psychiatric emergency room.

If you did not tell, why not?

TYPICAL RESPONSES
> No one will take you seriously when you have a mental illness diagnosis.
>
> I thought I would need a lot of proof and that without it no one would believe me.
>
> Everyone thought my psychiatrist was so great, they would have thought I was lying to get attention if I said he abused me.
>
> If I told on the nurses I would have gotten put in seclusion.
>
> I really thought that if I said anything it would come back to haunt me.

QUESTION 3

What are the specific abuses of the mental health system?

TYPICAL RESPONSES
> Having my confidentiality violated
> Being overmedicated
> Being put in restraints
> Being hit by a staff person

Having no part in decisions affecting my treatment
Having staff make sexual advances toward me
Being threatened by nurses
Being made fun of by psych techs
Having my privacy violated

ADDITIONAL QUESTIONS

1. How has the abuse changed your pattern of service use?
2. When dealing with the mental health system, how can you present yourself more effectively?

EXERCISE

The exercise from the main manual will be more relevant and useful if the situation is altered by asking members to imagine that they are in a personal crisis and are in an emergency room (ER). Each woman is asked to design her own protocol, detailing how she would like to be treated by the ER personnel.

TOPIC 19 Abuse and Psychiatric Symptoms

The session rationale, leaders' notes, and exercise remain the same as the session in the main manual. The questions are slightly altered to focus on symptoms that are seen as grounds for psychiatric diagnoses. This session addresses the most important issues in trauma recovery, particularly for women who have been diagnosed as mentally ill. For many women, their diagnosis and the mystery of how their symptoms began leaves them feeling helpless to move on in their recovery.

LEADERS' NOTES

QUESTION 1

Name the psychiatric symptoms you have experienced.

The discussion will begin with members' generating a list of psychiatric symptoms they have experienced. Leaders will make sure the list includes some of the following:

TYPICAL RESPONSES		
Depression	Panic Attacks	Anxiety
Delusions	Self-mutilation	Dissociation
Hypervigilance	Paranoia	Isolation
Substance abuse	Mania	Suicidality
Flashbacks	Hallucinations	Eating disorders
Rage	Insomnia	Excessive crying

QUESTION 2

What instance of abuse can you tie to each symptom?

QUESTION 3

In what way was the symptom a reasonable or understandable way of coping with the abuse?

The answers to these questions are used to help complete the Understanding Abuse chart. The chart helps group members understand the connection between trauma and coping strategies previously labeled as psychiatric symptoms. You should return to the member who gave a particular symptom to obtain the corresponding answers to Questions 2 and 3.

UNDERSTANDING ABUSE: TYPICAL RESPONSES

SYMPTOM (From Question 1)	ABUSE (From Question 2)	UNDERSTANDING (From Question 3)
Dissociation	My father having sex with me	To escape and survive the abuse
Paranoia	My family always protecting and covering up for the abuser	I had to be on the lookout to protect myself because I couldn't count on anyone else to help me. It wasn't safe to trust anyone.
Anxiety	Waiting for my father to get home and beat me	I was hyperalert so I could brace myself for the inevitable.
Depression	Being told I was evil again and again	I felt so hopeless and desperate.
Substance abuse	Watching my father beat my mother	I had to numb myself from the fear and pain.

ADDITIONAL QUESTIONS

1. Do you remember when you were first diagnosed as having a mental illness? Was abuse involved in any way?
2. What might the consequences be for relinquishing a particular symptom?

TOPIC 20-A Abuse and Homelessness

SESSION RATIONALE

Many women with serious mental illness, particularly those with a history of substance abuse, have experienced periods of homelessness. Often abuse and its aftereffects have played the major role in the loss of housing. Introducing women to the idea that homelessness has roots in their abuse and in their response to that abuse may help women expand their notion of alternative, safe housing options.

GOAL 1: Each member will begin to understand how abuse begins a process of alienation and exile that may end in homelessness.

GOAL 2: Each member will begin to understand her own choices about housing arrangements.

This session should be inserted between Topic 20, Trauma and Addictive or Compulsive Behavior and Topic 21, Abuse and Relationships in the core manual.

QUESTIONS

1. If you have ever been homeless, what do you believe caused your homelessness?
2. What are the differences between being on the streets and being in a shelter?
3. What have been the consequences of being homeless?
4. What do you believe would be the ideal living situation for you and what would it take to make that happen?

EXERCISE

Draw your ideal home. What would it look like, what would be in it, and who would be in it?

LEADERS' NOTES

QUESTION 1

If you have ever been homeless, what do you believe caused your homelessness?

TYPICAL RESPONSES   My father kicked me out.
I had to get away from my abusive husband.
I lost my job.
I burned down my house when I was drunk and fell asleep with a lit cigarette.
The street seemed safer.
Nobody knew me at the shelter.
I was too uncomfortable living with roommates and I could not afford to live alone.

You will want to help women look beyond the surface causes of their homelessness. By asking follow-up questions, you can focus on the role abuse and its aftereffects play in causing homelessness.

QUESTION 2

What are the differences between being on the street and being in a shelter?

TYPICAL RESPONSES   There are too many people in shelters.
I can't stand the rules in a shelter.
I want to be free to do what I want to do, when I want to do it.
I think the streets are safer.
People are always stealing my stuff at the shelter.
In a shelter I know there are people who want to help me.
Shelters give you dinner.
People are more generous in the streets.
Shelters won't let my dog in, he keeps me safe.

Try to link group members' responses to issues that may stem from abuse experiences. Not only will this continue to clarify the relationship between abuse and homelessness, but it will also help the women to understand why they make certain choices about housing.

QUESTION 3

What have been the consequences of being homeless?

TYPICAL RESPONSES

Positive	Negative
I don't have to use any of my check for rent.	My kids can't stay with me.
I got out of my abusive family.	I hate being cold.
I feel free.	I can't stay as clean as I would like.
I don't have to deal with anybody if I don't want to.	I don't like people staring at me.
It is easier to get drugs in the streets.	Sometimes I have to beg for money and food.
It's exciting out on the streets.	Sometimes I'm afraid.
	My clothes have gotten stolen.

Allow the women to speak freely. Many may see homelessness in a primarily positive light. It will be important to make sure women are realistic and do not idealize the street life. If some of the women in the group have not been homeless, this discussion may help them have a better understanding about their own housing choices.

QUESTION 4

What do you believe would be the ideal living situation for you and what would it take to make that happen?

TYPICAL RESPONSES   My own home—I would just need more money.
A one bedroom apartment—I want to get on the public housing list.

> Staying with a friend . . . I could afford it and I
>   wouldn't get so lonely.
> Having a rich husband and a house with a white
>   picket fence.
> I often dream about living in a palace.
> Any place that feels safe.
> Moving to a different part of the country where no
>   one knows me.
> With my daughter, she'll take care of me.

You may need to help women modify their fantasies to arrive at more realistic options. This is also a good opportunity to help women become more aware of the steps necessary to obtain an appropriate living situation. Some women will long for more independent living arrangements even though they do not have the skills to live without structure and support. You might gently point out the responsibilities that come with independent living.

ADDITIONAL QUESTIONS

1. What is the relationship between the abuse you have experienced and your homelessness?
2. What changes can you make in your life to prevent future homelessness?

EXERCISE

Have paper and markers or crayons ready for this exercise. Give members the option of doing a collage or describing their picture verbally. You will want to have magazines, tape, and scissors available if some women choose this alternative. After women have completed their drawings, they should discuss their ideal living situations. The focus of the discussion should be primarily who would be in the home and what would be in the home, not so much around what the home looks like.

TOPIC 21 Abuse and Relationships

ADDITIONAL LEADERS' NOTES

This may be a particularly difficult topic for seriously mentally ill women. These women are usually quite limited in their choices for partners in relationships. They tend to live in housing, receive services, and participate in day programs that are limited to the mentally ill. They are socially marginalized and frequently have no choice but to select a partner who is also mentally ill. In most cases, neither partner has the strengths or internal resources to manage the relationship over time.

The Prince Charming myth also may be particularly strong for women who suffer from serious mental illness. Their lives are generally impoverished and lonely. Many still dream of an escape from mental illness and see marriage as their best hope for a normal life filled with comfort and fulfillment. This fantasy leaves them anxious, frustrated, and vulnerable. Mentally ill women with disability incomes or subsidized housing may be susceptible to the charms of substance abusers or psychopathic predators looking for a free ride or a place to hide out. Be prepared to deal with these realities about relationships for mentally ill women. Women require empathy and understanding, balanced with guidance about what they can expect from others and how they can protect themselves.

TOPIC 26–A High-Risk Behaviors

SESSION RATIONALE

Women with serious mental illness and histories of abuse often engage in various types of high-risk behaviors. Their impaired judgment, lack of insight, loneliness, and impulsivity make these women likely to engage in quickly satisfying but potentially dangerous activities. These same factors also make them particularly vulnerable to the ill effects of high-risk behaviors. This session is designed to help women identify which of their behaviors may fulfill some of their needs initially, while bringing on greater problems in the long run. This session also asks the women to look at past experiences to see how they can change their behaviors to avoid serious repercussions.

GOAL 1: Each member will develop an understanding of which of her behaviors are dangerous.

GOAL 2: Each member will develop an understanding of the role dangerous behaviors play in her life.

This session should be inserted between Topic 26, Self-Destructive Behaviors and Topic 27, Blame, Acceptance, and Forgiveness in the core manual.

QUESTIONS

1. Can you identify some high-risk behaviors? What are they?
2. What are some of the consequences of engaging in high-risk behaviors?
3. Why do you think you have engaged in high-risk behaviors?
4. How can you modify your behavior so that you are safe?
5. Has there been an incident in your life that has led you to make your behavior more safe? What type of incident would it take to make you change your behavior?

EXERCISE

The group will develop a list of information women need about safe sex.

LEADERS' NOTES

QUESTION 1

Can you identify some high-risk behaviors? What are they?

TYPICAL RESPONSES   Unprotected sex
Prostituting my body
Shooting up dope
Owing a drug dealer money
Hitchhiking
Bingeing and purging
Shoplifting
Trying to kill myself
Cigarette smoking
Drinking

Keep the responses from the group in mind as the session progresses, making sure that the most prevalent behaviors are emphasized when going over subsequent questions. You will want to ensure that the group deals with the specific problems of the participants.

QUESTION 2

What are some of the consequences of engaging in high-risk behaviors?

TYPICAL RESPONSES   I became disorganized and got hospitalized.
I got AIDS.
I was raped.
I lost my children.
I got an infection and I can't have children anymore.

> I got arrested.
> I lost my home.
> I'm always sick . . . there is always something
>   wrong with me.
> Smoking makes me cough all the time; I can't catch
>   my breath.

The women may find it difficult to admit to losses they have suffered resulting from their own behavioral choices. Some women excuse their dangerous behaviors by calling them merely wild or daring. Help women see these behaviors for what they are, costly and destructive.

QUESTION 3

Why do you think you have engaged in high-risk behaviors?

TYPICAL RESPONSES Low self-esteem
        Peer pressure
        Loneliness
        Pressure from my boyfriend
        The need to escape my problems
        Being stupid
        Wanting some excitement in my life
        Needing to act out my anger
        Wanting to get rich
        Wanting to belong

This close examination of underlying motives may be difficult for group members. Leaders may need to think back to stories they have heard from women in previous sessions. Reminding the women of these stories will help them to answer this question.

QUESTION 4

How can you modify your behavior so that you are safe?

TYPICAL RESPONSES   By using condoms
By having only one sex partner
By going into a program to get off drugs
By staying home after 11:00 P.M.
By trying to think about what bad could happen to
me if . . .
By making new friends

Some women may see the process of altering their lifestyles as too inhibiting or difficult. Therefore, they may deny the possibility of change. Leaders can help members to see change is possible if they break down general behaviors (being impulsive) into a series of identifiable actions. Women may feel that it is easier to change one link in the chain than to alter their whole lifestyle. This more modest approach helps women to develop confidence in their own abilities to make safer choices.

QUESTION 5

Has there been an incident in your life that has led you to make your behavior more safe? What type of incident would need to take place to make you change your behavior?

TYPICAL RESPONSES   I got into a stranger's car and he pulled a knife; I'll
never do that again.
After I got raped, I didn't have sex for a year.
My brother died of AIDS so I stopped shooting
drugs.
I would stop drinking if I ever hit my kid.
If my husband left me, I would get my act together.
They pumped my stomach in the emergency
room—I'll never swallow pills again.
I fell asleep and set the bed on fire with my ciga-
rette. I won't smoke in bed anymore.

This question asks the women to connect behaviors and consequences to determine where change is healthy and possible. It also reminds the women of the value of examining the past, and making connections between actions and outcomes to develop a better understanding of themselves and their vulnerable areas.

ADDITIONAL QUESTIONS

1. How will changes in your behavior affect current relationships and activities?
2. How would you talk to a partner about having safe sex?

EXERCISE

During the exercise, you may need to fill in the gaps with information about safe sex as clients may not be knowledgeable about safe sex practices. Be prepared to teach a safe sex class, which may need to include instructions and practice in putting a condom on a penis. Be sure to have condoms and/or a penis model available.

INCARCERATED WOMEN

Catherine M. Anderson, M.Ed.

Deborah Bankson, M.S.W.

Evelyne Zephirin-Atkins, M.A., M.S.W.

RATIONALE FOR TRAUMA WORK WITH INCARCERATED WOMEN

The number of women incarcerated in local, state, and federal jails has risen during the past two decades. One study reports that since 1980 the incarceration rate for women has grown 400 percent, twice that of men (Thomas, 1996). Overwhelmingly, women being sent to prison are African-American, young (between age 25 and 30), undereducated, and poor. They also have a history of trauma. A study by the American Correctional Association published in 1990 found that over half the incarcerated women interviewed had histories of physical abuse and more than a third reported histories of sexual abuse. A Massachusetts study suggested that the rate was much higher, with nearly 90 percent of the women interviewed having experienced either childhood or adulthood trauma (Watterson, 1996). Not only have most incarcerated women experienced trauma prior to their incarceration, but studies show that there is an increased prevalence of abuse against incarcerated women. These abuses, which range from sexual and physical abuse to harassment, are committed by prison officers, workers, and other inmates (Thomas, 1996).

Because of the prevalence of trauma in the lives of women entering the criminal justice system, it is appropriate for clinicians to consider doing recovery and empowerment work with this population. For incarcerated women, however, the prison environment poses serious impediments to recovery goals, necessitating that leaders modify the emphasis throughout the core sections of *Trauma Recovery and Empowerment*.

THE PRISON CULTURE—
THE INMATE'S PERSPECTIVE

In general, daily life for a prisoner starts at 5:00 A.M. when a guard unlocks her cell, allowing her to file into line for breakfast. Before she enters the cafeteria, she must be frisked for weapons or contraband. She is given only 20 minutes to eat. After breakfast she is frisked again and then returned to her cell. In an hour, if she is fortunate enough to have qualified for one of the few activity placements, she is given a pass to go to a work site, a therapy group, or a Graduate Equivalency Degree (GED) class. Even these activities may be interrupted during the day by several lockdowns for inmate counts. During each such count, inmates are mandated to return to their cells until the count is completed. In such an environment, it makes no sense to talk with women about taking control of their lives. The routine of prison life is designed to take control away from women and place it in the hands of guards and officers. Unfortunately, for women who have been traumatized, a lack of control is an all too familiar feeling.

Prison culture demands hypervigilance. Guards are on the look out for violations and often enforce rules arbitrarily. All institutions have long lists of inmate-prohibited activities that may include the following—adulteration of food or drink, tampering with locks, loaning or borrowing between inmates, altering or damaging government property, giving another inmate medications, faking an illness, failing to follow sanitary regulations, using abusive or obscene language, and having physical contact with other inmates. Rule violations are recorded in a woman's record that determines if she is eligible for early release. If the rule violation is deemed severe, a woman may be taken from her cell or activity immediately and placed in segregated confinement, a punishment which could last from one day to several months. When group leaders ask members to consider relaxing their paranoid stances—often developed after years of abuse—leaders must remember that the prison culture demands the same hypervigilance for a woman to survive.

Prisons are becoming increasingly overpopulated so that two or three women may be assigned to a cell originally intended for one inmate. More women are competing for fewer work positions and GED classes; overcrowding deprives women of the opportunity for solitude in the leisure areas where many are required to spend their days. Even when a woman goes to her room to use the bathroom, she is deprived of the most basic privacy as frequently no door separates the toilet area from her cell mates. Furthermore, the door to the cell may have a window so that she can be observed by the guards. This lack of privacy makes it difficult for incarcerated women to create the personal space necessary for processing and integrating new thoughts, feelings, and behaviors as part of a healthy trauma recovery. The lack of personal space also makes it difficult for clinicians to conduct a productive discussion about managing interpersonal boundaries because incarcerated women do not control the space in which they must live.

Survivors of sexual abuse go to great extremes to ensure that they have control over their environment in an effort to keep themselves safe from future abuses. In prison a woman is stripped of her autonomy; she is told what to do and how to do it. She has no choices and must comply with the often capricious decisions made for her. When her opinions are invalidated and dismissed, these circumstances feel reminiscent of abusive family patterns.

Prisons are established to contain, control, and punish those who have committed crimes. In such an environment, guards and treatment staff place a premium on maintaining security and safety. Gratifying an inmate's physical, emotional, or even therapeutic needs takes a necessary backseat. Even in progressive institutions where rehabilitation is valued, the prison environment remains sterile and unforgiving. It is difficult for a woman in this setting to experience feelings, become emotionally vulnerable, and contemplate new ideas generated from her participation in therapy groups.

Developing healthy strategies for comforting oneself is an important part of trauma recovery work. Many trauma survivors developed maladaptive coping strategies, such as using drugs and alcohol or engaging in promiscuous sexual behavior to self-soothe. Generally, as women begin to consider healthier options, they explore listening to music, going for long walks, and writing in journals. Regrettably, the lack of privacy and personal space, and the pervasiveness of prison rules limit an incarcerated woman's options for self-soothing, forcing her to return to dysfunctional strategies.

When a woman is incarcerated, she is removed from her family and friends, causing her to lose needed emotional supports. However, she may ingeniously create a new social network within the prison consisting of an intimate partnership, friendships, a family, and a gang or clique to meet various physical and emotional needs. Although some of these relationships are exploitive and hurtful, others can be supportive and nurturing. Sometimes the abusive dynamics experienced prior to incarceration are perpetuated in new relationships formed in prison. Even if healthy relationships are developed, most of these are discontinued when a woman is released because probation and parole regulations prohibit contact between convicted felons. Trauma recovery work demands that a woman not only understands past interpersonal patterns but also works to establish new ways of relating. Prohibitions on forming friendships and the prevalence of predatory inmates make it difficult for the incarcerated trauma survivor to overcome abusive patterns of relating.

Because of abuse, a woman may have lost or never developed a sense of ownership and control of her body. When a trauma survivor enters the criminal justice system, this feeling of not having control of her body is reinforced and perpetuated by a range of invasive prison protocols. When a woman becomes incarcerated, everything she brings into the prison, including herself, becomes government property. Women in prison are subjected to random frisks and strip searches for weapons and contraband. They have no recourse but to tolerate these invasive procedures that may only intensify the sense of powerlessness they already have about their bodies. Of particular concern for trauma survivors, incarcerated women have no control over their own bodies with respect to sexual expression. Any sexual activity, including self-stimulation, is often against the rules. Moreover, incarcerated women do not have the usual choices other women have regarding how they choose to care for their bodies. Medical care in prison is often poor and women may elect to postpone medical treatment until release. A woman does not have control over her diet as meals are standard, and menus are altered only if a woman has a medical dietary restriction.

The development of a positive sense of self is a primary goal of trauma recovery work. Trauma survivors who are incarcerated often enter prison with their self-esteem severely battered. This negative self-image is further reinforced by the prison experience. Incarceration is a daily reminder of a woman's badness and need to be isolated from society. Prison culture robs a woman of her essential humanness; she is referred to as an inmate identified by a number, not as a woman with a name. Women often define themselves by their social roles (i.e., mother, wife, lover, daughter, sister). Incarceration interrupts a woman's opportunity for fulfilling her various role obligations, thus decreasing her sense of womanhood and promoting feelings of failure and inadequacy. In prison, a woman's crime, not her positive accomplishments, defines who she is. For trauma survivors who already feel guilty for having been abused, the sense of being bad is only intensified by incarceration.

THE PRISON CULTURE—
THE CLINICIAN'S PERSPECTIVE

There are many prison systems where rehabilitation is offered. Nonetheless, treatment failure is almost certain if all facets of the institution are not in support of the rehabilitation philosophy. For example, treatment can be impeded by officers not giving women passes for therapy groups, or removing them from groups for other routine prison operations such as medication call. A woman often is forced to choose between therapy groups and GED classes, work, or going to the commissary for a weekly supply of snacks.

Group therapy work is complicated by boundary issues resulting from interpersonal relationships and the fact that group members often live with one another. Women may bring an ongoing conflict they are having with one another into the group, creating tension that disrupts the group's agenda and intimidates or distracts other members. Moreover, women are asked to share personal experiences, ideas, and feelings in the group. By doing so they become vulnerable to members who might choose to use this information in an abusive manner outside the group. All these complications raise issues of trust and safety for a woman doing trauma recovery work in prison.

Individual progress also can be impeded by the dual roles many treatment staff must play in a prison environment. Treatment providers are assigned not only the task of offering an opportunity for personal growth and change but also of making ongoing assessments of inmates' progress. The concept of confidentiality within a therapeutic relationship can be confounded when treatment takes place under the auspices of the criminal justice system, where what you say can and will be used against you. Medical records, therapeutic assessments, and progress reports are accessible to institutional staff and may be used in determining recommendations for status changes within the institution, work release, or parole reviews.

EMPOWERMENT WORK IN PRISON

While in prison a woman's self-esteem is under assault even if she chooses to obey all the rules. Women who do as they are told are rewarded by positive reports and the possibility of an early release for good behavior. Yet passive compliance often depletes a woman's sense of integrity and self-determination. An inmate who actively opposes what she feels is an unjust rule suffers the consequences of being reported, being segregated or locked down, and jeopardizes her opportunity for early release; yet she manages to maintain a sense of integrity and self-determination (Watterson, 1996).

Obviously, the concept of doing empowerment work in prisons seems contradictory because it is difficult to instill power in a woman who lives in an institution where she has no power. However, empowerment work can be done in prison if a woman is encouraged to believe that real personal power comes from valuing herself. When a woman trusts her own intuitions and makes choices that are self-affirming, she feels more powerful regardless of whether she is living with an abusive spouse or residing in a prison. A woman must be helped to see that although she has little control over externals she does have some control over herself. In controlled institutions like prisons, women must be more creative in how they attain a sense of personal power. A woman, for example, can choose how she will respond and react to others. If an inmate feels mistreated by an officer, rather than using old coping mechanisms, she can report the mistreatment to the appropriate personnel. Voicing discontent appropriately, whether or not it changes the situation, can feel empowering, even to a woman with a long prison sentence.

NOTES TO THE CLINICIAN

Often clinicians are not prepared for the personal impact of doing therapy work with incarcerated women. Clinicians sometimes report feeling depressed and disillusioned after beginning the work. Listening to the women tell stories of violence in which they were perpetrators as well as victims often creates moral and philosophical dilemmas. Additionally, clinicians can feel hopeless and demoralized by the overwhelming number of problems these women present. Yet it is vitally important to maintain the belief that change is possible, regardless of whether it occurs by incremental steps or major insights. During the groups, leaders have the opportunity to introduce concepts that the women may remember and use later to help change their behavior.

Working in a prison environment also may leave clinicians feeling personally disempowered. Group leaders who are not part of the prison staff are not generally given keys, and are dependent on the officers to be let in and out. Work in prisons may be unpredictable; inmates may be released without any notice, and group sessions can be shortened or canceled because of lockdowns or other overriding prison priorities. Clinicians doing work in prisons must have a support system and supervision to counter these feelings of personal powerlessness.

Clinicians providing services in prisons also may bring with them certain preconceptions about incarcerated women. For example, some group leaders might overemphasize the crimes women have committed and see group members as bad. These leaders will have difficulty establishing a therapeutic atmosphere in which women can learn to feel valued and respected. Other clinicians may begin with the assumption that all women are victims, making it difficult to set limits and confront group members about taking responsibility for their actions. It is important for clinicians to be aware of their biases and to strive to see each incarcerated woman as a whole person. Inmates need to be seen realistically as women who, while they may have experienced a range of socioeconomic difficulties, have chosen to cope with these difficulties through maladaptive and criminal behavior.

It is common for inmates to believe therapists and other prison staff possibly have influence over their sentences. Consequently, inmates may choose to participate in treatment solely to receive credit and a good evaluation. Group leaders must repeatedly remind the women that the goal of the treatment is not to reduce their sentences, but to learn skills that prepare them to return to the community and to help them enhance their ability to remain out of prison.

The likelihood of having women with antisocial or even psychopathic character styles participating in therapy groups is obviously greater when doing groups in a prison setting. Unlike the popular stereotype, women with psychopathic personality styles are not usually serial killers, nor are they outwardly hostile and aggressive. They may not be the inmates who have committed the most serious crimes. Instead they can be quite charismatic in groups and appear to be the most active participants. Because of her charm, a woman with psychopathic traits can dominate the group process and prevent the group from having an honest discussion. Often such women agree to participate in a group to collect information and improve their manipulative style rather than to gain any personal insight. It can be dangerous to allow psychopathic women an opportunity to witness other inmate's vulnerabilities because they can use that information to gain an advantage outside the group. If at all possible, the leaders should screen all potential group referrals for psychopathy and deny membership to any woman who scores high on an objective checklist (Hare, 1993).

The group process also may be hampered and the goals of the group session derailed by women with highly aggressive, provocative, or extremely passive behavioral styles. These styles may be defensive postures developed to cope with feelings of vulnerability and powerlessness; therefore they need to be acknowledged and addressed by the leaders who should consider each situation carefully prior to confronting a woman. If certain behaviors become too disruptive, the leaders may choose to respond by talking to the woman outside of the group in an effort to avoid shaming her in front of her peers. If this initial approach does not work, the leaders need to determine if the woman should continue the group or should be asked to leave.

Clinicians should be sensitive to linguistic and cultural diversity among incarcerated women. Women who have been part of urban gangs may use idiomatic speech that group leaders find difficult to understand. Clinicians need to respect, clarify, and understand diverse communication styles. If they fail to do so, group members may feel frustrated, devalued, and misunderstood. Members may respond to this frustration by remaining silent during the group, leaving the session prematurely, missing sessions, or becoming verbally aggressive to the leaders.

MANUAL MODIFICATIONS FOR INCARCERATED WOMEN

In addition to the "General Instructions to Group Leaders" in the core manual, clinicians working with an incarcerated population should remember the following instructions:

1. Empowerment and trauma recovery groups function best when conducted in a supportive therapeutic setting. Ideally, each group member should have someone available to help her process the group material and deal with any upsetting feelings between group meetings. Because of the relative unavailability of therapists in a prison setting, group leaders should be prepared to give extra time to a woman who needs it.

2. Clinicians should be advised that doing this group with a captive audience does not necessarily mean the attrition rate will be lower than in a community-based group. Even incarcerated women find ways to self-select out of the group or miss sessions that they feel are too threatening or overwhelming.

3. During each session of the group, the women should be instructed to consider the topics in relation to their lives both prior to and during imprisonment. For example, consider session two, "What It Means to Be a Woman." In this session each woman should discuss what her feelings were about being a woman in her life prior to her incarceration, how she feels about being a woman now, and how being incarcerated may have altered her sense of womanhood.

4. In particular, several sessions have been modified to address the special needs and issues of women in prison.

TOPIC 5 Emotional Boundaries: Setting Limits and Asking for What You Want

SESSION RATIONALE

Women in prison often suffer from having too many emotional barriers. Having emotional boundaries that are too restrictive may keep a woman safe and protected but it also interferes with her ability to build relationships and meet her emotional needs. Women in prison are generally proficient at setting limits, but have difficulty letting others in and depending on others to meet their emotional needs. Often when women in prison cannot get the physical distance they need from one another, they may use psychologically manipulative tactics to achieve this.

GOAL: Members will gain an understanding of the distinction between emotional boundaries and emotional barriers.

This session needs to be altered from its original form to focus more on getting one's emotional needs met rather than saying no and setting limits. Generally women in prison have no problem saying no. The following questions and exercise should be substituted for the questions and exercise listed in the core manual.

QUESTIONS

1. What are emotional boundaries?
2. How do you maintain your emotional boundaries?
3. Have you ever noticed that these boundaries or barriers make it hard for you to get your emotional needs met?
4. What do you think the link is between your trauma experiences and the pervasiveness of your emotional barriers?

EXERCISE

Each member will think of a situation in which she has set limits that were too constricted and resulted in her not being able to have certain emotional needs met. The group will choose one or two of these situations for discussion, focusing on how a woman can protect herself from vulnerability and yet get some emotional satisfaction.

LEADERS' NOTES

QUESTION 1

What are emotional boundaries?

> TYPICAL RESPONSES   The walls I put up so no one can get close to me
> Keeping everything (thoughts and feelings) locked up so no one can use them against me
> Holding on to feelings in order to avoid confusion in my life
> Hiding my emotions from others so no one will think I am weak
> Saying no to a friend who wants to use me
> Keeping my distance until I feel safe

You will need to help members distinguish between healthy boundaries and defensive barriers. Members may begin to discuss how barriers make it difficult to get emotional needs met.

QUESTION 2

How do you maintain your emotional boundaries?

> TYPICAL RESPONSES   I keep to myself, mind my own business, and no one bothers me.
> I keep all my thoughts and feelings to myself.
> I tell people I'm fine, even if it is not true, so they leave me alone.

> I look mean so no one wants to get close to me.
> I don't trust anyone, so I don't let anyone know me.
> I only show part of my personality to others, there
>   are parts of me that no one sees.

You will want to distinguish between those strategies that allow for eventual closeness and those that end a relationship before it has a chance to get started.

QUESTION 3

Have you ever noticed that these boundaries or barriers make it hard for you to get your emotional needs met?

TYPICAL RESPONSES   I don't care, it is not worth the risk of being
    vulnerable.
Sometimes I feel alone, but it is safer than risking
    being hurt.
I do not recognize that I have emotional needs.
I often feel isolated and alone but I don't think that I
    can get close to anyone.
I have missed out on some relationships that could
    have been something special.
My difficulty trusting people makes it hard for me
    to accept help and support from others.

Members may begin to consider the price they have paid for keeping a distance. Even when they crave intimacy, members may feel that they have no choice but to keep a wall around themselves.

QUESTION 4

What do you think the link is between your trauma experiences and the pervasiveness of your emotional barriers?

TYPICAL RESPONSES   I learned not to trust anyone.
I learned not to let anyone know how I was feeling
    so I would not get hurt.

>My mother used to tell me to stop crying or she
>would give me something to cry about. So I
>learned to hide my emotions.
>
>Because of the abuse, I can't seem to trust that any-
>one would really want the best for me.

For most women, this connection is an obvious one. Women who are still in denial about the impact of the trauma will have more difficulty with this question.

EXERCISE

Help group members think of situations where their emotional boundaries interfered with getting needs met. Focus the discussion on how a woman can protect herself from vulnerability without sacrificing her needs. For example, a woman may talk about feeling trapped in a violent relationship and how she has cut off contact with her support system because of her shame about the abuse, and fear of being blamed. The group should generate a list of alternative resources that would allow her to have her emotional needs met in a nonjudgmental way.

TOPIC 7   Developing Ways to Feel Better: Self-Soothing

SESSION RATIONALE

Many women in prison, whether convicted of drug offenses or not, have a history of using alcohol and other substances as a way to self-soothe. Lack of both privacy and personal space limits an incarcerated woman's options for self-soothing. Her options are further limited by the institutional setting and prison rules.

The session will be used as it is in the core manual with the addition of the following question and exercise:

QUESTION

How have you had to alter your soothing techniques because of your confinement in prison?

EXERCISE

Each member will generate a list of things she can do for herself when she is in need of comfort while incarcerated.

LEADERS' NOTES

QUESTION

How have you had to alter your soothing techniques because of your confinement in prison?

TYPICAL RESPONSES   I can't take a walk in the woods now, so I just fantasize that I am walking through the woods.
I have a cell mate, so it is hard to get time alone in my room. Sometimes I go take a shower just so I can be alone for a few minutes.

> I used to like to go for a run when I was upset, so
> now I just exercise in my cell.
> I'm learning to write down my thoughts and feel-
> ings in a journal instead of running from them
> like I did when I was using cocaine.
> I used to feel better when I was holding my son,
> now I look at his picture when I feel sad.
> I don't know what to do when I feel upset, I always
> used drugs before.
> I have started reading the Bible.

Many soothing strategies are still viable in a prison setting; others need to be modified. By sharing creative strategies, women can get ideas from one another. Negotiating for space and privacy with a cell mate is especially relevant to this discussion.

EXERCISE

Often bringing supplies for creating Comfort Cards into the prison is too difficult. If creating Comfort Cards is not possible, as an alternate exercise, each woman can generate a list of things she can do for herself when she is in need of comforting. The women can take their lists back to their rooms to use for future reference.

TYPICAL RESPONSES   Write in my journal
Write letters home
Fantasize about walking in the woods like I used to
    do before being incarcerated
Reread letters from home
Look at pictures of my kids
Do sit-ups and other exercises I can do in my room

TOPIC 9   Female Sexuality

SESSION RATIONALE

Because their first sexual experiences were under someone else's control, many trauma survivors are unaware that they can control their own sexual pleasure. Trauma survivors often see sex as taboo and their sexual responses as bad. This belief is reinforced by prison rules that not only prohibit any form of sexual activity but also may limit the extent to which a woman can wear make-up and clothes that may help her to feel sensual and feminine. It is common for trauma survivors to opt out of having sexual lives and become almost asexual. However, many women in prison have histories of involvement in commercial sex and/or trading sex for drugs or other favors. They may be experiencing shame and guilt related to both abuse and their consensual sexual behaviors. The session allows women to discuss sexuality in an open non-shaming format. The group allows a woman to see her own sexual responses as normal and to begin the long process of accepting her body and its sensuality.

The session will be used as it is in the core manual with the addition of the following goal and questions:

GOAL 2: Members will explore how being incarcerated has broadened and/or altered their definition of female sexuality.

QUESTIONS

1. How has your incarceration affected your sense of yourself as a sexual being?
2. Has being incarcerated altered the way in which you express yourself sexually? How?

LEADERS' NOTES

QUESTION 1

How has your incarceration affected your sense of yourself as a sexual being?

TYPICAL RESPONSES   It is hard to think of yourself as sexual in here.

I don't see myself as a sexual being right now.

I'm not interested in sex anymore.

I just learned to block it out since I can't be with my partner.

Many women continue their sexual activity in prison. Some may select a female partner; others continue to write erotic letters or engage in phone sex with an outside lover. Regardless, women do tend to see a split between their lives outside the prison and the way they behave on the inside.

QUESTION 2

Has being incarcerated altered the way in which you express yourself sexually? How?

TYPICAL RESPONSES   Well if you are going to have sex, you have to sneak around to do it.

My girlfriend and I actually talk more about sex now that I'm locked up.

Even though I'm not sexually active here, I can still feel sexual by wearing make-up, doing my hair, and dressing attractively.

I masturbate a lot more since I cannot have my boyfriend near me now.

I never thought I would have sex with another woman, but I find that it is really good.

Since I cannot be physically intimate with my partner, we write letters and say erotic things to each other.

You will want to encourage an honest discussion without encouraging a how-to session. Some women will report that they now engage in activities that they would not have considered before.

Some women may be reluctant to talk openly because of the close living quarters and lack of privacy. A discussion in the third person may be easier for members.

TOPIC 16 Physical Safety

SESSION RATIONALE

In general, this topic is better suited to a more vulnerable population. Women in prison tend not to see themselves as vulnerable to danger despite their often violent lifestyles. In fact, many women have overcompensated and become aggressive in an effort to protect themselves. Also women may have developed a false sense of security and safety by carrying weapons, being in a gang, or becoming aggressive. A woman involved in drug use and drug dealing often disregards her own personal safety.

The session will be used as it is in the core manual with the addition of the following questions:

QUESTIONS

1. How do you know when you are in a dangerous situation?
2. When you are in a dangerous situation, how do you protect yourself?
3. What are the factors that impair your ability to know when a situation is dangerous?

LEADERS' NOTES

QUESTION 1

How do you know when you are in a dangerous situation?

TYPICAL RESPONSES   My body tells me; my heart starts pounding and my palms sweat.

When I go to certain neighborhoods and I start feeling nervous.

Sometimes I don't know until after the fact and someone else tells me how dangerous it was.

When I feel like I have to protect myself.

Some women may have difficulty identifying danger. The discussion may need to begin with an open discussion about what constitutes danger.

QUESTION 2

When you are in a dangerous situation, how do you protect yourself?

TYPICAL RESPONSES   Carry a weapon.

Get prepared to fight.

Make sure I am not alone.

I try to look intimidating so no one bothers me.

I strike first, to get the jump on them, that way I
have the advantage.

I try to find an out as quickly as I can.

I do whatever I am asked to do by the person who
has put me in danger.

You will need to discourage expressions of bravado. Members should be
helped to see that many strategies for self-protection do not involve violence.

QUESTION 3

What are the factors that impair your ability to know when a situation is dangerous?

TYPICAL RESPONSES   When I am drunk or high.

When I am in a dissociative state.

When I do not care what happens to me.

When I am heated and angry.

When I need drugs, I'll go anywhere and do anything to get them.

Many women in prison have a history of drug use. Make sure that drugs and
alcohol are included in the discussion. Many women have learned to numb
themselves to chronic danger; you will want to include a discussion of how
women can begin paying attention to situational cues.

TOPIC 18 Institutional Abuse

SESSION RATIONALE

The percentage of incarcerated women abused by prison authorities is high. Because prisons are meant to be punitive, officers can justify and frequently get away with abusive behavior. Women frequently feel they have no recourse and consequently keep silent about the abuse. In this session participants may for the first time have a safe and supportive setting in which they can talk about abuse in prison. The group can then suggest appropriate ways for addressing the abuse.

The session will be used as it is in the core manual with the addition of the following questions:

QUESTIONS

1. How do you distinguish between what is abusive behavior by an officer or other prison workers and what is prison protocol?
2. How do you cope with the many physical and emotional intrusions justified by the prison protocol?
3. How can you respond appropriately to abuse in a way that can help you feel empowered?

LEADERS' NOTES

QUESTION 1

How do you distinguish between what is abusive behavior by an officer or other prison workers and what is prison protocol?

TYPICAL RESPONSES   When an officer comes down on you for no apparent reason.

If you have broken a rule and an officer writes you a ticket, that's not abuse.

268

> When an officer writes you a ticket, and you have
> done nothing wrong, that is abuse of power.

It is important to make the distinction clear between what may be perceived as abuse and what is real abuse. The prison protocols may feel abusive to the inmates; however, they may be deemed necessary to maintain safety and security.

QUESTION 2

How do you cope with the many physical and emotional intrusions justified by the prison protocol?

TYPICAL RESPONSES   I remind myself I won't be in jail forever, I can put up with it.
I dissociate when I am strip-searched or frisked.
I say the Serenity Prayer.
I remind myself that I got myself here by my actions, and this is the consequence.
I can only take it so long then I blow up and talk back to an officer.

Members will see that how they cope with intrusions parallels how they cope in general. You may want to ask which of these strategies works well and which does not.

QUESTION 3

How can you respond appropriately to abuse in a way that can help you feel empowered?

TYPICAL RESPONSES   Report it and write-up the officer.
Stand up for myself and confront the officer who mistreats me.
Tell my grandmother if I am mistreated. She will get things stirred-up.

> Choose your battles. If it's one you cannot win, you
> just have to accept it.

Begin by asking members if they know the protocol for reporting abuse within the prison. Even when women cannot change their circumstances, they may gain a sense of empowerment from making their concerns known.

TOPIC 20 Trauma and Addictive or Compulsive Behavior

SESSION RATIONALE

Many incarcerated women have a history of addiction and other compulsive behaviors. Addiction or compulsion often is seen as a primary form of coping with trauma issues; however, this form of coping is self-abusive. Many incarcerated women are in prison for drug-related offenses. This session gives women an opportunity to see connections between early abuse and the adult behavior patterns that lead them into the criminal justice system.

The session will be used as it is in the core manual with the addition of the following questions:

QUESTIONS

1. What is the relationship between your addictive or compulsive behavior and being incarcerated?
2. How has your addiction or compulsion affected your relationship with family and friends?

LEADERS' NOTES

QUESTION 1

What is the relationship between your addictive or compulsive behavior and being incarcerated?

TYPICAL RESPONSES My addiction is what got me here. I'm in for possession and distribution.

I needed money to get my drugs, that's why I started robbing people.

> I wrote bad checks and stole from my employer to pay my credit card bills. I was a compulsive shopper.
>
> I loved the thrill of shoplifting and could not stop myself. Then I got caught.

Be careful not to shame members. Some members may need help making the connection between their crimes and their addictions.

QUESTION 2

How has your addiction or compulsion affected your relationship with family and friends?

> **TYPICAL RESPONSES**
>
> My family cut me off because of all the harm I did to them when I was using.
>
> No one trusts me anymore because of my stealing from them when I was using.
>
> My mother filed for custody of my kids because of my drug use and the way I acted.
>
> I don't have any friends anymore. I'm trying to stay clean, so I had to give up all my old friends.

Families become vitally important to incarcerated women; they are the only link to one's outside life and one's past as well as being a source of needed resources. Members may have genuine anxiety about anything that threatens these all important connections.

TOPIC 21–A What Is Domestic Violence?

SESSION RATIONALE

Many women in prison have experienced a pattern of domestic violence in their relationships. Women often are perplexed and self-blaming about being involved repeatedly in abusive relationships. It is important for them to understand the link between early trauma and the subsequent development of relational patterns that are characterized by abuse. This session offers group members an opportunity to clarify any misconceptions they may have about domestic violence. Group members will also have an opportunity to acknowledge their own role as abusers, either as coinitiators of violence, or as defenders of themselves or their children.

This session can be best inserted in Part II: Trauma Recovery after Topic 21 / Abuse and Relationships.

GOAL 1: Each member will be able to define what constitutes domestic violence.

GOAL 2: Each member will begin to understand how power and control define relationships.

GOAL 3: Each member will gain an understanding of the cycle of violence.

QUESTIONS

1. What constitutes domestic violence?
2. How does one person come to have more power and control than the other in a relationship?
3. What behaviors, feelings, or situations triggered the violent episodes? How often did the violence occur?
4. What signals did your body send you before the violence began?
5. Did you ever try to leave the abusive relationship? If not, what kept you from trying?

LEADERS' NOTES

QUESTION 1

What constitutes domestic violence?

TYPICAL RESPONSES   Fighting between two people who are in an intimate relationship.

A husband forcing his wife to have sex.

A man or woman hitting his or her partner.

If they grew up in violent homes, violence may have become normal and members may have trouble identifying it. Members should be encouraged to see violence as more than just the act of hitting.

QUESTION 2

How does one person come to have more power and control than the other in a relationship?

TYPICAL RESPONSES   My husband would not allow me to work; since he was the only one making money, he had all the power.

My husband did not want to be bothered with having to make decisions about anything, so I had to take charge.

I was afraid of my boyfriend, he was so big and could throw me around.

My husband would tell me how ugly I was and that no one would want me.

I used to tell my husband that if he didn't like the way I ran things, then he could leave; I didn't need him.

I wasn't allowed to have any of my own friends, he wouldn't even let me see my family.

My husband would tell me no one would believe me if I reported him because I was a prostitute.

> My children's father used to tell me that if I didn't
> do what he said, he would take the children away
> from me.
>
> When my husband hit me, he used to tell me I was
> the only person who could make him act that way.

As women give examples, you may want to label the behaviors using the following categories:

Coercion, threats, and intimidation
Emotional abuse
Isolation
Minimizing, denying, and blaming
Using children
Male privilege
Economic abuse

QUESTION 3

What behaviors, feelings, or situations triggered the violent episodes? How often did the violence occur?

> TYPICAL RESPONSES   When my father came home drunk, he would walk
> in and just start yelling and hitting.
>
> Money was always the trigger. I learned to expect a
> big fight between my parents at the end of every
> month, bill-paying time.
>
> My boyfriend always thought I was messing around
> on him. If I went out with my girlfriends, he
> would beat me when I got home.

You can use this discussion to help members identify the chain of events that lead to violence. This discussion is facilitated by diagramming the sequence on a flip chart or chalkboard. This is especially useful when the chain includes events that are discontinuous in time. The chain also may include seemingly irrelevant events that contribute interpersonal tension.

QUESTION 4

What signals did your body send you before the violence began?

    TYPICAL RESPONSES   Nausea
          Urinating on myself
          The feeling of walking on eggshells
          Queasy stomach
          Sweaty palms

Members benefit from learning that their bodies give useful feedback. Many members may never have learned how to read their own physical responses accurately.

QUESTION 5

Did you ever try to leave the abusive relationship? If not, what kept you from trying?

    TYPICAL RESPONSES   I tried to leave but he kept finding me.
          I didn't think I had any place to go.
          I thought this was what I had to put up with.
          I thought he loved me.
          I kept remembering the good times.
          I did not want my family to know.

Be careful that women do not feel ashamed because they stayed in an abusive relationship. The same techniques that perpetuate abuse also serve to keep a woman trapped in a relationship. You also may want to remind members that it is never too late to make a decision to leave.

REFERENCES

Hare, R. D. *Without Conscience: The Disturbing World of the Psychopaths Among Us.* New York: Pocket Books, 1993.

Thomas, P. "Growing Female Inmate Population Facing Greater Assault Risk, Study Says." *Washington Post,* December 8, 1996, p. A18.

Watterson, K. *Women in Prison: Inside the Concrete Womb,* rev. ed. Boston: Northeastern University Press, 1996.

WOMEN WHO ARE PARENTS

David Freeman, Psy.D.

Lori Beyer, M.S.W.

Sharon Miller, M.S.W.

INTRODUCTION

This chapter describes a group intervention for seriously overwhelmed mothers who have already completed the trauma curriculum described in earlier chapters. In addition to having severe trauma issues of their own, women who are referred to this parenting group will have persistently struggled with the impact of trauma on their parenting skills and identity. Despite their participation in the trauma intervention, women referred to this parenting group will be unable, at the beginning of the group, to adequately prevent the transmission of the impact of trauma to their children. This group therefore focuses on containing the impact of trauma by reducing the multigenerational transmission of trauma experiences.

Multigenerational transmission of trauma can be expressed in many different ways. Some women will be overprotective of their children in the hope of preventing a repeat of the trauma experience. In other cases, trauma related disabilities will cause women to be absent or neglectful. Some women abandon their children because they are unable to cope effectively with the stressors associated with the prevention of trauma. Still, other women may be unable to manage the abuse of their children by others. Finally, some women will be more specifically involved in the perpetration of trauma through the physical and/or sexual abuse of their children.

This intervention is not a how-to on parenting for trauma survivors. Instead, group discussion promotes the development of a cohesive and stable identity as a parent so that mothers can provide adequately for the safety and care of children.

This curriculum will be useful for women requesting assistance with parenting issues after participating in the 33-week trauma intervention. Women who have come to the attention of mental health professionals through community-based therapy services, Child Protective Services, jail-based services, divorce and mediation services, employee assistance programs, and managed care organizations will find this group useful.

TOPIC 1   Who Raised You?

SESSION RATIONALE

It is important for group members to begin to look at the ways their parenting styles have been influenced by the way they were raised. This curriculum is not a guide on how to parent but an opportunity for members to begin to discuss the broader influences on their own parenting style and identify how those might have been influenced by their histories of abuse.

GOAL 1: Each member will describe the relationships she had with her primary caregivers.

GOAL 2: Members will begin to understand that parenting styles often are repeated in successive generations.

QUESTIONS

1. Who raised you?
2. How was your primary caregiver raised?
3. Who do you consider a role model for raising children?
4. With respect to your parenting style, do you want to be the same as or different from your parents and/or caregivers?

LEADERS' NOTES

Members will disclose a range of experiences with their own parents and caregivers. Some members will have experienced physical, sexual, and emotional abuse that may make it difficult for them to talk about their childhood experiences. Leaders should be alert to the possibility that members' caregivers may have had mental illnesses, addictive disorders, or other severe problems that contributed to their own difficulties in parenting. This session becomes highly charged as members disclose their own severe trauma experiences.

QUESTION 1

Who raised you?

TYPICAL RESPONSES My parents stayed together and raised me at the same time.

My mother and grandmother shared custody; my time was divided between the two.

It depended on whether my parents were fighting or not.

I raised myself.

My parents divorced and remarried so I had four parents.

My older sister raised me when my parents died.

My brother and I raised each other because my parents were both alcoholics.

Group members may describe complex family situations in which responsibility for child raising was shared among several people in the extended family network. Prompts that may help clarify the central caregiver are

Who did you live with?
Who took you to church?
Who took care of you when you were sick or upset?
Who helped you with school?
Who helped you solve problems with friends?
Who taught you right from wrong?
Who helped you when you were in trouble?

QUESTION 2

How was your primary caregiver raised?

TYPICAL RESPONSES My grandmother was weak and her husband was domineering.

My grandparents were drunk all the time.

> My grandfather died when I was two, I never knew
> him.
> My grandfather was abusive, we were all afraid of
> him.

This question enriches women's understanding of the multigenerational transmission of family problems.

QUESTION 3

Who do you consider a role model for raising children?

TYPICAL RESPONSES
> My grandmother, she was tough but she showed me
> love.
> Bill Cosby.
> My neighbor, she handles mothering and working
> with no stress.
> My mother, she was a single parent who was able to
> love us all.
> My best friend.
> My father's mother because she didn't drink.

These answers will give you a sense of how realistic the members are in their role models for parenting. Help women explore the feelings they have when they cannot identify a role model within their own personal experience.

QUESTION 4

With respect to your parenting style, do you want to be the same as or different from your parents and/or caregivers?

TYPICAL RESPONSES
> I want to be there for my children more than my
> parents were there for me.
> I don't drink.
> I want to raise my children without a man because I
> don't want them to be abused as I was.

I want to make my marriage work—no divorce.
My job will never be more important than my son.

The experiences one has of being parented influence greatly the development of parenting style. Members will be assisted in accurately assessing the ways in which their experiences of being parented have molded their styles. The influences may be positive or negative or both. When women were abused by parents, they often use their own parents as examples of how not to behave.

TOPIC 2 Becoming a Mother: Starting a Family

SESSION RATIONALE

The process of becoming a mother is one of the most powerful experiences in the life cycle. Fantasies and expectations about life after the birth of a child, adoption, or the reconstitution of a family can have an impact on the relationships women form with their children. The actual changes in a woman's life after becoming a mother also can have a far-reaching impact on relationships with their children. Women who are trauma survivors will share many parenting experiences with women who are not, but also may have unique attitudes toward and experiences of becoming mothers.

GOAL 1: Members will identify their feelings about starting a family and will develop stories of their experiences.

GOAL 2: Members will think about the ways life changed for them during and after the birth of their children.

QUESTIONS

1. Was it your choice to have children?
2. How did you feel when you found out that you would have a child?
3. Did the people in your support system treat you differently after you told them the news?
4. How did your life change after the birth of your children? Which changes were expected and which ones were surprises?
5. How do you think these changes affected your relationship with your children and others in your support network?

LEADERS' NOTES

This session will allow members to explore their feelings about becoming mothers and the way these feelings have influenced their relationships with their children, both in positive and negative ways.

QUESTION 1

Was it your choice to have children?

TYPICAL RESPONSES Yes, I had always wanted children, I couldn't wait to get pregnant.

No, I was raped by my father and gave the child away.

My husband and I made the decision together and then he left me alone to raise them.

My sister couldn't raise her children so I took them, there was no other choice.

It is important to begin with exploring the mother's role in the decision to become a parent. Trauma survivors who feel disempowered generally also may feel that they had no choice even in making the important decision to have a child.

QUESTION 2

How did you feel when you found out you would have a child?

TYPICAL RESPONSES I was so excited, I wanted to tell everyone.

I was scared.

I thought I would finally be loved for myself and not be alone anymore.

I started thinking about protecting the child and raising her the right way.

I was afraid someone would find out before I could have an abortion.

I was resentful that someone else would control my life.

Leave room in the discussion for both positive and negative reactions to becoming a mother. For some women, becoming pregnant elicits fears that the trauma will be passed to another generation.

QUESTION 3

Did the people in your support system treat you differently after you told them the news?

TYPICAL RESPONSES Yes, I was pampered for the whole nine months. My mother took care of me.

My parents weren't ready to be grandparents and were upset I was pregnant.

My mother told me to leave the house, and then I was on my own.

My husband got jealous of the attention I was receiving, and began to hit me.

My boyfriend dumped me.

Members' experiences with their family and friends influence the way they approach becoming mothers. Often when families have been shattered by trauma, they are not available to provide the customary support around major life events.

QUESTION 4

How did your life change after the birth of your children? Which changes were expected and which ones were surprises?

TYPICAL RESPONSES I wasn't alone anymore, it was wonderful.

It brought back all my old memories of being abused, I had no control in the situation.

It was a shock to me that I had no time to myself and that an infant is so demanding.

I expected to have lots of family support but I did not.

I think about the child I gave up every year at her birthday, I'm surprised that it never goes away.

Women will have a range of emotional responses to the changes that children bring to their lives. Group members can learn from each other that even the negative aspects of bringing children home are often shared by others.

QUESTION 5

How do you think these changes affected your relationship with your children and others in your support network?

TYPICAL RESPONSES   My parents focused on the baby and my husband and I felt left out.

I was angry with my son because I now had no time for myself.

I was afraid to leave my father alone with my daughter, I don't trust him.

I finally had approval from my in-laws.

Arrival of children often creates remarkable shifts in a woman's identity and in her roles in her social network. This discussion can help clarify the changes women have experienced and help women appreciate some relationship dynamics that shape their identity as parents. Women should be encouraged to consider how trauma in their own pasts might have influenced their responses.

TOPIC 3 Dealing with Your Children's Other Caregivers

SESSION RATIONALE

Many parents share child-raising responsibilities with extended family, neighbors, baby-sitters, teachers, and others. In some situations, the parent may not feel empowered to make decisions concerning her children's care. Open discussion about the patchwork of caregiving responsibilities is crucial to the understanding of the parenting role.

GOAL 1: Members will explore their children's alternate care giving situations.

GOAL 2: Members will begin to understand their relationships with these other caregivers.

QUESTIONS

1. Who shares in the responsibility for the care of your children?
2. Who makes the decisions about who will provide this care?
3. What are your feelings and concerns about the care your children receive from other caregivers?
4. What actions can you take to influence the care your child receives from others?
5. What would help you to feel that you had some control in these situations?

LEADERS' NOTES

You can increase the impact of this session by making a chart with columns headed by each question. After answering all the questions, the members will be able to see an integrated picture of how their children are being raised. As women confide their concerns about other caregivers, they may express some anxiety about who will have access to the information. They may worry that the leaders will report situations at home to Child Protective Services or another social service agency. At the beginning of the session, discuss with the women which behaviors constitute abuse and neglect and thus will need to be reported. Women can then have control over the information they choose to reveal.

QUESTION 1

Who shares in the responsibility for the care of your children?

TYPICAL RESPONSES Family: father, mother, grandparents, aunts, uncles, siblings, foster parents

Social network: teachers, baby-sitters, coaches, day-care providers, neighbors, friends

Members should be encouraged to think about formal as well as informal caregiver situations.

QUESTION 2

Who makes the decisions about who will provide this care?

TYPICAL RESPONSES My mother has decided that the children should live with her.

My husband and I make the decisions together.

The school system assigned my daughter to a teacher that I don't like but there isn't anything I can do about it.

The judge decided my husband and I would get joint custody.

I want to participate in the decisions but my husband won't let me.

This question helps members explore the authority they feel they have in the family situation. Women lose authority for many reasons depending on life circumstances, including: legal decisions, power relations within the family, illness, abandonment of authority by the woman herself, and a history of past abuse.

QUESTION 3

What are your feelings and concerns about the care your children receive from other caregivers?

TYPICAL RESPONSES My mother beat me and I'm afraid she will also hit my children.

I'm worried that my mom will fill my daughter's head full of crazy things about me.

I trust my mother completely, I have no concerns although she always comments on the way I raise my children.

My uncle abused me and I'm afraid he may hurt my daughter even though my aunt says he's never alone with her. I have no one else to care for her.

I can only relax fully when my husband is taking care of the children.

Mothers often are concerned about how children are being cared for when they are not with them. Assist members in sorting out real concerns from the normal concerns of not having full control over their children's care. Trauma survivors, because of their histories, may express an unusually high degree of concern.

QUESTION 4

What actions can you take to influence the care your child receives from others?

TYPICAL RESPONSES I fight with my husband over the way his new wife treats my daughter and I look like the mean one.

> I negotiated with my aunt so that my uncle will not
> be in the house when my daughter is there.
> I hired a lawyer to force the school to meet my son's
> special needs.
> I try to take a stand but always end up feeling pow-
> erless and that I'm imagining the problems.
> No matter what I do my grandfather is still in the
> house. He abused me and I'm afraid he'll abuse
> my daughter.

As participants brainstorm in response to this question they will describe more and less effective actions. Help members overcome shameful feelings they have about previous episodes of ineffective advocacy on behalf of their children. This may raise memories of ineffectual family members who failed to keep women safe when they were children.

QUESTION 5

What would help you to feel that you had some control in these situations?

TYPICAL RESPONSES   Find people who will listen to me respectfully
Persuade my husband to take my side occasionally
Organize my arguments before I start

Assist members in separating out real solutions from those that are impractical or impossible. If the members can be helped to see that there are ways that they can be more influential in their children's care, they may feel more able to make the effort.

TOPIC 4 The Impact of Forced Separations

SESSION RATIONALE

This topic helps members to see the importance of explaining the reasons for separations to children; to explore the impact of these separations on parent and child relationships; and to enrich their understanding of how these separations have affected their own image as parents. They will also begin to see the vulnerability their children may feel when they are away for even short periods of time.

GOAL 1: Members will explore the impact these forced separations have on their relationships with their children and on their own identities as parents.

GOAL 2: Members will clarify the extent of the knowledge that their children and families have about the reasons for separations.

QUESTIONS

1. How often and for how long are you separated from your children?
2. How do you explain these separations to your children?
3. How is your influence on your children's lives affected by these separations?
4. How can you protect your children when you are absent?
5. How have these periods of separation affected your sense of yourself as a parent?
6. How do you think your children are affected by these separations?

LEADERS' NOTES

Mothers who are overwhelmed due to multiple life stressors often are forced to be separated from their children for periods of time. They may be separated because of hospitalizations for substance abuse and/or mental illness, incar-

292

ceration, government intervention because of abuse and/or neglect, or divorce. There may be considerable sadness, frustration, and/or guilt about these separations.

QUESTION 1

How often and for how long are you separated from your children?

TYPICAL RESPONSES   I get hospitalized about twice a year for about two weeks each time.

I've gone to jail on drug charges twice in the last two years.

I'm only allowed supervised Saturday visits by Child Protective Services.

Every weekend—their father has them.

This information will give leaders and the other group members a context for understanding the reasons for the separations, the length of separations, and the seriousness of the issue for members.

QUESTION 2

How do you explain these separations to your children?

TYPICAL RESPONSES   I tell them that the hospital helps me to feel better.

I didn't tell them I was in jail, but they heard from the neighbor's child.

I told them the judge thought it was better for my aunt to care for them until I get myself together.

They understand that their father and I don't get along with each other.

Help members to decide the amount of information that should be given to children. You can take the opportunity to discuss the pros and cons of full disclosure and help the participants decide on an approach that is most helpful for them and for their children. Help facilitate group feedback when a member is holding secrets that are harmful to children. Members should be aware that they often have less control than they would like over what their children hear.

QUESTION 3

How is your influence on your children's lives affected by these separations?

TYPICAL RESPONSES   When I'm in the hospital it really hurts my children, the other kids tease them.

When my mom brings them to see me on visiting days we spend all our time getting acquainted all over again and no time discussing problems.

The case worker at Child Protective Services is always in my business and lets me have no influence.

I feel that I have less and less influence since my husband was awarded custody.

Members may have strong emotional reactions to this question. They may need to mourn the loss of the mothering role.

QUESTION 4

How can you protect your children when you are absent?

TYPICAL RESPONSES   I leave a very detailed plan about my child's daily schedule.

I have to be realistic, I can't offer full protection when I am away.

I try to get information from the sitter, but I have to rely on what my son tells me.

I make it clear to my aunt that I will report her if there are problems.

I can threaten my husband that I will go back to court to get custody.

This question may cause members to remember their own vulnerability because of an absent parent.

QUESTION 5

How have these periods of separation affected your sense of yourself as a parent?

TYPICAL RESPONSES   I feel like my addiction gets more of my time and attention than my kids do.
I feel like a failure.
I know I've been a bad parent.
The children listen to their dad and not to me, I don't even feel like a parent.

Parents often have a range of troubled feelings about their separations from their children. The guilt, frustration, and sadness that may accompany these separations can undermine the confidence members have in their parenting ability. This question gives members further opportunity to talk about their complicated feelings about separations.

QUESTION 6

How do you think your children are affected by these separations?

TYPICAL RESPONSES   My daughter is worried I'll never quit using and will always do these disappearing acts.
My son hates to come to the jail and often refuses to talk to me when I call, he's angry.
My kids call their grandmother "mom" now.
My kids are acting out their frustrations at school, the teacher is always sending home notes about their bad behavior.

Try to help the group members get in touch with the anger and frustration their children are probably feeling about these separations.

TOPIC 5 Returning Home After Long-Term Separations

SESSION RATIONALE

This session helps members discuss the fantasies they have about how they will resume their parenting roles when they return home. The discussion encourages the development of realistic plans for the actual circumstances they will face upon their return.

GOAL 1: Members will discuss their images of returning home after long-term separations.

GOAL 2: Members will develop more realistic expectations about their return home.

QUESTIONS

1. How do you imagine your homecoming?
2. What behaviors and attitudes do you expect from your children when you return?
3. What do you expect from your children's caregivers?
4. Do you have a plan for how to resume your role as parent? What will your parental responsibilities be when you return home? Describe your plan.
5. What do you imagine will be the greatest difficulty in being reunited with your children?

LEADERS' NOTES

This topic targets a subpopulation of women and may not be appropriate for all groups. Help the group participants focus on the difficult aspects of returning to their children's lives after stigmatizing events such as jail or hospitalizations due to substance addiction or mental illness.

You will need to be sensitive to the fact that some women have been separated from their children because they were abusive or neglectful mothers. Reunion, if there is to be one, clearly poses different issues for these women. These women might not be willing to talk about their criminal behavior toward their children. There may be secrets that the members and their families have kept hidden. If you know about these secrets, do not collude with the silence. On the other hand, you will want to avoid having the session become a retrial of a woman who has been abusive or neglectful of her children.

QUESTION 1

How do you imagine your homecoming?

> **TYPICAL RESPONSES**   There is going to be a huge party.
> They will ask me a hundred questions, some will be hard to answer.
> The kids will be excited, I don't know if the adults will be.
> Very emotional. I'm afraid the children will be angry.
> It will be like I never left.

If the difficulty of returning home is glossed over or whitewashed, ask about what happened the last time a member returned home, and why she left again. Group feedback can assist mothers in being more realistic about their plans.

QUESTION 2

What behaviors and attitudes do you expect from your children when you return?

> **TYPICAL RESPONSES**   They will expect me to prove myself to them, it will take time.
> I think my daughter will be very angry, she is already acting out.
> They will expect me to be there for them, I don't know if I can.

Help members focus on the difficult behaviors resulting from the anger and disappointment their children act out. Members will explore the struggles they may experience regaining their credibility. Children may be skeptical about their mothers' chances of success and afraid of future abandonments.

Question 3

What will you expect from your children's caregivers?

TYPICAL RESPONSES   Resentment.
They will be glad to give the responsibilities back to me.
They will be very skeptical of my abilities and my intentions.
They will give the care for the kids back to me slowly.

Some caregivers will be relieved to have the mother back, but others will be wary. Leaders will help members focus on how they will face the doubts and fears of the people who have filled in for them in their absence.

Question 4

Do you have a plan for how to resume your role as parent? What will your parental responsibilities be when you return home? Describe your plan.

TYPICAL RESPONSES   Pick up where I left off, minus the drugs.
I have stayed in the decision making, I was never cut out.
I think the kids will come to me.
I don't know, I'll have to sit down with my mom and we'll have to work it out.

Some members will underestimate the difficulties involved in resuming a meaningful role as a parent upon their return home. You will need to help those members develop strategies for negotiating resumption of parental responsibilities. Members may not be allowed to resume their parenting role without proving they can be responsible in the community.

QUESTION 5

What do you imagine will be the greatest difficulty in being reunited with your children?

TYPICAL RESPONSES   Facing time lost
Making my son feel safe, proving that I will be there
Starting all over with my baby
Dealing with my ex-husband

Members need an opportunity to share their fears and frustrations about being separated. Be supportive without giving simplistic assurances that everything will be OK.

TOPIC 6 What Is Important for Children to Learn from Parents

SESSION RATIONALE

This session helps members clarify what they want to teach their children. The discussion helps differentiate between idealized values and attitudes and more realistic expectations. The discussion also helps differentiate between what is said and what is actually done.

GOAL 1: Members will learn to identify, assess, and evaluate their own expectations, rules, and hopes for family living.

GOAL 2: Members will begin to understand the values they were taught and how that learning influences what they teach their children.

QUESTIONS

1. What were the spoken and unspoken attitudes in your family regarding:
   a. Money?
   b. Violence?
   c. Lying, secrets, avoiding problems?
   d. Religious values?
   e. Drugs, alcohol, sex?
2. What values and standards are most important for you to teach to your children?
3. Are there factors that will reduce your credibility as an authority figure?

LEADERS' NOTES

Ask members not only about the content of what they were taught but also how they felt about the lessons their caregivers imparted either directly or indirectly. For each of the content areas, leaders should ask about both positive and negative reactions to parental beliefs and messages. They also should question whether those reactions changed over time and if so, how they altered.

QUESTION 1

What were the spoken and unspoken attitudes in your family regarding:

a. Money?

TYPICAL RESPONSES   Mom put all my money in the bank.
My sister told me to save but I didn't.
Dad worked, brought his paycheck home, and turned it over to mom.
I had to help out with the bills because mom was raising us alone.
We lived off of credit cards.

Money is an issue that is difficult for most people to talk about, but if children are not taught how to handle money they can have serious difficulties with adult responsibility. Group members might identify how their own parents' confused messages affected them.

b. Violence?

TYPICAL RESPONSES   Mom said, "No fighting in the house," so we went outside and fought like cats and dogs.
Only fighting in our house was between my mom and dad.
No fighting was allowed between brothers and sisters, but my parents beat us when they felt like it.
Mom told me always to stand up for myself, but yelled when I got in trouble for doing it.
I watched my mom physically abuse my brothers.

Children sometimes experience mixed messages when it comes to violence. It is then left to them to make some sense out of the confusion.

c. Lying, secrets, avoiding problems?

TYPICAL RESPONSES   My uncle said he would kill me if I ever revealed our sexual relationship.

We weren't allowed to talk about our family's money problems.

I would get an ass whipping if I was caught in a lie.

We were taught what goes on in this house stays in this house.

They tried to keep it a secret when mom went to the hospital.

Mom tried to hide it from me when she was getting high.

Children are instructed not to lie, but are witnesses to their parents' lies and secret-keeping. Participants will see how confusing this was for them and will develop strategies regarding how to do it differently with their children.

d. Religious values?

TYPICAL RESPONSES   My mom was involved in a Bible study.

We went to church, but as soon as we got home mom started swearing and drinking.

My uncle never stopped talking about the Twelve Steps.

My parents disagreed about what religion we kids should be.

We only went to church for weddings and funerals.

I was abused by my priest.

Children may be hurt, troubled, and confused by the contradiction between religious values espoused by church and family and the actual behavior of churchgoers and family members. Sometimes religious rhetoric can camouflage abusive behavior. Members can be helped to differentiate between these misuses of religion and those religious and spiritual resources that can be instrumental in coping with a wide variety of life problems.

e. Drugs, alcohol, sex?

TYPICAL RESPONSES   Mom and dad could do drugs and alcohol but we couldn't.

Mom said I could talk to her about anything, but when I asked her for birth control pills she said I was too young to have sex. She couldn't accept that I was already doing it.

They told us no drugs, control your alcohol, and no sex until marriage.

I thought my mom's rules were too strict (curfew was too early and I wasn't allowed to go out with friends) so I ran away from home.

When mothers have a history of abuse, they often develop dysfunctional attitudes toward sex (i.e., promiscuity or total avoidance). Abusive experiences also can lead survivors to use alcohol and drugs to forget the pain of the past. Members may struggle with providing guidance to their children around these issues.

QUESTION 2

What values and standards are most important for you to teach to your children?

TYPICAL RESPONSES   Honesty
Consistency
Respect
Communication
Love
Stand up for yourself

Members are usually quick to mention what they want to teach their children, but at a loss as to how to do it. Explore with group members how these values and standards can be conveyed.

QUESTION 3

Are there factors that will reduce your credibility as an authority figure?

TYPICAL RESPONSES   My history of drug abuse.

I got married because I was pregnant.

My kids watched me in a relationship with an abusive boyfriend for two years.

My emotional problems make me less of a role model.

I don't have the confidence to teach my children about sex because I was sexually abused.

Sometimes parents think that they are not effective role models because they had so many of their own devastating problems. Members who believe their credibility has been damaged can use group feedback to evaluate the efficacy of the coping strategies they would like to teach their children.

TOPIC 7 Discipline Is Not Punishment

SESSION RATIONALE

Influencing children's behavior without abusive punishment is a central difficulty for parents. The purpose of this session is to help participants understand
the differences among discipline, punishment, and abuse; and to develop alternatives to punishment.

GOAL 1: Participants will learn the difference between providing discipline
and administering punishment.

GOAL 2: Participants will learn at least three alternatives to corporal
punishment.

QUESTIONS

1. What are the differences among discipline, punishment, and abuse?
2. Why do children disobey?
3. What are the elements of going too far with punishment?
4. What are the useful alternatives to punishment?

LEADERS' NOTES

Perhaps more than any other topic, the session on discipline raises questions
about abuse. Members may find it painful and difficult to consider that their
attempts to discipline their children sometimes become abusive, or more troubling still, that they commit abuse behind the facade of discipline. You will
need to walk a fine line, respecting familial and cultural differences and avoiding blaming and shaming members while at the same time helping members to
be honest and clear about how they discipline their children. You can offer support by acknowledging just how difficult it is to be a parent and how common
it is to feel frustrated when children are misbehaving or testing the limits.

QUESTION 1

What are the differences among discipline, punishment, and abuse?

TYPICAL RESPONSES   Discipline is correcting the child.

Discipline is knowing the rules beforehand.

Discipline is setting limits.

Punishment is striking the child.

Punishment is taking something away.

Abuse is when you're so angry you get out of control.

Punishment is causing injury to the child.

Members might find it difficult to differentiate between discipline and punishment. You will find it useful to have the dictionary definitions of punishment (suffering, pain, or loss that serves as retribution) and discipline (instruction or training that corrects, molds, or perfects the mental faculties) available for the group members. Members may strongly disagree with each other as they sort out the boundaries between discipline, punishment, and abuse.

QUESTION 2

Why do children disobey?

TYPICAL RESPONSES   Testing the limits

Want attention

Curiosity

Lack of supervision

Probe for all of the factors that influence the behavior of the child including: **parent factors** (inaccessibility, failure to explain rules, inconsistency, unreasonable demands, and problematic behavior by parents, stemming from substance abuse, mental illness, or domestic violence that causes acting out by the child); **child factors** (illness, developmental stage, emotional need, lack of skill, fatigue, hunger, bad behavior, peer pressure); and **situational factors** (instability, lack of supervision, neighborhood influences).

QUESTION 3

What are the elements of going too far with punishment?

TYPICAL RESPONSES   My mother used to humiliate me in front of my
friends.

My uncle locked me in the closet all day.

My father whipped me and then forced me to sit in
a salty bath.

My mother really enjoyed beating me. I could tell
by the look in her eye.

Members should explore the aspects of punishment that are abusive and emotionally scarring. Focus the discussion on the use of humiliation, punishment,
torture, public shame, and sadism.

QUESTION 4

What are the useful alternatives to punishment?

TYPICAL RESPONSES   Education: point out ways in which the child can be
more appropriate.

Express strong disapproval without attacking the
child.

State your expectations—are they age appropriate?

Show the child how to make amends.

Give children choices.

Allow the child to experience the consequences of
his or her behavior.

Time-outs.

Help members explore disciplinary methods that don't resort to punishment.

TOPIC 8 What Is Age-Appropriate Behavior for Children?

SESSION RATIONALE

Discussion of fair and reasonable expectations of children is assisted by accurate information about age-appropriate behaviors. A developmental framework can then provide a context for discussion of the goodness of fit between age-appropriate child behavior and parental responses and needs at each developmental stage. Women who have experienced trauma often report growing up too fast and consequently being unaware, as adults, of age-appropriate behaviors.

GOAL 1: Participants will identify age-appropriate behaviors in the intellectual, emotional, behavioral, moral, sexual, and relational domains.

GOAL 2: Participants will discuss the goodness of fit between their skills and interests and their children's needs.

QUESTIONS

For each of four age groups (ages 0–2; 3–5; 6–11; and adolescence) ask the following questions:
1. In what way do you expect too much of your child?
2. What are the most difficult aspects of children this age?
3. What are the most pleasurable aspects of children this age?

LEADERS' NOTES

Using a flip chart, develop a table for questions in each of the four age groups listed above. In the first column, list four age-appropriate behaviors in each age group. Then complete the table with members' responses. For example:

	Question 1	Question 2	Question 3
Age-Appropriate Behaviors (provided by leaders)	In what way do you expect too much of your child?	What are the most difficult aspects of raising children this age?	What are the most pleasur-able aspects of raising children this age?

As members discuss these questions, they may want to reflect on their own childhood experiences and discuss how they felt about their parents' various expectations of and reactions to them. Members' individual differences in personality, skill, and sources of emotional gratification and frustration enrich the discussion of these questions.

Do not assume that this one session will satisfy all of the members' questions about child-rearing practices. Be prepared to distribute articles and accessible references.

CHILDREN FROM BIRTH TO TWO

SOME AGE-APPROPRIATE BEHAVIORS

Poor sleep habits
Crying when they feel distressed
Exploring everything when mobile
Learning to eat

QUESTION 1

In what way do you expect too much of children younger than two?

TYPICAL RESPONSES   Sometimes I want my baby to leave me alone.
I wanted my baby to sleep through the night much sooner.
Wanting my child to be toilet trained.

QUESTION 2

What are the most difficult aspects of raising babies?

TYPICAL RESPONSES   It takes more effort to go places with a baby.

You never get any sleep when you have an infant.

The first baby is the hardest—I wasn't prepared for the responsibility.

QUESTION 3

What are the most pleasurable aspects of raising babies?

TYPICAL RESPONSES   I love holding babies.

When your baby smiles you fall in love.

I liked having somebody who was totally dependent on me.

Seeing how quickly they learn new skills and languages.

CHILDREN AGED THREE TO FIVE

SOME AGE-APPROPRIATE BEHAVIORS

Tantrums
Control struggles
Problems with sharing
Lots of questions
Toilet trained

QUESTION 1

In what way do you expect too much of children aged two to five?

TYPICAL RESPONSES   I want my two-year-old to do what I say without protesting.

I wanted my three-year-old to go to day care without crying.

I expected my daughter to be toilet trained at the age of two.

QUESTION 2

What are the most difficult aspects of raising children this age?

TYPICAL RESPONSES   Sending my daughter to day care made me really sad.

It's hard for me to keep my temper when my four-year-old is stubborn.

I have a tendency to spank my child instead of asking her what is wrong.

QUESTION 3

What are the most pleasurable aspects of raising children this age?

TYPICAL RESPONSES   I love having bedtime conversations.

My favorite part was playing outside with my son.

I liked playing silly games and laughing.

Struggles for power and control can emerge and reemerge during this age span. Nonviolent problem solving is sometimes difficult for parents who were the victims of violence in childhood.

CHILDREN AGED SIX TO ELEVEN

SOME AGE-APPROPRIATE BEHAVIORS

Learning to stay home alone
Much greater independence
Trouble with homework
New friendships

QUESTION 1

In what way do you expect too much of children aged 6–11?

TYPICAL RESPONSES   At first I expected my child to do homework without help.

I expected my daughter to baby-sit before I found out it was against the law.

I let my son play on his own without checking in and he got in trouble.

I expected my daughter to tell me when she was upset. I didn't recognize signs of trouble.

QUESTION 2

What are the most difficult aspects of raising children this age?

TYPICAL RESPONSES   This is the age I was when my uncle abused me. I'm worried I won't be able to protect my daughter.

When my children fight back, sometimes I want to smash them.

When teachers criticize my children I get extremely angry.

Sometimes their opinions differ from mine.

QUESTION 3

What are the most pleasurable aspects of raising children this age?

TYPICAL RESPONSES   They're so curious about so many things.

This is such a creative stage.

They like to explore new things.

They are becoming interesting people.

Issues of social adjustment often are prominent in these years. Parents with a history of traumatization may have difficulty role modeling and teaching effective social problem-solving skills.

ADOLESCENTS

SOME AGE-APPROPRIATE BEHAVIORS

Rebellion or independence
Driving
Exploring sex
Asking about drugs
Need for privacy
Able to baby-sit
Becoming assertive
Becoming more responsible

QUESTION 1

In what way do you expect too much of your teenager?

TYPICAL RESPONSES   I expect them to be able to follow rules without asking me questions all the time.
I expect my daughter to act as an adult.
I expect my son to respect me like he used to. Now he thinks I don't know anything.

QUESTION 2

What are the most difficult aspects of raising teenagers?

TYPICAL RESPONSES   I have a hard time when my teenaged children are so mean and rejecting.
My son has a group of friends I simply can't stand.
I don't feel comfortable discussing sex.
I can't control my children with physical force anymore.
Validating their opinions when they differ from mine.
Being consistent with rules.

QUESTION 3

What are the most pleasurable aspects of raising children this age?

> **TYPICAL RESPONSES**   Every once in a while we have a really nice talk.
> I'm very proud of my child's accomplishments.
> Being able to do more adult things with them.
> Teaching family values.
> Having their friends over.

The discussion of development in the teenage years is always stimulating and exciting for group members. Many are still struggling with issues about independence, relationships, and sex in their own lives and have vivid memories of their own adolescent experiences.

TOPIC 9 Communication with Your Children: Learning to Listen

SESSION RATIONALE

A careful study of listening skills facilitates the development of good communication that is a central component of good parenting. Trauma survivors may have difficulty with communicating because they remember not being heard as children.

GOAL 1: Participants will learn the basic elements of good listening.

GOAL 2: Participants will identify the emotional impediments to good
listening.

QUESTIONS

1. How did your parents listen to you?
2. Are there things your parents could not hear?
3. How do you listen to your children?
4. Are there things you cannot hear?

LEADERS' NOTES

This session is an especially good tool for skill building. As women become clearer about what are and what are not good strategies for communication, ask them to consider what stops them from using the more positive strategies when they are communicating with their children. You would be wise to assume that it is not solely a skill deficit but also individual psychological barriers impeding good communication.

QUESTION 1

How did your parents listen to you?

TYPICAL RESPONSES   They did not listen well at all, they didn't take the time.

I had a big family. We got attention according to what we needed.

My mother drank and wasn't available.

They used tired clichés.

They assumed they knew what I was talking about.

They bossed me around and yelled at me.

They gave me invitations to talk:

- A smile and a motion to sit down
- A hand on the shoulder or a hug
- A statement: "You look as if something is bothering you. Want to talk?"
- A concerned look and gesture

Assist members to distinguish between helpful and unhelpful listening strategies.

QUESTION 2

Are there things your parents could not hear?

TYPICAL RESPONSES   They often ignored me when I needed things like clothes, because we didn't have any money.

My mother pretended I never asked for birth control even though I was born when she was 15.

My parents didn't want me to grow up and deal with adult issues.

My mother couldn't hear me when I told her my father raped me.

Help group members focus on the various dynamics that created barriers to communication. Perhaps the issue at hand was too provocative or perhaps the parent or caregiver was preoccupied with problems of her own.

QUESTION 3

How do you listen to your kids?

TYPICAL RESPONSES   I listen to every word my daughter says.

You have to listen for the cry for help.

With only one ear—I'm too tired at night to give her much more.

I listen to the tone of voice and watch their body language.

Participants may initially portray their own skills in an overly positive manner. You will want to gently encourage participants to be more realistic as they describe their own skills. Humor can be effective in this session if used judiciously. Some participants will relax when they realize there is no such thing as a perfect listener. You also might help participants discuss their ability to absorb information, probe topics at a greater depth, and tolerate more complete exploration of the topic at hand.

QUESTION 4

Are there things you cannot hear?

TYPICAL RESPONSES   You're mean.

You're not here for me when I need you.

I hate you.

You're a bad mother.

I'm going to kill myself.

When they want to talk about their sexual encounters.

How bad their drug use is.

That my boyfriend abused them.

The issue of blame is often one of the most emotionally charged for parents. There may be a sense of guilt for having done something wrong; and there may also be a deeper sense of shame about an alleged inadequacy in the self.

TOPIC 10 Communication with Your Children: Knowing How to Respond

SESSION RATIONALE

Communication between parent and child can raise very difficult emotional issues for all parties. Especially when children's questions probe areas in which their parents are uneasy or uncertain. Understanding of the emotional issues involved will help parents develop, sustain, and support richer and more meaningful conversations with their children.

Parents should be alert to possible problems when children are not asking difficult questions. Parents can assume that normal curiosity prompts children to ask embarrassing questions.

GOAL 1: Participants will learn various options for responding to their children in conversation.

GOAL 2: Participants will learn how their own feelings and behaviors can facilitate or stifle good communication.

QUESTIONS

1. What do your children ask you about?
2. What kinds of advice and information can you provide in response to your children?
3. What kinds of emotional support can you provide in response to your children?
4. What kind of tangible support do your children need?

LEADERS' NOTES

Use questions 1–4 in combination to construct a table that demonstrates connections among questions children ask and categories of possible responses. First, generate a list of questions children ask (question 1). Second, from this list, the group can select four topics for more detailed discussion. Third, explore possible responses using questions 2–4 and complete the chart as you go along. When completed, the chart will illustrate the scope of possible responses available to parents.

QUESTION 1

What do your children ask you about?

> **TYPICAL RESPONSES**   What happens when you die?
> My boyfriend wants to have sex. What should I do?
> How come I can't use drugs but daddy can drink?
> Why do you and dad fight all the time?

QUESTION 2

What kinds of advice and information can you provide in response to your children?

QUESTION 3

What kinds of emotional support can you provide in response to your children?

QUESTION 4

What kinds of tangible support do your children need?

The answers to questions 2–4 are used to complete the Responding to Children chart.

RESPONDING TO CHILDREN
TYPICAL RESPONSES

Children's Questions from Question 1	Advice and Information from Question 2	Emotional Support from Question 3	Tangible Support from Question 4
What happens when you die?	You go to heaven.	You'll be remembered.	Take child to a minister.
	I don't know.	God will take care of you.	Develop rituals for acknowledging anniversary of death.
	You're just dead.	It's scary to think about.	

TYPICAL RESPONSES

Children's Questions from Question 1	Advice and Information from Question 2	Emotional Support from Question 3	Tangible Support from Question 4
My boyfriend wants to have sex. What should I do?	Wait until you're 18. Learn about safe sex.	I tried to help her understand the difference between sex and love. I told her what happened to me when I didn't say no.	I gave her extra money for birth control. I took her to the clinic. I got her some good books on the subject. I keep listening to her.
How come I can't use drugs but daddy can drink?	Drugs and alcohol are dangerous. Your father is an adult and can make his own decisions.	I try not to get frustrated about the topic. I let her know that I think her father needs help with his problem.	I get her pamphlets from AA/NA and Alateen.
Why do you and dad fight all the time?	I let her know it's not serious. I tell her about the times we get along.	I let her know we both love her even though we fight. I try to listen to her concerns.	I don't fight in front of the kids. If a fight is brewing I send the kids to my mother's.

The purpose of the chart is to illustrate for parents that answering children's questions is a complex task that may require more than one type or level of response. In some cases, parents will learn a new way of organizing their thinking about what they already do. In other cases, the chart will help parents develop additional flexibility and expand their repertoire of responses.

TOPIC 11 Decision Making with Children

SESSION RATIONALE

Decision making between parents and children is a complex task that requires a sophisticated sense of self and other. Flexibility regarding expectations about who has authority for decision making is important, because these expectations can change over time and across situations.

GOAL 1: Participants will learn decision-making skills.

GOAL 2: Participants will learn how to use these decision-making skills in their roles as parents.

QUESTIONS

1. Which decisions are yours?
2. Which decisions are your child's?
3. What is really worth struggling over and what can you live with?

LEADERS' NOTES

The distribution of responsibility for decision making often becomes more of an issue as children get older. Focus on how decision making and compromise becomes more complicated as mothers try to negotiate with adolescents. Women may voice differences in how far they are willing to go in setting limits on their children's acting out. Are they more or less protective because of their own experiences? Are they worried that their children will repeat the mistakes they made? Do they have issues about which they will not compromise?

Questions 1 and 2 will be answered together using two columns on a flip chart.

QUESTION 1

Which decisions are yours?

TYPICAL RESPONSES I decide how to manage money for the family.

I tell the kids they have to go to school, no matter what.

My kids would never go to the doctor or dentist on their own.

Sometimes it seems like I only have control over the petty things like haircuts.

QUESTION 2

Which decisions are your child's?

TYPICAL RESPONSES They're allowed to pick their own clothing—within limits.

They get to choose how they will spend time on Saturday.

I wish it wasn't true because I think they're too young, but my children make their own decisions about when to have sex.

This question helps members sort out and differentiate their own domain of responsibility from their children's. At first parents may assume that children have very little responsibility in decision making. Help parents focus on the reality of a child's influence on the family decision-making process.

QUESTION 3

What's worth struggling over and what can you live with?

TYPICAL RESPONSES I don't trust my son's ability to make decisions about drugs and alcohol.

I am strongly encouraging my children to postpone their first sexual experience.

I put my foot down when my son was caught stealing.

My daughter and I worked out a good compromise about her cigarette smoking.

Initiate a discussion of lose-lose versus win-win strategies in negotiating with children. Help members be mindful of the long-term problems that can result from not negotiating or from being heavy handed. The child's loss of opportunity to take responsibility for decision making is one unfortunate consequence.

WOMEN WHO ABUSE

Carolyn Duca, M.S.W.
Ellen Arledge, M.S.W.

INTRODUCTION

This psychoeducational group intervention provides a forum for female trauma survivors who commit abuse to discuss abusive behavior. A general discussion of abusive behavior often gives way to a more specific discussion of members' abusive actions. Additionally, members' knowledge regarding abusiveness is derived from their experience as both perpetrators and victims of abuse. While reducing members' abusive behavior is a desired outcome of group participation, the emphasis of the intervention is on increasing group members' awareness and understanding of the dynamics of abusive behavior.

Participation in the intervention demonstrates to members that they can think about the precipitants to and consequences of abusive behavior rather than merely reacting to circumstances. The group further introduces the idea that the women can choose to behave nonabusively if they are sufficiently motivated to do so.

Referrals to this intervention may come from employee assistance programs, prison diversion programs, community mental health centers, substance abuse programs, or child protective services. All women will have completed the Trauma Recovery and Empowerment intervention.

The Abusers' Group intervention is 7 to 13 weeks long; Topic 1 usually requires only one 75-minute session whereas the remaining topics (2–7) take either one or two sessions each.

Not surprisingly, working with female trauma survivors who also abuse presents special challenges for group leaders. The first challenge is the content of the intervention—the inappropriate and destructive expression of aggression—and the individuals for whom the intervention is targeted. It is realistic for group leaders to be concerned about the possibility of triggering strong, potentially uncontainable affect or behavior in doing this group. This would be a particular concern in working with abusers who also are disturbed characterologically. The presence of intense aggression and the concurrent absence of reliable internal constraints on the expression of that aggression is a potentially dangerous combination found in many personality disorders (Kernberg, 1992). The fact that this intervention is psychoeducational, not psychotherapeutic, in nature does not guarantee that a storm of affect or threatening behavior or a psychiatric decompensation will not be touched off inadvertently by the intervention. To deal with these potential developments most effectively, it is important that group leaders are experienced master's-level mental health professionals who are knowledgeable about serious character pathology and have access to clinical and administrative supports. Group leaders should carefully prescreen members via personal interviews and a review of each individual's mental health and legal history. As a general guideline, exclusion from group participation should be considered for individuals who have pronounced narcissistic or borderline traits and would clearly be called for with individuals who have pronounced psychopathic traits.

A second challenge, not necessarily unrelated to serious character pathology, is the tendency of abusive individuals to deny that they are in fact abusive. Often, women participate in the group only after some form of real or perceived arm-twisting by the referral source or primary treatment provider. As a result, leaders may be faced with members who assert that a mistake has been made and that they do not belong in the group. Or, leaders may encounter women who are more motivated by the possibility of receiving a particular tangible benefit from being in the group (e.g., earlier release from prison, a recommendation to have visitation restored with children) than by any real commitment to changing their abusive patterns. A group member is more likely to get something useful from the intervention if she acknowledges that she has a problem with violence and sincerely wishes to understand and change her behavior. Leaders can utilize the pregroup screening interview to assess the degree and nature of motivation shown by potential group members.

A third challenge concerns confidentiality. Leaders are faced with having to report actual or suspected child abuse by group members to appropriate outside parties. They also have a duty to warn an individual whom a group member threatens to injure. These exceptions to holding information in confidence promote the important goal of protecting victims and potential victims. However, these exceptions to the rule of confidentiality may further compromise a member's ability to be honest about her aggressive impulses and actions. Members should be informed of the limits of confidentiality when they start the group.

A fourth challenge for group leaders concerns countertransference. Leaders should expect to have strong reactions to the abusive acts described by group members and to members' specific characterizations of those acts (e.g., their lack of remorse, blaming the victim, minimization of harm done, denial or diffusion of responsibility). Coleaders should be prepared to take time with each other before and after the group to process their emotional responses. Doing so lends mutual support, provides safe catharsis of feelings, and facilitates the constructive use of leader responses in the service of the group. For example, a leader's anger and outrage at the abusive behaviors described in the group might form the basis of modeling to group members how anger and outrage are appropriate responses to abusiveness. This point is not lost on group members who have not only perpetrated abuse but also been victims of abuse.

At other times, leaders may feel unnerved by similarities they perceive between themselves and the women in the group or by having to reevaluate their own capacity for violence. Leaders should discuss these issues as well.

Two closing comments: First, we believe that members will be better able to participate in and derive benefit from the Abusers' module if they have completed participation in the core Trauma Recovery and Empowerment group. It is helpful for members to know from experience what is entailed in focusing on difficult emotional material in the company of others. Squarely facing one's own aggression is a complex emotional task, requiring motivation, courage, and psychological strength. The Trauma Recovery and Empowerment module fosters the development of these internal resources.

Second, leaders should be mindful of members' educational and cultural backgrounds to better tailor the intervention to the specific needs of the group members. Leaders should take care to define key words and ideas introduced throughout the intervention and not assume that these concepts already are known by the members.

TOPIC 1   Introduction to the Group

SESSION RATIONALE

The purpose of the introductory session is to present members with the framework and rules of the group. The information presented, and the manner in which it is presented, both convey that this is a carefully thought out, structured intervention. Consistent with the topic at hand, the leaders' tone should be serious, but not stern or punitive.

GOAL 1: Each member will introduce herself to the group.

GOAL 2: Each member will understand the agenda, format, and rules of the group.

QUESTIONS

As this initial session is strictly informative in nature, the format of this session differs from that of the remaining sessions. There are no questions for this topic.

LEADERS' NOTES

The group begins with brief introductions by all participants. Provide name tags and markers for members to write their names. Each participant should wear a name tag.

Inform group members that the group is referred to as a Violence Awareness Group and/or as an Abusers' Group. Members have been referred to the group because they have been identified by themselves or others as being abusive. A number of reactions can be anticipated:

Members may deny, with or without anger, any personal association with violence or abuse, other than perhaps being victims of it.

Members may begin to tell stories of when and how they have been abusive, focusing on how they were provoked or merely defending themselves.

Members may brag about being abusive.

Members may acknowledge having a problem with violence.

Be prepared to respond to these reactions by acknowledging that most people who are abusive find this difficult to admit.

The group requires that members reflect on their own values and beliefs as well as their decision-making and conflict-resolution skills. This process may be unfamiliar, difficult, or taxing for members.

Engage members to give feedback about how the intervention is affecting their feelings and their functioning. You may need to set aside time at intervals to address how members are managing. However, you will want to avoid deviating too far from the designated format.

The group is structured to focus on a weekly topic related to abuse and violence and associated questions. Within this structure, encourage members to express their thoughts and feelings.

Present the following rules of the group:

1. A given session will be closed to a member if she arrives 20 or more minutes late to that session.
2. Members should come to the group prepared to stay for the entire session.
3. All information disclosed in the group is to be held in confidence by both the group leaders and the participants. However, leaders are required to disclose information pertaining to or shared by a participant in some exceptional circumstances. For example, leaders will disclose information to appropriate third parties when a participant is a danger to herself or others. Leaders are required by law to report suspected or actual child abuse or neglect. Members who are not able to maintain confidentiality will be asked to leave the group.
4. Abusive and/or disruptive behavior will not be allowed within the group. Some examples of abusive behavior that may occur in the group are direct or indirect threats, put-downs, and intimidation. Disruptive behavior is any behavior that seriously interrupts the flow of the group process; for example, whispering to others while a group member is speaking.

The firmness with which you respond to abusive/disruptive behavior should correspond to the severity of the problem with which you are presented.

The interaction between the leaders and the transgressing group members will be watched carefully by all members. An appropriate and effective response (one that addresses the problem without replicating abuse) helps to establish your credibility with group members.

Present the topic headings of the remaining sessions to give members an idea of the scope of the intervention. Encourage members to voice questions or concerns they may have at this point.

TOPIC 2   What Is Abusive Behavior?

SESSION RATIONALE

Often, people who behave abusively do not view their behavior as such. This distortion typically is accomplished through some form of self-justification. In this session, members are invited to begin to articulate where and how they draw the line between abusive and nonabusive behavior.

GOAL 1: Members will identify behaviors that are abusive.

GOAL 2: Group members will identify attitudes, beliefs, and thoughts that accompany abusive behavior.

QUESTIONS

1. What do you consider abusive behavior? What do abusive people do?
2. What factors do you consider when you are deciding whether a behavior is abusive?
3. What things do abusive people have a hard time doing?
4. What are some of the attitudes, beliefs, and thoughts that accompany abuse? What is going on in the abuser's mind? (Leaders prepare scenarios of abuse beforehand.)

LEADERS' NOTES

QUESTION 1

What do you consider abusive behavior? What do abusive people do?

TYPICAL RESPONSES		
Insults	Criticism	Hurtful words
Hitting	Neglect	Threatening
Intimidation	Bullying	Degrading or
Name	Scaring	humiliating
calling	Using people	someone

Members typically have little difficulty identifying blatant, physical forms of abuse. Therefore, you will want to help members identify more subtle areas of abuse involving manipulation, control, threats, and intimidation. Prepare examples and descriptions of each prior to the group.

As they respond to the question, members usually begin to debate whether certain behaviors or attitudes described are in fact abusive. If they do not, you might try to get this debate going using some examples that you have prepared before the group. (What if a person did _____, would you consider that abuse? Why? Why not?) Members are usually quick to say that, for many scenarios, the answer to the question of whether a behavior is abusive is, "It depends." The leaders should help members begin to articulate factors they take into consideration when deciding whether an action is abusive.

QUESTION 2

What factors do you consider when you are deciding whether a behavior is abusive?

TYPICAL RESPONSES Whether the person meant to be mean
Whether the person was pushed to act abusively
How badly the victim was hurt—"no harm, no foul"
Whether the person was defending himself or herself at the time
Whether the victim deserved the abuse
Whether the person usually acts that way

At this time, you want to avoid influencing members' thinking on these issues. For example, refrain from asserting common abuse maxims such as "There is no provocation that gives a person the right to hit another person" or "No one deserves to be abused." Rather, highlight the process of evaluation and decision making that members use to determine when a behavior is abusive. There will be opportunities for leaders to challenge members' beliefs and engage in constructive dialogue about those beliefs at later points in the intervention.

QUESTION 3

What things do abusive people have a hard time doing?

TYPICAL RESPONSES   Nurturing
Thinking rationally when stressed out
Taking responsibility
Respecting boundaries
Reacting creatively to conflict
Accepting that no means no
Not flying off the handle when feeling angry or upset
Admitting they are wrong
Giving and taking in relationships
Considering others' feelings and needs
Caring about anything or anyone, including themselves

This question underscores the idea that abuse is a function of not only what the abuser does but also what she does not do.

In addition, the way this question (and many other questions in the intervention) are asked gives group members a choice about whether to "story" themselves into their responses. They can discuss abusive people, not necessarily themselves. In this way, members are given the space to begin to explore abusiveness without having to expose too much of themselves.

The intent of this approach is not to reinforce existing denial and dissociation, although that is always a risk. Rather, the approach reflects a recognition that members may need time before disclosing negative aspects of themselves.

If some self-disclosure does take place in the group, members may be comforted to see that others have similar problems with self-management and interpersonal relationships. This reduces the sense of isolation members are likely to feel, an important early group task. On the other hand, you should also be aware that there may be a pull within the group to ostracize or scapegoat a group member who reveals something of herself. Be prepared to step in and keep further abuse from taking place within the group. Model empathy and limit setting.

QUESTION 4

What are some of the attitudes, beliefs, and thoughts that accompany abuse? What is going on in the abuser's mind? (Leaders prepare scenarios of abuse beforehand.)

TYPICAL RESPONSES   The abuser thinks that someone is threatening or
hurting her.

The abuser is insecure.

The abuser is jealous and feels that she can't trust
her partner.

My needs are more important than your needs.

They always think that they are being disrespected.

Abusers believe that other people are their property.

Weakness is wrong and deserves to be punished.

Someone else's behavior is a reflection on me.

If members are not getting this question, present the vignettes or scenarios of abuse you prepared beforehand and ask members to speculate about what is going on in the abuser's mind. For example:

> A couple—a man and a woman go to a party together. Once they arrive, the woman goes up to the bar to get drinks for them both while the man takes a seat at their table. The man sees the bartender smiling and reaching out to shake hands with his girlfriend. She returns the smile and her manner suggests that she knows him. When she sees the boyfriend watching her, she quickly glances away. Later that night, the boyfriend accuses his girlfriend of cheating and begins to beat her.

This question helps members begin to articulate various reasons why abusers abuse, setting the stage for the next session.

ADDITIONAL QUESTIONS

1. What do you do that is abusive?
2. On a scale of 1 to 10, with 1 meaning "no problem" and 10 meaning "very big problem," how bad a problem would you say you have with being abusive? Does this rating reflect an improvement or a worsening of the problem? How do you account for the change?
3. When is behaving aggressively or abusively justified?

TOPIC 3 Why People Abuse: Motivations for and Precipitants to Abuse

SESSION RATIONALE

This session begins a formal discussion of the steps that precede abusive behavior. Frequently abusers will say that they are abusive because that is just the way they are, that they don't know why they explode, or that they go from 0 to 100 on the anger meter in a split second. Consideration of this session's questions helps members to clarify the processes that precede aggressive and abusive behavior.

GOAL 1: Members will articulate motivations underlying abusive and aggressive behavior.

GOAL 2: Members will be able to identify precipitants to abusive and aggressive behavior.

QUESTIONS

1. Why do people behave abusively or aggressively?
2. What are the primary feelings involved for the abuser while behaving abusively or aggressively?
3. What can an abuser gain from being abusive?
4. What can an abuser avoid by being abusive?
5. What events or situations trigger episodes of abuse?

LEADERS' NOTES

QUESTION 1

Why do people behave abusively or aggressively?

TYPICAL RESPONSES

I was abused all my life.	Provocation.
I was raised that way.	Revenge.
Bravado.	Justified retaliation.
Fear.	Self-defense
Because it works.	The best defense is a
To cope with feeling	good offense.
vulnerable.	Not caring.
Lack of empathy.	Impulsivity.
Because they are mean.	

I hold things in and then it all comes out against
someone else.

They don't have alternatives to violence to deal with
problems.

Lack of consequences for being aggressive.

Being aggressive = being strong and tough.

They enjoy the feeling of power over others.

The wording of this question references both abuse and aggression. Both terms are used because although abuse and aggression are distinct terms, people tend to use them interchangeably. Aggression can be an easier term for members to understand when beginning this discussion. Leaders then can help members apply what they know about aggression to abuse.

This question does not require much prompting. It does require that the leaders watch what is transpiring in the group with a mind to gauging how defensive and/or evasive members are about their motivations. At times, members will be disarmingly frank.

QUESTION 2

What are the primary feelings involved for the abuser while behaving abusively and aggressively?

TYPICAL RESPONSES

Anger	Frustration	Relief
Fear	Anxiety	Vulnerability
Nothing	Excitement	Paranoia
A sense of smugness		

It is important that members begin to recognize that their feeling state while abusing may suggest underlying motivations for their behavior. In addition, while this question may seem elementary, you should not be surprised to learn that some members have never given much thought to the feelings accompanying their abusive behavior.

QUESTION 3

What can an abuser gain by being abusive?

TYPICAL RESPONSES   A sense of power.
A sense of control.
It helps the person get their feelings out.
Safety—no one bothers you because they can see
   you are tough.
Satisfaction because you've evened the score.
Whatever they want.
Sex.
Respect.

QUESTION 4

What can an abuser avoid by being abusive?

TYPICAL RESPONSES   Avoid feeling small
Avoid feeling guilty about all the other times they
   have abused
Avoid having to do what other people tell me to do
Avoid being frustrated
Avoid taking responsibility for their actions
Avoid facing myself
Avoid letting anyone know how scared I am
Avoid boredom
Avoid feeling scared or insecure

The previous two questions suggest that abusive behavior is supported by a range of possible gains for the abuser. To change her behavior, an abuser may need to develop substitute satisfactions, alternative ways to cope, or greater resolve in the face of frustration. You can point this out but should take care that your comments are not prescriptive or preachy. You also should keep in mind that later in the intervention an entire session is devoted to the issue of how to change abusive behavior.

You may find that you need to spend more time helping members to identify what they are avoiding instead of what might be gained by being abusive. Often these feelings are so painful that the women have buried them and resist thinking about them.

QUESTION 5

What events or situations trigger episodes of abuse?

TYPICAL RESPONSES	If someone cheats in a relationship.
	Getting drunk or high.
	Being rejected or excluded.
	Being disrespected.
	Being angry.
	I really go off when someone messes with my head.
	Any conflict.
	Being challenged.
	It seems to come out of nowhere.

Members are often quick to comment that certain triggers mentioned are offered by abusers as excuses for their behavior. In fact, if members learn nothing else in the Trauma Recovery and Empowerment module it is that their abusers' explanations for abuse were nothing but excuses designed to shift responsibility away from themselves and onto the victim. Leaders should facilitate a discussion of the difference between an explanation and an excuse, keeping in mind that excuses are designed to lessen the perception of being responsible for a harmful outcome in the minds of the wrongdoer and others (Weiner, 1995).

End this session by giving group members a homework assignment to help set the stage for the next week's topic. The assignment is to think of three recent incidents that made them angry.

ADDITIONAL QUESTIONS

1. Why do you behave abusively and aggressively?
2. What is the difference between an explanation and an excuse?
3. What is your understanding of the relationship between having been abused and subsequently becoming abusive yourself?

TOPIC 4 Responsibility and Anger

SESSION RATIONALE

The aim of this group is to spell out the relationship between deciding that someone is responsible for a harmful outcome you have suffered and becoming abusive or aggressive in response.

GOAL 1: Members will explore the thought processes involved in holding someone responsible for a negative event.

GOAL 2: Members will make the connection between inferring responsibility and becoming retaliatory.

QUESTIONS

1. Think of a situation, circumstance, or event that made you angry recently. What aspect of the situation in particular made you angry?
2. How do people determine that someone is responsible for a harmful event? What factors come into play?

LEADERS' NOTES

As Bernard Weiner, Ph.D., a leading contributor to the field of attribution theory outlines in his book, *Judgment of Responsibility: A Foundation for a Theory of Social Conduct,* there is a strong, pervasive tendency in humans to try to determine who or what is responsible for the difficulties they experience. Someone who is the victim of a negative event will seek to determine its cause.

A first step in this process is evaluating whether the harm was caused by the actions of another person. If so, and if this act is perceived as subject to the person's volitional control and there are no mitigating circumstances involved, then the author of the misdeed is inferred to be responsible for his or her actions. Drawing this conclusion, an inference of responsibility, in turn evokes feelings of anger and gives rise to the impulse to retaliate against the person who is now seen as a perpetrator. Simply put, people are apt to respond angrily and wish to retaliate when they perceive that others intend to harm them.

In this model, aggression is viewed as the product of a thinking-feeling-action sequence. However, it is important to note that not all aggressive behavior is retaliatory or reactive in nature. On the other hand, given that some of it is, a discussion of the Responsibility Model is a worthwhile undertaking in the group.

QUESTION 1

Think of a situation, circumstance, or event that made you angry recently. What aspect of the situation in particular made you angry?

TYPICAL RESPONSES

SITUATION	ANGER
My roommate keeps taking my stuff.	Because I told her before not to touch my things—she knows better.
This girl bumped into me and didn't stop to say "Excuse me," or to apologize.	Because she was disrespecting me—there was no reason she couldn't have at least acknowledged me.

Let members present their examples and then carefully ask what exactly about the situation made the member angry. It is useful to organize members' responses as shown above.

You can, for the sake of the discussion, manipulate different aspects of the members' stories and ask if this results in their feeling more or less anger.

To illustrate this process, you might ask:

What impact would it have on your anger if the girl who bumped into you had just been told that her mother had been seriously injured in a car accident, and she was rushing to get to the hospital? Would you be more or less angry? Why?

- or -

What if the roommate who was taking your belongings was barely managing to scrape by while you were doing quite well? Would you be more or less angry at her? Why?

As one might expect, members generally have little difficulty generating examples of things that make them angry. You will want to guard against the group devolving into a gripe session where members complain about being continually mistreated and provoked. Try to keep members focused on the task at hand that is exploring which factors increase and decrease their level of anger.

QUESTION 2

How do people determine that someone is responsible for a harmful event? What factors do they take into consideration?

TYPICAL RESPONSES	Whether the person meant to cause the negative event
	Whether the person had any choice about how she behaved
	Whether there were good reasons for what he did
	Whether it was an accident
	Whether their behavior was neglectful versus intentional
	Whether they understood the consequences of their action when they acted
	The age of the person

Constructing this list is made more manageable by discussing Question 1. However, members may resist the idea that aggression is the product of a decision-making or rational process.

If this is the case, you will want to explain that the process being described often does occur quite rapidly and outside of conscious awareness. Take this opportunity to say that this is precisely why it is important to slow things down and deliberately focus on the thoughts that precede aggression.

TOPIC 5   Seeing Others as Intending Harm

SESSION RATIONALE

This session helps group members begin to gauge the extent to which they presumptively hold the belief that others mean to harm them. It facilitates discussion of the cues that members rely upon to draw this conclusion and challenges group members to examine the relative reliability of their interpretations of these cues. This session also helps members begin to see that making assumptions about others' motivations and intentions leaves considerable room for misunderstandings and anger.

GOAL 1: Members will begin to identify their own predisposition to assume that others intend or mean them harm.

GOAL 2: Members will begin to examine critically the nature of the cues that they use to conclude that others mean them harm.

QUESTIONS

This session relies on the following exercises, drawing on members' experiences in and out of the group, to help members begin to recognize and examine the characteristic negative way they perceive other people's intentions toward them.

EXERCISES

1. Gauging the Extent to Which We Expect Harm
2. Examining Cues That Indicate Others' Intentions
3. Misinterpreting Cues of Intention

LEADERS' NOTES

Begin the group by summarizing the Responsibility Model outlined in the last group. This time around, it is useful to ask the group members to recall the thinking-feeling-action sequence of the Responsibility Model presented and discussed in the previous group and to outline it once again on the flip chart. If group members have trouble with this task, you should quickly step in. You may need to spend more time on the Responsibility Model, emphasizing practical examples. Keep in mind the main point you are trying to get across—that becoming angry at someone and wishing to retaliate is often a function of whether we perceive that the person has intended us harm.

This session takes this basic idea a step further. In short, it introduces the idea that some individuals are predisposed to believe that others will behave in a hurtful manner toward them. These individuals possess what is termed a *hostile attributional bias,* that is, they are decidedly inclined to attribute hostile motivations to others. This bias, in turn, may account for individual differences in the tendency to behave aggressively (Weiner, 1995).

EXERCISE *1:* Gauging the Extent to Which We Expect Harm

Ask members to answer the question: "How much (frequently, often) do you feel that others mean to harm you?" You should direct members to answer the question by rating themselves on a scale of 1 to 10, with 1 meaning not very much and 10 meaning very much.

The follow-up questions, "Do you feel this way more or less than you used to?" and "What accounts for any change?" help members to refine their own estimation of where they stand in relation to the problem.

Be prepared to challenge members' self-rating based on their own knowledge and past experience of group members. Group members may underestimate their tendency to attribute malevolence to others to project an image of being unflappable or being disinterested in what others think.

EXERCISE *2:* Examining Cues That Indicate Others' Intentions

Ask members to describe the cues that they look for or rely on to determine that another person means to harm them. List members' responses.

What should quickly become obvious (hopefully to members as well as leaders) is that people cite a variety of cues that they believe can be relied on to ascribe malevolent intent to others. What should also become clear—and is certainly a topic for group discussion—is that many cues that members present as obvious, inviolable indicators of intended harm are at best neutral or ambiguous cues of intent.

Members typically find it difficult to entertain the idea that they misjudge others' intentions or that they misinterpret cues in the interpersonal environment. At times, members not only find the exercise difficult, but they also become offended that leaders would challenge their understanding of interpersonal events. This exercise implicitly suggests that much of the hostility that group members perceive in the interpersonal environment is literally misplaced, and may in fact more rightly belong to the member. This places, at times uncomfortably, more responsibility on group members for the hostility they project onto others. At other times, members will voice concern that reevaluating how they process interpersonal cues will leave them more open to victimization by others.

You may have to answer these objections directly. Be prepared to explain to members that the purpose of carefully considering our perception of external events is to enhance our ability to see situations as realistically as possible. The more realistically we see other people and situations, the better able we are to respond appropriately. This could in turn reduce the likelihood of being abused or of acting abusively. Also be prepared to acknowledge that taking more responsibility for one's negative or hostile way of interpreting other people's actions and motivations might produce some discomfort for the group members.

Exercise 3: Misinterpreting Cues of Intention

Having worked through some of their resistance and objections to examining their perceptions of others as meaning harm, hopefully members will be in a better position to participate in the following exercise:

> Think of an instance where you concluded that another person meant to harm you and you were wrong. What part of the interaction did you misinterpret? What helped you to see that you were wrong in how you understood the other person or situation?

You should not merely emphasize what was misperceived, rather you should help members articulate their ideas about how and why the misperception occurred. Moreover, you want to help members express as fully as possible what enabled them to correct themselves. Members generally appreciate having their preexisting adaptive skills and strengths highlighted.

TOPIC 6 Changing Abusive Behavior

SESSION RATIONALE

Once a woman can recognize how the perception of intentional harm relates to aggressive reactions and how she may be predisposed to see others as intending harm, the stage is set to examine ways of changing abusive or aggressive behavior. The questions of this session correspond with some of the most obvious points of intervention suggested by the Responsibility Model. As Weiner (1995) notes, aggression theoretically can be reduced (1) if inferences of malevolent intent are reduced, (2) if emotions other than anger can be elicited in spite of perceptions of responsibility, and/or (3) if an individual can learn to behave nonaggressively even in the face of feeling angry and wishing to retaliate.

GOAL 1: Members will begin to identify various choice points where they can potentially change their abusive reactions.

GOAL 2: Members will begin to articulate what might help them to reduce their abusiveness.

QUESTIONS

1. How might you reduce or change your perception that someone means to harm you?
2. What feelings, other than anger, could be going on for you when you think that someone has intentionally harmed you?
3. Without being abusive, how might you behave differently even if you are still feeling angry at the person who harmed you?

EXERCISES

1. Empathy: Feeling for and Feeling with Another Person
2. Comparing the Costs of an Injury and a Retaliation

LEADERS' NOTES

QUESTION 1

How might you reduce or change your perception that someone means to harm you?

TYPICAL RESPONSES   Look at the big picture—the larger situation.
Talk to the person and check out what they are thinking.
Look at what they are reacting to besides just me.
Try to remember that kids can't really control their behavior that well.
Consider that maybe they just weren't paying attention to what they were doing.
Maybe they are going through a personal difficulty.
It might help just to catch myself in the process of making the assumption.

Depending on the responses generated by members, you can take the opportunity to note the link between stopping oneself to reflect and the ability to perceive a situation in a different and more realistic manner.

QUESTION 2

What feelings, other than anger, could be going on for you when you think that someone has intentionally harmed you?

TYPICAL RESPONSES   Shock
Hurt
Betrayal
Pity
Indifference
Frustration
Guilt
Shame
Concern

A discussion of this question can help members begin to appreciate that one reason they respond so quickly and frequently with anger may be to avoid other, potentially more painful emotions. You may want to acknowledge to the members that ultimately resolving this dilemma takes courage and time.

Question 3

Without being abusive, how might you behave differently even if you are still feeling angry at the person who harmed you?

TYPICAL RESPONSES   Blow it off
Keep my mouth shut
Walk away
Count to 10
Be patient
Talk to a supportive friend
Talk it out with the person
Let them know that I don't like how they are treating me
Pray
Punch my pillow
Remember that what goes around comes around

You may want to ask what experience members have had with their strategies.

Additional Questions

1. What would be an effective deterrent to your behaving abusively?
2. What would motivate you to refrain from behaving abusively?

Exercise 1: Empathy: Feeling for and Feeling with Another Person

Ask members to recall an incident where they were treated abusively. Then assist the women to break down their reactions to that event and to examine closely what they were feeling at the time. Ask members to recall a recent incident where they, in their own judgment, treated someone else abusively. Ask members to imagine how the other person felt during and after the abuse. Compare the two reactions in an effort to help the members put themselves in the other person's place. Discuss how empathy is a process of feeling for or feeling with someone else and is integral to curbing hurting behavior between people. If group members have difficulty relating personal experiences, you can give an example of an abusive interaction from popular literature (e.g., *The Color Purple*) and ask members to speculate how the victim in the story feels.

EXERCISE 2: Comparing the Costs of an Injury and a Retaliation

Ask group members to think about a recent situation where someone hurt them and they retaliated. Then elicit responses to the following questions:

> What was the cost to you of what they did?
> What was the cost to them of what you did back?
> How do the two lists of costs compare?
> Are the costs equal?

Members frequently appeal to the concept of fairness to justify their abusive behavior. They say that they only gave back to a person who harmed them an equal measure of what was done to them. The above exercise provides a way of critically examining the veracity of this claim. Once confronted by feedback from other group members and by the fact that her retaliation caused harm disproportionate to what she suffered, a member may reconsider how she handles herself the next time she feels she has been crossed.

TOPIC 7 Making Amends

SESSION RATIONALE

This session is intended to help women explore the possibility that they cannot undo the harm they have done to others. The group will include a discussion of the nuances and complexities of asking forgiveness and making amends. Often, perpetrators of abuse fail to recognize the tremendous presumption and continued emotional burden they place on their victims with their expectation that the victim will forgive them for their misdeeds. Often perpetrators have not given thought to making amends in ways that address the practical and emotional needs of their victims.

GOAL 1: Members will consider whether and how they can repair the damage they have inflicted on others.

GOAL 2: Members will understand the difference between asking for forgiveness and making amends.

QUESTIONS

1. What are the practical and emotional consequences for you if the victim of your abusive acts does not forgive you?
2. How can you make reparation for the abuses you have committed? What ways are of the most help to a victim of abuse?
3. What are your perceptions of a victim of abuse who refuses to forgive the abuser?
4. What is the difference between asking for forgiveness from someone and making amends to them?

LEADERS' NOTES

QUESTION 1

What are the practical and emotional consequences for you if the victim of your abusive acts does not forgive you?

TYPICAL RESPONSES   I will still feel guilty.
                               I'm angry at him for not getting over it.
                               I said I'm sorry; what else does she want?
                               She is trying to punish me by withholding
                                     forgiveness.

This question helps the women consider why they may be asking for forgiveness in the first place. What is it that they are hoping to accomplish? Further, the members may not be prepared for the possibility that their victims may not forgive them. A discussion of this possibility helps members to prepare themselves and to respond respectfully should a victim choose not to forgive the abuser.

QUESTION 2

How can you make reparation for the abuses you have committed? What ways are of the most help to a victim of abuse?

TYPICAL RESPONSES   I can say I'm sorry and mean it.
                               I can make financial reparation.
                               I can pay for therapy, medical bills, etc.
                               I can listen to what the experience was like
                                     for her.

Leaders stress the importance of the perpetrator's acknowledging that she has done something that needs to be repaired. This question encourages the members to consider that indeed there are ways to express remorse for their abusive behavior, and further that there are concrete ways in which they can try to repair the damage they have done. By asking the women, "What ways are of the most help to a victim of abuse?" the members must realize that the reparation is for the victim and not to make the abuser feel better or to save face.

QUESTION 3

What are your perceptions of a victim of abuse who refuses to forgive the abuser?

TYPICAL RESPONSES   She's a bitch.

He can't let go of the past.

She's using this to hold over my head to get me to do what she wants.

He is still hurting.

It's her right to decide when and if she is ready to forgive me.

Members' responses to the victim who refuses to forgive are often negative and highlight the extent to which members continue to advance a self-centered agenda. They are willing to see the victim as bad and themselves as good. Indeed it replicates the abusive situation where the victim is to be used for the abuser's needs. Ask members to consider their own choices regarding forgiving their abusers. It is important that the leaders emphasize that this is a very personal choice for each woman and that there is no right or wrong answer on the victim's part.

QUESTION 4

What is the difference between asking for forgiveness from someone and making amends to them?

TYPICAL RESPONSES   They're the same thing.

Forgiveness is the person saying they don't hold you responsible any more.

Forgiveness is the person saying they aren't mad at you any more.

Making amends is saying you're sorry.

Making amends is trying to fix what you did wrong.

Making amends is giving a gift to say you're sorry.

You will want to help members make the distinction clearly. Making amends is something the abuser does for the victim. Forgiveness is something the victim may or may not choose to do for the abuser. Further, forgiveness may be more closely related to the victim's process of healing than to a process of releasing the abuser from her responsibility or sense of guilt.

ADDITIONAL QUESTION

Did you forgive your abuser? What connection, if any, do you think exists between your desire for forgiveness and your willingness to forgive?

REFERENCES

Kernberg, Otto F. *Aggression in Personality Disorders and Perversions.* Yale University Press, 1995.

Weiner, Bernard. *Judgment of Responsibility: A Foundation for a Theory of Social Conduct.* New York and London: The Guilford Press, 1995.

MALE SURVIVORS

Roger D. Fallot, Ph.D.

David W. Freeman, Psy.D.

Stephen Zazanis, M.S.W.

John Dende, M.A.

INTRODUCTION

This adaptation of the Trauma Recovery and Empowerment approach helps male trauma survivors to develop skills necessary for coping with their trauma experiences and with the multiple problems often related, sequentially or concurrently, to abuse and violence. It retains the general philosophy and structure of the women's model. However, the distinctive trauma-related concerns of men, especially in a disadvantaged population, are reflected in significant differences in the emphases and priorities of this group. Because of these content differences, the men's group is outlined in some detail.

STRUCTURE

The men's group topics are divided into two parts. The first (comprising 11 topics) addresses primarily men's issues, problem-solving styles, and recovery themes while dealing with specific trauma experiences secondarily. The second part (comprising five topics) focuses more directly on trauma, its effects, and the processes of recovery. In practice, each topic may, and usually does, involve more than one group meeting. The entire program usually involves about 40–45 group meetings.

POPULATION

This group model was developed for male trauma survivors who also have experienced significantly decreased functioning related to one or more of the

following factors: severe mental illness; substance abuse; perpetrating violence; homelessness; criminal incarceration. Other groups of men may benefit from a similarly informed and structured model but these specific
guidelines assume that the group members have experienced problems severe
enough to interfere with their daily lives to a significant degree.

THEORY

The model is based on an experiential set of five themes considered central to
men's development and to trauma recovery in particular: self-esteem, self-
protection, self-direction, mutuality, and responsibility. Our operating hypoth-
esis is that trauma can produce specific developmental disruptions and
vulnerabilities along these core dimensions. Further, each disruption consists
of polar opposites along a continuum in which one end represents a
deficit/weakness experience and the other an experience of power/strength. In
this way, self-esteem may yield a continuum with extremes of shame and
grandiosity; self-protection divides into vulnerability and invulnerability; self-
direction into rigid self-control and impulsivity; mutuality into dependence and
independence; and responsibility into under- and over responsibility. The five
core recovery themes and the related 10 polar extremes provide an organizing
content structure for the group.

TOPIC 1 Introductory Session

SESSION RATIONALE

Three factors make this an effective and relatively nonthreatening opening session. First, rather than focusing too directly on trauma issues, these concerns are placed in the larger context of men's lives and identities. Second, having the participants list potential areas of interest to men serves to build a sense of group coherence and shared experience. Third, the collages complement this emphasis on commonality by drawing attention to individual differences and unique viewpoints; they do so in a less anxiety-producing way than that of purely verbal, face-to-face contact.

GOAL 1: Each member will understand the purposes of the group.

GOAL 2: Each member and group leader will introduce himself to the group.

AGENDA FOR OPENING COMMENTS

1. Group leaders present the two main purposes of the group: *(a)* to discuss experiences of trauma in members' lives, and *(b)* to explore resources for problem solving, empowerment, and recovery, with special emphasis on those resources and styles most characteristic of men. This opening statement of purpose makes it clear that the group's understanding of trauma is broad and may include physical and sexual abuse, community and institutional violence, and combat experiences.

2. Group leaders outline the overall agenda and structure for the group. Here, leaders discuss the division of the group into two parts; the first addresses issues of male identity and relationships, and the second focuses more directly on trauma. In this way, leaders may emphasize that trauma issues will be addressed primarily in the context of understanding the men's current life situations, recurring difficulties, and personal strengths and weaknesses. The leaders' roles in providing specific topics, questions, and/or exercises for each session also are discussed.

3. Group leaders describe expectations and norms for group process: confidentiality and its limits; physical and emotional safety guidelines (prohibition on violence; importance of mutual respect in dealing with personal differences); regular attendance.

QUESTIONS

1. What issues are most important for a men's group to discuss?
2. What would you like to say about yourself to introduce yourself to the group?

EXERCISE

Each group member and leader develops a predominantly visual collage depicting important aspects of themselves they would like others in the group to know about them. Leaders provide large sheets of poster paper, magazines, newspapers, markers, scissors, and glue. After the collages are completed (about 20–30 minutes), each participant describes the contents of his collage to the group and says something about why he included various items.

LEADERS' NOTES

Leaders should use a flip chart or chalkboard to list the various responses to this question.

QUESTION 1

What issues are most important for a men's group to discuss?

TYPICAL RESPONSES   Family and family relationships
Relationships with women
Being responsible
Being a protector or defender
Problem solving

        Relationships with men
        Anger, violence, and self-control
        Making money and being a provider

You may use such responses to discuss more fully the agenda for the group, showing how the content planned for later sessions will address these concerns. This group process of generating topics also permits the leaders to highlight shared interests and experiences.

QUESTION 2 / EXERCISE

What would you like to say about yourself to introduce yourself to the group?

    It is important to select magazines and other materials sensitive to the composition of the group, taking into account such issues as the culture, race, social class, religion, sexual orientation, education, age, and likely interests of its members. Including a wide range of visual images permits active participation by those whose literacy level may be lower than that of other group members. Encouraging group members to use primarily visual images and only secondarily to use text (to label or fill in something for which an image is unavailable) provides concrete materials for discussion and minimizes potentially embarrassing differences in writing ability.

    TYPICAL RESPONSES   Pictures of favorite activities (e.g., sports, music, painting)

Pictures of goals (e.g., cars, money, relationship with a woman, weight loss)

Pictures of central roles (e.g., father, son, brother, husband, lover)

Pictures representing core values (e.g., church or spirituality, prayer, leadership, bravery)

Pictures representing problem areas (e.g., smoking, being overweight, controlling temper)

Words or sentences capturing ideas difficult to image

Labels clarifying an image or highlighting a relevant aspect of the image

Assist each person to describe and explain his collage, inviting others to share their responses, and appropriately limiting discussion. There are opportunities in this relatively structured exercise to concretely demonstrate group expectations for participation, for listening, and for responding to others.

TOPIC 2 What Is a Man?
The Cultural Perspective

SESSION RATIONALE

Cultural definitions of idealized masculinity form an important context for men's self-images and self-esteem as well as for their understanding of traumatic experiences and their sequelae. Of the core experiential dimensions informing this model, images of independence, invulnerability, and overresponsibility may be stereotypically invoked in picturing the ideal man. Racial, social class, and other subcultural differences in such ideals are important to note to facilitate the widest range of participation in the group and to acknowledge differences among members. Finally, the men's core values, commitments, or hopes may be best explored by way of the images of their heroes.

GOAL 1: Each participant will discuss generalized cultural understandings of the ideal man.

GOAL 2: Subcultural differences in these understandings will be acknowledged and described.

QUESTIONS

1. Who are your heroes? What do you admire most about them?
2. Who were your heroes when you were growing up? What made them unusual?
3. What is the most outstanding and admirable thing you have heard of a man doing?
4. Do heroes have flaws or weaknesses? If so, what are they?

LEADERS' NOTES
QUESTIONS 1, 2, 3, AND 4

Question 1 (Who are your heroes?) is the central focus of this session. The others may be used as necessary and helpful to clarify or facilitate further discussion of the responses to this initial question.

TYPICAL RESPONSES My father—or other family member (taught me responsibility, worked, sent me to college, was not abusive, knew how to deal with people)

My teacher (really cared)

Sports figures—for example, Michael Jordan (team player, excellent player, cares about others, responsibility for family, national hero for blacks and whites)

Religious leaders—for example, Louis Farrakhan (strength, power, leadership, belief in God) or Martin Luther King, Jr. (courage under pressure)

Inventors (create things that are helpful and useful)

Friends (able to stay sober, never give up, go to work, serve in military)

People who can manage anger and violence

Heroes are people who overcome something (family problems, staying sober, money problems)

Myself (overcome image of a loser, overcome psychosis, have faith)

You can facilitate this session most effectively by being sensitive, on one hand, to common themes among the heroic traits described by participants and, on the other, to issues of cultural diversity among members. The foremost process goal is to assist the development of a sense of member similarity and group cohesiveness that is realistic enough to recognize differences in values, styles, and backgrounds openly.

In terms of content, you will want to help draw out themes defining key attributes of ideal masculinity. This discussion is enriched by contrasting current heroes with former heroes; by exploring the limits, weaknesses, or flaws of heroes; and/or by seeing the similarities and differences between public and private figures as heroes. It is also possible to make connections between themes discussed in the introductory session and images of the ideal man.

TOPIC 3 What Is a Man?
The Personal Perspective

SESSION RATIONALE

Trauma and abuse, especially in familial contexts, often disrupt and distort the victim's psychological, social, and sexual identity. This session moves from the cultural to the personal level in exploring members' individual experiences of themselves as men. Recognizing their defining moments in becoming men helps members to describe key moments in this process of identity formation. The session also specifically asks members to take a developmental perspective on their lives, noting times of movement and change.

GOAL 1: Each member will discuss some personal experience related to his sense of male development and identity.

GOAL 2: Each member will identify some key marker in establishing his sense of being a man.

QUESTIONS

1. When did you become a man?
2. How did you know you had become a man? What were your personal rites of passage in becoming a man?

LEADERS' NOTES

QUESTIONS 1 AND 2

When did you become a man? How did you know? What kind of passage did you go through?

> **TYPICAL RESPONSES** Bodily changes (growth of body hair, changes in genitalia)

> Social independence (could be on my own, joining
> the service)
> Thinking about or actually fighting back with abu-
> sive parents
> Smoking, drinking and/or drugging
> Making a baby

Use columns on the flip chart or chalkboard to help organize the various responses to these questions. For example, themes may be extracted and used to show how certain experiences—of being strong, of being independent, of making one's own decisions, of observing one's own body, of standing up for or defending oneself—may mark something recognizable about being a man.

Men describe positive and negative ways of marking the passage into manhood. You will want to explore the accomplishments in seemingly negative benchmarks of passage and search out the unnoticed strength in seemingly negative behavior.

TOPIC 4 What Is a Man?
The Biological Perspective

SESSION RATIONALE

The clinical sequelae of trauma include physical and psychological numbing and dissociation. Recovery can be facilitated by an increased awareness of bodily processes. Initial exploration of the sources of pleasure and of discomfort or pain set the stage for developing coping skills around physical health, nutrition, and exercise.

GOAL 1: Each member will describe some thoughts and feelings about his own body.

GOAL 2: Each member will describe some of the bodily changes associated with adulthood and middle age.

QUESTIONS

1. What makes you feel good? What are your favorite experiences? What are your favorite nondrug experiences?
2. What stresses you out? What makes you feel uncomfortable?
3. How do things change for you as a man as you get older?

EXERCISE

Plan a day that includes all your favorite physical sensations and pleasures.

LEADERS' NOTES

QUESTION 1 AND EXERCISE

What makes you feel good? What are your favorite experiences? What are your favorite nondrug experiences?

TYPICAL RESPONSES   Sex
                      Good food (eating out at a restaurant, home cook-
                         ing)
                      Drugs (crack cocaine, alcohol)
                      Playing sports (exercise, working out)
                      Music or art (relaxing)
                      Watching TV
                      Burning incense

Draw attention to the various senses involved in pleasure such as tasting, touching, hearing, seeing, and smelling.

QUESTION 2

What stresses you out? What makes you feel uncomfortable?

TYPICAL RESPONSES   Conflict (arguing with women, with family mem-
                         bers, with lovers)
                      Fear (of drug dealers, of street violence)
                      Boredom (nothing to do so may as well use drugs)
                      Loneliness (hanging out by myself)
                      Problems with work (losing a job, arguing with a
                         supervisor)
                      Problems with medication (premature ejaculation,
                         impotence)

Use these responses to direct attention to the physical correlates of negative emotions: heart beating fast, sweating, fatigue, difficulty sleeping, and restlessness.

QUESTION 3

How do things change for you as a man as you get older?

TYPICAL RESPONSES   Feel more pain
                      Body can't do the things your mind wants to do
                      Hang out with younger people

> Sexual problems (can't ejaculate, can't have sex
> whenever you want)
> Gain weight
> Illnesses (arthritis, prostate trouble, cramps)

Again, you may facilitate this discussion by using categories (e.g., normal aging, illness-related, or reversible or irreversible) or themes to organize members' responses. Asking about positive aspects of aging as well as the often more spontaneously offered negative ones helps members develop a fuller sense of the various shifts that may occur throughout the life span.

This session can be overstimulating for some men. Men who are more loosely organized and impulsive may describe experiences that are frightening to men who are more constricted. You should exercise tactful but firm influence on the group to provide a sense of safety.

TOPIC 5 Goals and Empowerment

SESSION RATIONALE

This session focuses on two dimensions of trauma recovery: self-direction and self-esteem. Trauma often leaves men with an inability to set positive and realistic goals for themselves. It also distorts their assessment of their capacity to pursue and accomplish even the most realistic goals. Participants can give other members feedback not only about their goal-setting but also about the skills and abilities needed to achieve those goals.

GOAL 1: Each member will describe a particular goal he has set for himself.

GOAL 2: Each member will recount some experience in which he felt a sense of accomplishment.

QUESTIONS

1. What is your most important goal for the future?
2. Of which life accomplishment are you most proud?

LEADERS' NOTES

QUESTION 1

What is your most important goal for the future?

TYPICAL RESPONSES   Want to get my own apartment
Want to get a car of my own
A love relationship
Get more work
Have a better relationship with family (e.g., with estranged son, with mother)

> Stay sober or stay off drugs
> Want to put abuse to bed, let sleeping dogs lie
> Want to think before I act

Some members may offer unrealistic or clearly delusional goals while others may find it impossible to imagine even setting an explicit goal, having renounced any hopes of achievement. You need to be aware of this dilemma so that apparently grandiose goals can be acknowledged and also broken down into more attainable, and still valued steps.

QUESTION 2

Of which life accomplishment are you most proud?

TYPICAL RESPONSES   Staying clean (off drugs and/or alcohol)
Being a responsible father to my son
Holding down a job
Playing well in sports (high-school athletic accomplishments)

As with goal-setting, you need to be cognizant of extreme responses reflecting grandiosity or self-denigration. Some men may grossly exaggerate their achievements while others may find it difficult to see any significant accomplishments in their lives. You can assist men at each of these extremes to move toward a more balanced sense of self-esteem.

TOPIC 6 Problem-Solving and Coping Skills

SESSION RATIONALE

The dimensions of self-direction and responsibility are the focuses of this session. Trauma often carries with it difficulties in achieving a consistent sense of self-direction; planful and deliberate problem solving is undermined by rigidity or impulsiveness. Similarly, taking too much responsibility (and feeling overwhelmed) or too little responsibility (and feeling little sense of obligation or integrity) are dangers. This session addresses some of the fundamental capacities and skills necessary for dealing with everyday problems and obstacles in group members' lives.

GOAL 1: Each member will identify a specific problem that has kept him from achieving a particular goal.

GOAL 2: Each member will contribute to the group's catalog of coping skills and resources.

GOAL 3: Each member will begin to understand some of the skills necessary for effective problem solving.

QUESTIONS

1. What specific problem or obstacle has kept you from achieving an important goal?
2. What has been helpful in coping or dealing effectively with this problem or obstacle?
3. What skills go into making this problem-solving or coping strategy work?

EXERCISE

Develop a list of problems and a set of corresponding coping or problem-solving strategies.

LEADERS' NOTES

QUESTION 1 AND EXERCISE

What specific problem or obstacle has kept you from achieving an important goal?

TYPICAL RESPONSES
> Anger; often out of control; use violence
> Going too fast; acting without thinking things through
> Drinking and/or drugging
> Difficult childhood; physical abuse
> Getting confused or upset
> Hanging out on the streets
> Don't know how to handle conflict
> Spending money unwisely
> Wanting too badly to belong, to feel accepted
> Housing loss due to drug use

Because group members may present either a vague and apparently overwhelming problem (e.g., I just can't do anything right) or a long list of interwoven difficulties, leaders should help each member identify a single, specific, and concrete problem for further discussion (e.g., I can't hold down a job when I drink). This begins the process of modeling effective strategies for problem solving by labeling and listing problems that are not trivial but are amenable to solution.

You also should monitor the problems listed to ensure adequate internal (e.g., I get too angry) or mutual (e.g., My mother and I can't get along) framings of the problems without simply dismissing external ones (e.g., My partner won't do what I want). The process of reframing problems in ways that give group members more control over their possible solution is a key step in the overall problem-solving approach.

QUESTION 2

What has been helpful in coping or dealing effectively with this problem or obstacle?

TYPICAL RESPONSES Stopping and calming down before doing anything else

Staying in control; concentrating

Maintaining independence; solving problems within myself

Being able to walk away from conflict and violence

Talking out conflicts directly with the people involved

Taking small steps in solving a problem

Making a plan and sticking to it

Here you should adopt two separate approaches. First, assist individual group members in identifying any instances in which they handled particular problems effectively. Often participants fail to recall such times. Revisiting these moments not only serves as a source of hope for future problem solving but also sets the stage for Question 3 in which the group works toward identifying the helpful elements in the coping strategy (i.e., what *specifically* contributed to the success of this technique). Second, engage the group in brainstorming other possible approaches to each problem, in sifting and identifying the most promising responses, and in breaking those down into steps of manageable size.

QUESTION 3

What skills go into making this problem-solving or coping strategy work?

TYPICAL RESPONSES Self-control: being able to step back and think about the problem; modulating anger; no impulsive drug use

Planning: weigh the pros and cons of the decision; always have a backup plan if the first one doesn't work

A sense of spirituality and perspective: can control self more effectively; recognize that problems can be approached positively; be calm and collected

> Collaborate with other people: sit back and listen; work with professionals; negotiate differences directly; treat others with respect

Help group members identify the key attributes of effective coping methods. By labeling these skills, abilities, and resources in specific and concrete ways, you actually contribute to members' convictions that they are capable of solving problems more readily. You also will want to facilitate discussion of making realistic plans, monitoring follow-through and effectiveness, and evaluating progress with appropriate expectations.

TOPIC 7 Friendship with Men

SESSION RATIONALE

While the trauma recovery dimension of mutuality is most directly addressed in this session, issues of self-protection and responsibility also emerge with some frequency. Trauma often disrupts a sense of trust and makes the development of friendships a potentially risky and complicated process. Because others may be seen primarily as sources of tangible or emotional support (self-as-dependent) or as sources of betrayal and hurt (self-as-isolated or independent), establishing mutuality is often difficult.

GOAL: Each member will explore some of his feelings about friendships with other men.

QUESTIONS

1. Have you had friendships with other men? What have they been like?
2. Are there any particular strengths or problems you see in friendships with men?

LEADERS' NOTES

QUESTIONS 1 AND 2:

Have you had friendships with other men? What have they been like?
Are there any particular strengths or problems you see in friendships with men?

TYPICAL RESPONSES   Can get advice from other men about problems; about being grown-up
Competition (over lovers, sports, money)

373

Need to sort out sexual and nonsexual relationships
Can talk about same interests (movies, sex, girls)
Can trust other men
Can have guys to get high with
Can be more honest with other men
Want to hang out and be like each other; similar
    goals
Can joke with other men

The two questions for this session are treated together because the second is simply a way of elaborating and organizing responses to the first. Actively trace the positive and negative aspects of relationships with other men. Using columns with labels such as "pro" and "con" or "advantages" and "dangers" allows for a stark rendering of the usually expressed interpersonal dilemmas here.

TOPIC 8 Friendship with Women

SESSION RATIONALE

Relationships with women may tap into virtually all the dimensions of male development affected by traumatic experience. Men with histories of abuse may have particular difficulty in maintaining an adequate sense of mutuality with women, in preserving an appropriate sense of responsibility, in maintaining the capacity for self-direction, and in preserving self-esteem. This session facilitates the exploration of these dilemmas and helps men to place extreme responses in a more balanced perspective.

GOAL: Each member will explore some of his feelings about friendship with women.

QUESTIONS

1. Have you had friendships with women? What have they been like?
2. Are there any particular strengths or problems you see in friendships with women?

LEADERS' NOTES

QUESTIONS 1 AND 2

Have you had friendships with women? What have they been like?
Are there any particular strengths or problems you see in friendships with women?

TYPICAL RESPONSES   **WOMEN AND ASSOCIATED FEARS AND DANGERS**
Once you're obligated to women, you can't get free.
Women want too much, emotionally and financially.
Women are stronger than men mentally; they're the boss.

Women can make you do what they want; they have stronger wills.

Some women steal from you.

Some women draw you into using drugs and drinking with them.

Can get sexually transmitted diseases.

If you have a baby, it's a lot of responsibility.

WOMEN AND ASSOCIATED SUPPORTS

If you both work, you can help each other out financially.

Women can help keep a place; prepare food.

Women can be good friends; it's easy to talk to them.

Can enjoy shared interests with women (e.g., going out to movies).

Sex is enjoyable.

You will want to be aware of the many needs and dangers that attend relationships with women for male trauma survivors. The intensity of these feelings often jeopardizes mutually caring relationships (sexual or otherwise) that can be sustained over time. Leaders need to offer a viewpoint acknowledging both the fears and hopes of group members while keeping or placing them in a larger context. Sorting through the possible sexual aspects of a relationship may be discussed here though the following session addresses sexual intimacy more directly. For many men in this session, sexuality seems secondary to other wishes and fears.

TOPIC 9 Sexual Intimacy

SESSION RATIONALE

Especially for survivors of sexual abuse but for other trauma survivors as well, sexuality carries with it many intense and complicated associations. This session is intended to offer a further opportunity for exploring the members' feelings about sexuality. Because of the powerful emotional responses many participants bring to this topic, its implications may be seen in many of the core dimensions of trauma recovery. Issues of sexual orientation and differences in sexual interest among group members may emerge or reemerge quite clearly here.

GOAL: Each member will begin to clarify his feelings about sexuality.

QUESTION

What are the joys and problems that go with sexual relationships?

LEADERS' NOTES

QUESTION 1

What are the joys and problems that go with sexual relationships?

TYPICAL RESPONSES   **POSITIVE FEELINGS ABOUT SEX**
Sex is fun, good feeling of arousal.
Dream and daydream about sex.
Can get more creative with sex as you get older.
Sex is always pleasurable; even better with drugs.

NEGATIVE FEELINGS ABOUT SEX
Sex involves too much obligation.
Sexual relationships can cause pain, envy.
Jealousy about sex can lead to violence.

DIFFERENCES BETWEEN SEX AND LOVE

Sex means no responsibility; love means responsibility.

Acceptance and concern most important in love; sex not so important.

Sex is only OK if you love the person and want to have kids.

A good relationship brings inner peace—that's love.

If there is either a paucity or monolithic set of responses, a specific contrast between sex and love may be helpful in clarifying feelings in this session. This serves not only to introduce an idea clearly related to development along many of the core dimensions but also to focus on what is unique to sexual relationships.

Finally, although many men will assume heterosexual behavior as universal, this session permits discussion of a variety of sexual experiences. You can demonstrate respect for these differences by encouraging their expression in group discussion and by treating any criticism of the differences in a way that offers the best possibility for resolution and mutual acceptance.

TOPIC 10 The Next Generation

SESSION RATIONALE

Because trauma and its sequelae often contribute to relationship difficulties, many men have experienced problems in relating to younger people as a father, older brother, uncle, and/or older friend. This session permits a review of individual strengths and weaknesses in this area and draws especially on the dimension of responsibility as men sort through the legacy they see themselves leaving to the next generation.

GOAL: Each member will discuss his role in a relationship to the next generation and describe his thoughts and feelings about this role.

QUESTIONS

1. What relationships do you, or have you had, with younger people?
2. What advice would you give the next generation?

LEADERS' NOTES

QUESTION 1

What relationships do you, or have you had, with younger people?

TYPICAL RESPONSES   Not much of a relationship. I see them on the street and they seem more violent.

Able to talk to my son about his experience in the Marines—a dream come true.

Renewed contact with son after several years—it's wonderful.

I don't have much influence on my nephew but I try to tell him some things.

> I tell my son to listen to his mother, not to me.
> Since I'm working, I can buy some things for my son; it makes me feel good.

As with the other relationship-focused sessions, this one draws both positive and negative instances of connections to younger people. Attend to themes of responsibility and obligation, whether members feel they have fulfilled or neglected their roles as father, mentor, and so on. For some men, their own deficits may make, or have made, it difficult for them to function consistently in these roles. For others, it is hard to imagine having any positive impact on a younger person.

QUESTION 2

What advice would you give the next generation?

TYPICAL RESPONSES Respect other people.
Stay in school—you'll go farther in life with a good education.
Don't put women on a pedestal; they come down, the balloon breaks, and men get violent.
I would tell them about the dangers of drug use.
Urge them to grow up and get a family.
Tell them how to stay safe; keep off the streets at night.
They ask for advice about drugs and women—I tell them don't be like me.
Trust your senses.

Even members who initially think they have little to say or to offer the next generation usually are able to become actively engaged in this advice-giving exercise. You can enhance this discussion by tailoring it to the specifics of the members' life situations and backgrounds. Having someone imagine a conversation with a specific person, for example, a son, nephew, kid from the neighborhood, or someone in a situation such as theirs 20 years ago, can make this process lively and informative.

TOPIC 11 Summary and Transition

SESSION RATIONALE

Previous sessions have addressed issues of members' understanding of what it means to be a man, of problem solving and coping, and of various relationships. Leaders have developed thematic materials related to the five key dimensions of trauma-related experience. Members' specific trauma histories have been discussed only in the context of these other topics. This session draws together materials from previous sessions in anticipation of exploring trauma more directly in the following sessions.

GOAL: The group will summarize its discussions to this point before moving to the more direct discussion of trauma.

QUESTION

What have been the most important issues discussed so far in this group?

LEADERS' NOTES

QUESTION 1

What have been the most important issues discussed so far in this group?

TYPICAL RESPONSES   Men and violence
Different ways to solve problems
That it's OK to have feelings
Talk to other people when you're in trouble
The importance of being responsible (e.g., as father)
To think about the future and consequences of my actions

Though trauma has been a secondary aspect of previous sessions, it is quite common for men to address issues of trauma in this summary. You can support this process by acknowledging these topics as significant ones and by beginning an agenda for the following sessions that includes not only general categories (e.g., physical abuse, sexual abuse) but also specific concerns of group members (e.g., how to deal with an abusive parent).

TOPIC 12 What Is Abuse and Trauma?

SESSION RATIONALE

Men often minimize the impact of abuse in their lives. This session maintains continuity with earlier sessions by drawing on the experiences of abuse and violence discussed in previous groups. It introduces the specific purposes of later sessions by defining and labeling abuse and trauma and by discussing some of the relationships among trauma, its effects and correlates, and recovery skills.

GOAL 1: The group will develop a shared definition of abuse and trauma.

GOAL 2: Members will begin to look more systematically at the relationships among trauma, other problems, and recovery and coping skills.

QUESTIONS

1. What are the experiences of abuse that we have mentioned in the group so far?
2. What are the effects of this abuse?
3. What makes an experience traumatic?
4. How do men cope with trauma?

LEADERS' NOTES

QUESTION 1

What are the experiences of abuse that we have mentioned in the group so far?

TYPICAL RESPONSES   Being beaten by a parent or other relative
Childhood sexual abuse by a relative or other adult
Street or community violence (e.g., being shot at or
threatened with death)

Drug-related violence (e.g., being beaten by a drug
dealer)
Institutional violence (e.g., in psychiatric hospitals
or jails, perpetrated by other patients or inmates
or by staff)

The purpose of this question is to maintain a sense of continuity between previous and future sessions both in content and in process and tone. Members' anxieties about addressing trauma directly are minimized if leaders communicate that the same overall approach will be taken in the sessions focusing on trauma as in those dealing with other topics.

QUESTION 2

What are the effects of this abuse?

TYPICAL RESPONSES   Anger
Confusion
Think about revenge a lot
Sexual confusion
Has hurt my sexual functioning
Withdrawal from other people; can't trust them
Nothing much

Group members are more likely to specify short-term effects of abuse than long-term ones. Depending on the overall functioning of the group, you might want to introduce the idea of long-term, less readily seen, sequelae of trauma. This notion will be developed more fully in the following sessions but speculating with the group at this point about connections between, for example, physical abuse and later drug use, can be a useful way to orient the group's thinking for subsequent discussions.

QUESTION 3

What makes an experience traumatic?

TYPICAL RESPONSES   Feeling like you're going to die

Being overwhelmed by something
Too uncertain about what's going to happen
Fear
Betrayal of trust
No control

Men often tend to rationalize even severe physical abuse in childhood as appropriate discipline and sometimes frame sexual abuse as simply early training or mutual exploration. Focus here on some of the immediate concomitants (e.g., extreme fear, including fear for one's life; confusion; or betrayal of trust) and short-term effects (e.g., inability to get the experience out of one's mind, flashbacks, or nightmares) in helping the group arrive at a shared understanding of trauma. For combat veterans and victims of street violence, these experiences may be more readily available. For victims of childhood sexual abuse, they may be less accessible. You will need to respect the different levels of awareness, different clarity of memories, and different degrees of openness to controlled discussion so that neither individual members nor the group as a whole is retraumatized in the course of this exploration.

QUESTION 4

How do men cope with trauma?

TYPICAL RESPONSES Ignore it
Just get tougher
Think about how to get back at the abuser
Talk with someone about it
Break the problem down into smaller pieces

This question is intended to emphasize some of the problem-solving and coping skills from earlier sessions and to facilitate the connection between specific skills and specific trauma sequelae.

Throughout this session, you need to monitor the intensity of individual self-disclosure and its impact on the group. Some members may feel an urgency to recount more details and emotional aspects of their trauma experiences than they or the group can assimilate. Be clear and direct in tactfully limiting such potentially harmful and premature disclosure.

TOPIC 13 Physical Abuse and Recovery

SESSION RATIONALE

This topic elaborates on many of the experiences discussed more briefly in earlier sessions. It explicitly attempts to draw out some of the probable short- and long-term effects of physical abuse, to outline some connections with the members' other problems, and to review and apply coping skills from earlier sessions. For many men, violence is an accepted part of growing up; this session is designed to stimulate discussion of the impact of violence, whether it is seen as acceptable or excessive in its cultural context. The central themes for trauma recovery also may be addressed explicitly in this session.

GOAL 1: Each group member will begin to consider the various effects of physical abuse.

GOAL 2: Each group member will begin to explore the possible connections between physical abuse and other problems in his life.

GOAL 3: Each member will begin to examine recovery skills appropriate to physical abuse and its related difficulties.

QUESTIONS

1. What are some of the reactions men have to physical abuse?
2. What are some of the relationships between physical abuse and other problems?
3. What are some useful coping skills for dealing with physical abuse and its effects?

EXERCISE

Leaders present vignettes tailored to the group's reported experiences of abuse as well as to its racial, cultural, educational, and social class characteristics. For example, the following vignettes have been used in groups of inner-city men with a history of severe mental disorders and substance abuse problems:

1. Eleven-year-old Johnny spills a glass of milk and his father hits him in the face.
2. When Bill was eight, he broke a family rule and his father made him go get a belt for a whipping.
3. Stella is having a big party and chases five-year-old Richard with a knife when he crawls under the table looking for some money.

Discussion questions may include the following:

1. Is this physical abuse? What about the situation is abusive or not?
2. What thoughts and feelings would the person in this situation have?
3. What would this person do in response to this experience?
4. What effect will this experience have on this person in the future?
5. What alternative coping strategies could he use?
6. What skills would this person need to deal with the long-term effects he might experience?

LEADERS' NOTES

QUESTION 1

What are some of the reactions men have to physical abuse?

TYPICAL RESPONSES **Short term**
Get toughened up.
Can handle anything after what my father put me through.
Run away from home.
Shame at marks of beating.
Nothing really matters because you get beaten anyway.

Long-term
Sense of invulnerability (e.g., I can do anything I want—nothing will happen to me that I can't handle.)

> Struggle with self-control (e.g., trying not to hit own son even when angry.)
>
> Need to belong to groups for protection and acceptance (e.g., I would do anything they wanted just to fit in.)

Men often have more difficulty discussing physical abuse by women, usually because of some perceived additional shame associated with it. While men often depict abuse by men as more understandable, they portray abuse by women as something that should have been avoidable or minimal if they had only asserted themselves more (regardless of their age at the time). You will need to be clear about the power differences involved in abusive relationships as key factors in the group's definition.

QUESTION 2

What are some of the relationships between physical abuse and other problems?

> **TYPICAL RESPONSES**   Self-endangering behaviors (e.g., feeling invincible and taking inordinate risks)
>
> Becoming abusive to others (e.g., spouses/partners, own children)
>
> Substance abuse to deal with problems and difficult emotions
>
> Get beat up on the street
>
> Get beaten by drug dealers
>
> Anger easily; think about revenge a lot
>
> Have physical reactions to stress

The flip chart can be used here to visually depict the possible relationships between abuse or trauma and other adult difficulties. Again, diagrams should be designed to capture the specific experiences of group members. For example, in a group of inner-city men, a four-sided figure was drawn with the corners labeled "trauma," "homelessness," "symptoms of mental illness," and "substance abuse." Arrows were then drawn connecting each problem label with every other label. Group members were readily able to see and discuss the various ways one problem connects to others in this kind of diagram.

QUESTION 3

What are some useful coping skills for dealing with physical abuse and its effects?

TYPICAL RESPONSES   Pray
Talk to family about it
Write a letter
Learn to talk with other people rather than doing everything on your own
Walking away from conflict
Learning to be safe on the streets

Leaders should make active connections between the coping skills inventory developed in earlier sessions and the sequelae of abuse discussed under this topic. Leaders also should summarize any of the core recovery domains, such as self-esteem, self-protection, self-direction, mutuality, and responsibility, as they become significant in this discussion. For example, leaders may point out the self-protection involved in learning how to be safe on the streets and ask for other examples of self-protection. Or they may highlight the sense of self-esteem that comes from being able to handle situations effectively without violence. In any case, these domains can be helpful handles for group members to label and retain key ideas from the session.

TOPIC 14 Sexual Abuse and Recovery

SESSION RATIONALE

Because of the often intense shame and denial around sexual abuse for men, indirect methods of approaching this topic may be especially useful. At the same time, this session allows men the opportunity to address explicitly their experiences of sexual abuse, to place them in a larger context, to examine their impact, and to discuss attendant recovery skills.

GOAL 1: Each group member will begin to consider the various effects of sexual abuse.

GOAL 2: Each group member will begin to explore the possible connections between sexual abuse and other problems in his life.

GOAL 3: Each member will begin to examine recovery skills appropriate to sexual abuse and its related difficulties.

QUESTIONS

1. What are some of the reactions men have to sexual abuse?
2. What are some of the relationships between sexual abuse and other problems?
3. What are some useful coping skills for dealing with sexual abuse and its effects?

EXERCISE

As with the topic of physical abuse, leaders present vignettes tailored to the group's reported experiences of sexual abuse as well as to its racial, cultural, educational, and social-class characteristics.

For example, the following vignettes have been used in groups of inner-city men with a history of severe mental disorders and substance abuse problems:

1. Janice fondles her five-year-old nephew's penis while giving him a bath and later takes the boy, Sam, into her bed and pulls him on top of her.
2. Eleven-year-old Frank was forced to have sex by his neighbor, John, who was 16.
3. Uncle Mike takes 10-year-old Andy fishing and camping and introduces him to a special game. Later on, Andy figures out that the game was sex.
4. Paul says he will give Matt some crack cocaine if Matt will have sex with him.

Discussion questions may include the following:

1. Is this sexual abuse? What about the situation is abusive or not?
2. What thoughts and feelings would the person in this situation have?
3. What would this person do in response to this experience?
4. What effect will this experience have on this person in the future?
5. What alternative coping strategies could he use?
6. What skills would this person need to deal with the long-term effects he might experience?

LEADERS' NOTES

QUESTION 1

What are some of the reactions men have to sexual abuse?

TYPICAL RESPONSES   **Short term**
Fear
Feeling weird
Feeling turned-on sexually but not knowing what to make of it
Feeling like a man, being sexual with a woman

Long term
Confusion
Anger
Shame

You need to be sensitive to, and responsive to, the ways in which group members may move between discussing the vignettes and discussing their own experience. If some members of the group are more psychologically disorganized, this boundary often becomes unclear. Use your clinical judgment in deciding about how much and when to encourage direct as opposed to indirect exploration of sexual abuse experiences. Also keep in mind, and remind the group if appropriate, that the goal of this group is primarily to develop trauma recovery skills and that trauma stories are told to clarify related problems and possible coping techniques.

QUESTION 2

What are some of the relationships between sexual abuse and other problems?

TYPICAL RESPONSES   Forced sex is common when using drugs; especially if you can't pay.

Not any problems—helped me to become a man.

Being homeless is risky; you can get abused sexually.

Recurrent nightmares.

Can't talk about it—it goes too far back.

Physical stress.

Fear of others finding out.

Unclear about own sexual orientation and feelings.

A diagram of possible related problems is also helpful here in facilitating discussion related to the vignettes and to the members' own experiences. As in the previous topic, this diagram should reflect those specific problems that characterize the group members' expressed concerns.

QUESTION 3

What are some useful coping skills for dealing with sexual abuse and its effects?

TYPICAL RESPONSES   Forgetting about it

Having to learn to trust other people

Learning to relax when stressed
Learning that feelings are OK

Feel free to draw on many of the previously discussed coping and recovery skills. Members should be encouraged to make specific links between feelings, thoughts, problems, and possible responses. Brainstorming alternative possibilities is often useful if the formerly applied ideas begin to seem stale at this point.

The core recovery themes also may be used to summarize coping skills here. For example, pointing out the importance of mutuality in learning to trust other people may lead to a helpful discussion of the role of power in relationships, including its positive and negative uses.

TOPIC 15 Community and Institutional Violence and Recovery (Optional)

SESSION RATIONALE

This topic is a necessary one for many groups of men. Their experiences of trauma often have been part and parcel of their community setting and then later have been woven into relationships with other problems (substance abuse, psychiatric hospitalizations, etc.). If these events are not part of the experience of the target population or if they have been adequately covered in the three previous sessions, this topic may be deleted.

GOAL 1: Each group member will begin to consider the various effects of community and institutional violence.

GOAL 2: Each group member will begin to explore the possible connections between such violence and other problems in his life.

GOAL 3: Each member will begin to examine recovery skills appropriate to violence and its related difficulties.

QUESTIONS

1. What do we mean by community and institutional violence and what are their effects?
2. What coping skills are most helpful in dealing with these kinds of violence?

EXERCISE

This session is labeled optional because these experiences may have been discussed adequately under the previous two topics. If not, then leaders present vignettes tailored to the group's reported experiences of community or institutional violence.

For example, the following vignettes have been used in groups of inner-city men with a history of severe mental disorders and substance abuse problems:

1. Tom, who is 10 years old, is shooting some hoops on the playground. He hears a gunshot and turns around to see that his friend, Jerry, is bleeding from a wound in his stomach.
2. James, an adult, hides in a closet while a drug dealer roams through the apartment looking to kill him.
3. John is picked up by the police, handcuffed, and taken to a psychiatric hospital where attendants beat him up while putting him in restraints.

Discussion questions may include the following:

1. Is this really community (or institutional) violence? What do we mean by those terms?
2. What thoughts and feelings would the person in this situation have?
3. What would this person do in response to this experience?
4. What effect will this experience have on this person in the future?
5. What alternative coping strategies could he use?
6. What skills would this person need to deal with the long-term effects he might experience?

LEADERS' NOTES

QUESTION 1

What do we mean by community and institutional violence and what are their effects?

TYPICAL RESPONSES   **EXPERIENCES**

Being part of the drug scene gets you into violent situations.

Everyone seems to have weapons these days—and uses then.

You can't walk down the street without getting hassled.

People at the hospital don't care about whether they
    hurt you or not.
Guys in the service would just as soon kill you as
    look at you.
The drill sergeant would just spit on me.

EFFECTS
Scary
Don't know where to go to be safe
Got to get them before they get you
Learn to fight back
Don't ever want to go in the hospital again

This session tends to elicit more adolescent (e.g., gang-related) and adult (e.g., street or drug-related) experiences with violence. It also tends to elicit more stories of men as perpetrators as well as victims of violence. Be attuned to the ways in which being either a victim or a perpetrator of violence, or both, are connected with other experiences of trauma and the problems outlined under the topics of physical and sexual abuse.

QUESTION 2

What coping skills are most helpful in dealing with these kinds of violence?

TYPICAL RESPONSES   Learning to fight (e.g., karate or other self-defense)
Having to learn to be safe—where and when to go
    to certain places
Not hanging around with negative people—the ones
    who use drugs and deal
Not hanging out on the street at all when you have
    nothing to do—find something to do
Making plans and sticking to them—don't get
    dragged into doing other things
Staying off drugs—then you won't be in that kind of
    trouble

Again, you should offer a step-by-step problem-solving approach to these dangers by identifying specific risk factors and situations, generating positive alternative solutions, and addressing the obstacles to implementing those solutions. For many men, these dangers are ongoing ones, regardless of when they first experienced community violence. This affords leaders the opportunity to focus clearly on day-to-day problems and the alternative coping styles group members bring to issues of violence as well as the underlying domains of recovery. Self-protection and self-direction themes have been especially common in these group meetings.

TOPIC 16 Review and Summary of Recovery Skills

SESSION RATIONALE

This session is designed to review and summarize the group's work in trauma recovery by focusing its content on both the level of skills learned and recovery themes addressed. Its process permits men to say what they have learned from each other and to explore the value of collaborative problem solving.

GOAL: Each group member will have an opportunity to review and consolidate the core recovery skills discussed by the group.

QUESTIONS

1. What has been the most important thing you have learned in this group?
2. What is the most important thing you plan to do now that the group is ending?

LEADERS' NOTES

QUESTIONS 1 AND 2

What has been the most important thing you have learned in this group?
What is the most important thing you plan to do now that the group is ending?

TYPICAL RESPONSES
How important it is to work with other people in solving problems
How important it is to stay away from drugs—because it's all tied in with other problems
That I can do more than I thought I could to solve problems
How important it is to have a plan and stick to it

Organize the responses to these questions according to the recovery themes, thus grouping specific skills under the headings of the central theme to which it seems most tied. For example, "working with other people" might be listed under "mutuality" while "doing more than I thought" could be placed under "self-esteem." Following these themes throughout the session enhances consolidation of the group's content learning.

Group process, at the same time, should encourage members to express gratitude to others for their contributions, to express feelings about the group's ending, and to discuss any disappointments or unfulfilled expectations as well as sources of satisfaction. You will want to model an openness to the full range of members' reactions to the termination and assist in arranging plans for appropriate follow-up.

PART VI

Appendix

KAPITEL

Appendix

ITEM A *TRAUMA GROUP NOTEBOOK*

Topic 3: What do you know and how do you feel about your body?

Date: _____

QUESTION 1

Do you think you have a good understanding of how your body works? How would you rate your knowledge on a scale of 1–10?

QUESTION 2

What were you taught about your body at home? At school? On the streets? From the media?

MEMBER RESPONSES

FROM FAMILY: Once you start your period, you've really got to watch it because now you can go out and get yourself pregnant

My mom wouldn't talk to me about my body, my period, or anything . . . it was all shameful and private

Grandma said if a boy touched me I would get pregnant

I wasn't taught anything so when I got my period I thought was going to die

FROM SCHOOL: I didn't get much from the movies they showed us in school

I had a girl scout leader who told me about my period and what I should do about it

FROM THE STREETS: I didn't know much about my body until I got pregnant at age 13

My friends told me some stuff but I wasn't sure how much it was true

We played nurse and doctor

QUESTION 3

Are there things about your body that confuse you?

MEMBER RESPONSES

I don't understand what menopause is or when it happens.

I had a hysterectomy but I'm not completely sure what the doctor did.

I had a tumor in my uterus and I didn't know how it got there.

Other questions concern bladder infections, vaginal infections, birth control, conception, giving birth, and hygiene.

QUESTION 4

How do you feel about your body?

MEMBER RESPONSES

Ashamed.

Angry.

Disgusted.

Disappointed.

Embarrassed, because I've never looked good.

Mad, because I'm never thin enough.

I wish I were invisible.

Mad, because my body is misshapen—I never had the right shape.

Sad, because people have always said negative things about my body . . .
that I'm a butterball . . . too fat.

Ashamed, because all anyone ever wanted me for was my body.

I'm disgusted by my body—I'm too fat—and people don't like fat people.

I've never wanted breasts because I was raised that men want big-breasted
women for sex.

QUESTION 5

What are the messages others have given you about your body? What were
your reactions?

MEMBER RESPONSES

Disgust.

Self-hatred.

Shame.

Secrecy.

Confusion about my body.

I do not want to be a woman.

I dislike having a woman's body . . . I hate having my period . . . I hate
having breasts.

FURTHER THOUGHTS AND FEELINGS

_____

_____

_____

_____

_____

_____

ITEM B *SELF-ESTEEM THERMOMETER*

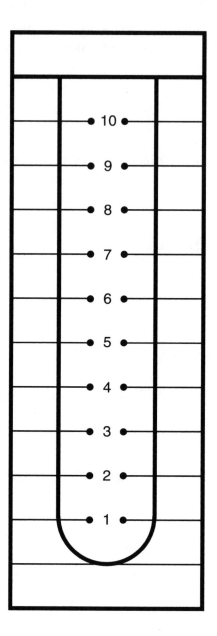

ITEM C *SELF-ESTEEM ACHIEVEMENT CHART (EXAMPLE)*

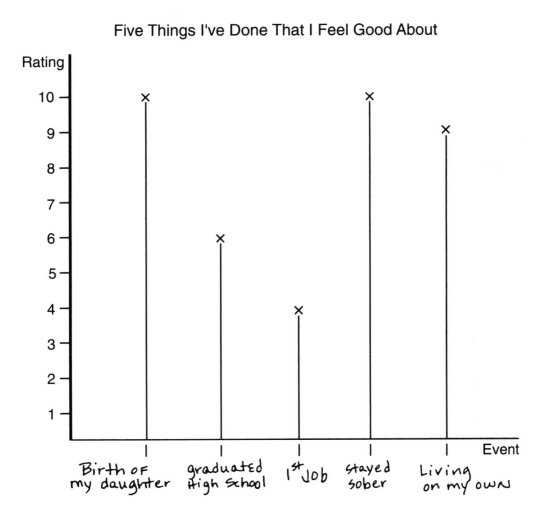

Five Things I've Done That I Feel Good About

ITEM **D** *SELF-ESTEEM ACHIEVEMENT CHART*

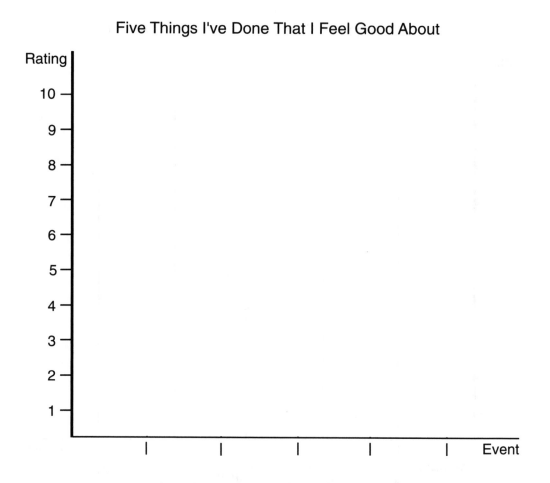

Five Things I've Done That I Feel Good About

ITEM **E** *COMFORT STRATEGIES*

Taking a bath

Listening to music

Reading a book or magazine

Watching TV

Meditating

Exercising

Going window shopping

Fantasizing

Going to the movies

Socializing

Distracting myself

Taking a nap

Being with a pet

Shopping

Talking on the telephone

Having a philosophy to live by

Having some privacy

Talking to someone who is calming or compatible

Eating soothing foods (avoiding sugar and caffeine)

Reflecting on self-knowledge

Counting

Taking a walk

Swimming

Being outside

Talking to a wise voice

Being with family

Imagining a soothing scene

Reflecting

Doing jigsaw puzzles

Playing an instrument

Being quiet

Deep breathing

Sitting in front of a fire

Looking at the stars

Drinking water

Crocheting, knitting, sewing

Going for a ride

Item F *INTIMACY NETWORK*

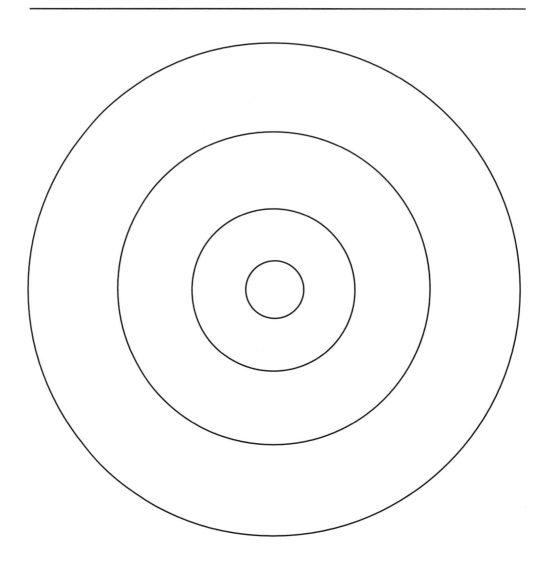

Item G *ROAD MAP*

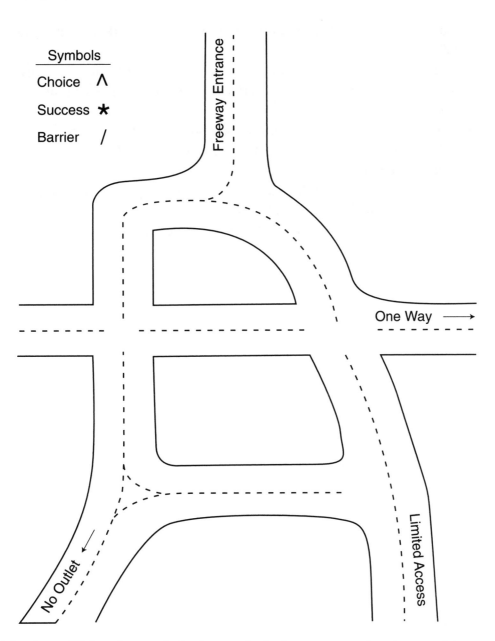

Symbols

Choice ∧

Success *

Barrier /

Freeway Entrance

One Way →

Limited Access

No Outlet ←

Members: Using the symbols shown, include successes, barriers, and important choices made in your lives.

ITEM **H** *LITERATURE SOURCES*

Angelou, Maya. *I Know Why the Caged Bird Sings.* New York: Bantam Books, 1969.

Bass, Ellen, and Louise Thornton, eds. *I Never Told Anyone: Writings by Women Survivors of Child Sexual Abuse.* New York: HarperCollins, 1983, 1991.

Danica, Elly. *Don't. A Woman's Word.* Pittsburgh: Cleis Press, 1988.

Fraser, Sylvia. *My Father's House: A Memoir of Incest and Healing.* New York: Harper & Row, 1987.

McNaron, Toni, and Yarrow Morgan. *Voices in the Night: Women Speaking About Incest.* Pittsburgh: Cleis Press, 1982.

Morris, Michelle. *If I Should Die Before I Wake.* New York: Dell, 1982.